Confessions of a Serial Celibate

Mysteries from an Irish Catholic Rosary
Book One: The Joyful Mysteries

By

J.G. McAllister

*For Catherine
and the next cohort
of Catholic warriors.*

J. Hughy'auster

7/15/2011

ISBN: 1-4107-6012-X (e-book)
ISBN: 1-4107-6013-8 (Paperback)

Library of Congress Control Number: 2003093453

This book is printed on acid free paper.

Printed in the United States of America
Bloomington, IN

1stBooks – rev. 08/21/03

Dedicated to all us Catholic warriors.

May we find peace.

ACKNOWLEDGMENTS

Deep thanks to all those who gave me encouragement to publish this book:

To my seminary friends and classmates, especially Mike Anderson, Pat Browne, Jeff Burns, Bob Carroll (R.I.P.), Don Carroll, Paul Feyen, Bill Finnegan, Ed Gaffney, Conrad Gruber, Al Larkin, Bob Leger, Mike McLaughlin, Mike McNamara, Gil Mata (R.I.P.), Gene Merlin, Larry Moorman, Bob Murnane, Jim Pulskamp, Tom Sheehan, and Mike Sullivan, some of whom were major players in these memoirs, others who graciously read the manuscript and encouraged me to continue.

To Pat Barnett and Kathleen Marvin, two non-Catholic friends who patiently endured my endless ramblings about Irish Catholicism and then encouraged me to exorcize those particular demons by writing them down.

To Fred Ramey for his insightful edits, suggestions, and reassurance.

To Lee Coleman and Bonna Gayhart for their meticulous proof-reading.

To Ed Skoglund for his photographic help.

PROLOGUE

As I write these words, I am, in fact, a practicing celibate. This, for many reasons, seems strange to me. I have not always been a celibate, nor, God willing, do I intend to remain one forever. My attitude toward celibacy has fluctuated radically over the years, beginning with enthusiastic embrace, then angry rejection, and now bemused acceptance.

When I entered a Catholic seminary at age 16, I considered celibacy to be the highest state to which a human being could aspire, and I assumed that I would be celibate for life. However, nine years later, when I was actually required to take the vow of celibacy in order to become a subdeacon, I had become so opposed to the concept that I cheated during the oath-taking ceremony, crossing my fingers, not really placing my hand on the Bible, and only mouthing the words rather than saying them out loud. By then, celibacy had become for me a symbol of everything that had gone wrong with Jesus' church.

Even today, celibacy is not something I intentionally choose; it's more like an accident, something I fall into periodically. Like catching a cold. Except that it tends to last longer. Often for years.

My chronic celibacy has made me curious, not only about the nature of celibacy itself, but also about why I seem to be so susceptible to it.

Webster defines the word "celibate" simply as "unmarried or single," and cites as its source the Latin word, "*caelebs*." The Follett Classic Latin Dictionary defines "*caelebs*" in a similarly minimalist fashion: "unmarried, single." The only reference to an earlier etymological root is the Sanskrit word "*kevalas*," meaning "alone" or "private." There's no reference to sex in this definition, even though, in modern usage, celibacy is often confused with virginity and chastity. Technically, a celibate person does not necessarily abstain from sex, merely from marriage. (In fact, during the Middle Ages, celibate priests were so promiscuous that their congregations often petitioned the bishop to mandate clerical marriage just to protect the women of the village.)

Hoping to put a positive spin on my own celibate condition, I tried to find some connection between "*caelebs*" and "*caeles*," the Latin word for "heavenly." There turned out to be no connection – probably just as well, since the Greek root for "*caeles*" turns out to be "*koilos*" – which means "hollow."

I did, however, find one reference in the Latin dictionary that made me feel better about being celibate. It was a derivative definition of "*caelebs*," which Follett included after his official entry. Horace, in one of his odes (II, 15), was bewailing the gentrification of his neighborhood by rich Romans and referred to their newly planted trees as "celibate." The term Horace used was "*platanus caelebs*," which Follett translates as "*a tree to which no vine is trained.*" Evidently the anal Roman gentry preferred the free-standing plane trees to the vine-cluttered elms.

"*To which no vine is trained.*" Now here was a description of celibacy which finally made sense to me, for I have been in several prolonged relationships (I have even fathered children), and yet, I have always ended up feeling like an old elm (a "*platanus*") so entwined with ivy that I can hardly find my own trunk. I think the therapists call it "enmeshed." In any case, it comes from having poor boundaries, more concave than convex. My romantic relationships thus far have left me feeling trapped and bewildered, with no memory of myself as an individual. Eventually I become depressed and then angry.

Why is this? Why do I always seem to lose myself in relationships and then end up feeling claustrophobic and angry? And why do I then default to celibacy, which, though liberating on some level, and comfortable, eventually leaves me pining for intimacy? Perhaps it has something to do with being raised Catholic (though millions of people are raised Catholic and don't seem to share my proclivity to celibacy). It may also have something to do with spending nine years in a Catholic seminary (though most of the ex-seminarians I know left the seminary primarily to escape celibacy). Conceivably it has something to do with being Irish (though typical Irish families aren't exactly testaments to celibacy). Perhaps it's because I was an only child and developed an appreciation of privacy and solitude at an early age.

Although all of these factors have no doubt contributed to my persistent (and often reluctant) celibacy, they don't totally explain it. I believe there is a deeper, more radical, cause – a particularly virulent strain of Catholicism which I contracted through my grandmother. Variously called "Manichaeism," "Jansenism," and later

"Puritanism," this viral strain within the Christian tradition imprints its hosts with the genetic message that <u>abstinence is always preferable to physical pleasure</u>. The philosophical basis of this message is the notion that the physical body is intrinsically evil, thereby posing a constant threat to the spiritual integrity of the soul. In this scenario, celibacy emerges as the lifestyle of choice, the ultimate Spartan hedge on our spiritual bets.

My Grandmother's stern Irish Catholicism was permeated with a righteous horror about sex and the body, and she conscientiously programmed this "saintly" attitude into my youthful psyche, emphasizing to me the importance of abstinence and "self-denial" in the life of a good Catholic. Since the ultimate form of self-denial for a young Catholic male in the 50s was to enter the seminary and become a priest, I eventually mounted my knightly steed at age 16 and rode off to the seminary, like Shane into the sunset, leaving family and friends – especially <u>girl</u>friends – in the dust.

In her youth my grandmother had wanted to be a nun. Why she didn't, no one ever knew, least of all her long-suffering husband, my grandfather. She truly believed that celibacy was the highest state to which a human being could aspire. It freed the individual from those worldly obligations (such as marriage) that distract one from the pursuit of God, and, more importantly, it signified a victory over the carnal desires of the flesh. The body, in my grandmother's view, was a weak and unreliable instrument, which had to be disciplined constantly lest it give in to its sinful inclinations. "Sin," in her lexicon, was synonymous with "sex," and the latter was so despicable that she never even uttered the word, lest its very sound on her tongue defile her in some way. If her thirst for God's presence was almost mystical in its fervor, her contempt for the body reflected a deep distrust of God's wisdom as Creator.

She wasn't alone in this attitude. An ascetic tradition has run through Judeo-Christianity since its inception, though it didn't become specifically anti-sex and anti-body until Manichaeism entered the scene in the fourth century. Early Judaism, whose covenant with God was focused on earthly prosperity, had little use for asceticism and considered procreation a religious duty. Only the Jewish Nazirites had any kind of ascetic practices, and these had nothing to do with sex. They dealt with such practices as abstaining from wine, avoiding contact with the dead, and not cutting their hair, but even these restrictions usually lasted only thirty days. Full-bore asceticism entered only after the Pharisees and scribes introduced the Eastern notion of life after death into the Jewish tradition, much to the displeasure of the conservative Sadducees.

Buddhism of course had had a long tradition of asceticism, based on the idea that Nirvana could be reached only by letting go of all earthly desires. Chastity was obligatory for all Buddhist priests and monks. The first Jews to adopt this type of other-worldly self-denial were the Essenes, who withdrew from society and abstained from everything that ordinary Jews relished – sex, wine, meat. John the Baptist was an Essene, and Jesus probably came from that same tradition, though He never seemed to push abstinence as much as his Essene brethren. But even the most extreme Essenes never taught that the body was _evil_, simply that spiritual goals were more important.

This was not the case with Manichaeism, a movement that originated in Persia in the third century and was practiced by St. Augustine before his conversion to Christianity. Its founder, Mani, taught that all matter was evil, created by a demon rather than by God. Since matter was intrinsically evil, procreation was to be avoided, lest more matter be brought into existence. Augustine eventually rejected Manichaeism, but that didn't keep him from dragging its worst elements into Christian theology. His doctrine of Original Sin created a sexual Catch-22 from which future generations of Christians have yet to escape. Original sin, he decreed, is a moral flaw transmitted to our offspring through the very act of intercourse. Without intercourse, original sin would have nowhere to go. This, of course, makes it pretty hard to feel righteous about sex, even when it is practiced strictly within the sacramental context of marriage.

Somewhere along the line, my grandmother got a pretty heavy dose of Augustine's Manichaeism, probably from the nuns at St. Benedict's Academy in Minnesota. She parlayed their Benedictine Manichaeism into a North Dakota Puritanism that would have made Calvin wince, and directed her righteous indignation at her brothers, most of whom, by that time, had fallen prey to alcohol, that tragically-ineffective vaccine often used by the Irish to counteract the devastating effects of Augustine's sexual Catch-22.

Long before the world had ever even heard of "computers," my grandmother intuitively knew that any effective system of control was based on a series of on/off, yes/no decisions. Her own binary moral system was based on an ontological byte choice that reflected Mani's basic dualism of Spirit ("On") versus Matter ("Off"), usually defaulting to the "OFF" position. In this earthly "vale of tears," the only way to achieve salvation was by turning off worldly pleasures and embracing suffering, thereby freeing the spiritual soul from the clutches of languid flesh. Eventually, the material body would pass away, and the soul, having the last vestiges of gross matter burned off in Purgatory, would enter Heaven, where, according to my grandmother, we would finally get a clear explanation of why things were so screwed up on earth.

The upshot of this programming was that, at an early age, I cultivated a deep distrust of "the world" and an almost pathological fixation on "the next life." This attitude didn't make the mysteries of puberty any less disturbing, but it certainly made the gratuitous discipline of the seminary easier to accept. When I got to the seminary, I found that my grandmother's elementary notion of "self-denial" had been elevated to the seminary's more exalted concept of "dying to the self," and that this entailed an unquestioning obedience to the "Will of God," (i.e., to one's superiors). As seminarians, we were expected to die to our own desires and submit completely to a celibate hierarchy. Only then would we be deemed worthy to become a priest, "another Christ," "God's representative on earth." We were expected to accept this role with deep humility, though the very title "priest" paradoxically created a subtle narcissism, in which we "chosen ones," set apart from our less worthy fellows, became the celebrated centers of our own universe. This narcissism, unfortunately, often thrives more easily in celibacy than in the married state.

While others chafed under what they correctly perceived as purely arbitrary rules, I blissfully submitted, convinced that everything had meaning only in relation to the next life anyway. The seminary's *Rule* was a clearly defined code of conduct intended to strengthen our mind and our will, and subordinate our emotions and feelings. No surprise here, since mind and will are the faculties most amenable to the on/off, yes/no demands of digital programming, whereas emotion and feeling, with their often contradictory shades of gray, create a complex analog wave pattern that doesn't easily reduce to an unambiguous code. The *Rule* gave us clear directives that the mind could grasp and the will could choose. The only emotion the *Rule* encouraged was "loving obedience," the emotion of a suitably subservient child.

I loved it. Everything was all very clear and I was a very obedient child.

The *Rule* began its hegemony at 5:40 in the morning, when "the bell" first sounded. This was not the deep-throated bell of the village church or the soft meditation bell of the Buddhist monastery. This was a blaring electric alarm, which ripped us from sleep with all the delicacy of an injured bobcat. The bell was reverentially dubbed "Vox Dei," the "voice of God," and we were expected to respond to it lovingly and enthusiastically, leaping nimbly from our beds with a prayer on our lips. Any sense of personal boundaries disappeared with the sound of that bell. It was our first opportunity of the day to prove our mettle and "die to ourselves."

I excelled in this dying to the self, probably because of all that early training at the hands of my grandmother. Only later did I realize that what worked in the seminary did not necessarily work well in other life situations. Dying to the self may be a necessary ingredient for success in male hierarchies, but it is not a good preparation for love or marriage relationships (unless, perhaps, one plans to mate with a vampire). No woman wants to wake up one day and realize she's been living with someone in an emotional coma.

There's an old Latin phrase we learned in the seminary: "Nemo dat quod non habet" ("No one gives what he does not have"). We were told that the phrase had some theological significance, but I have found that it is much more useful as a way of explaining my love relationships. After dying to my self in my relationships, I often find that the only thing I have left to give is my old encrusted sense of duty, hardly an exciting prize in the bingo game of romance.

It's at this point – when I find that I have reduced love to the ashes of resentful self-denial, and consequently feel hobbled and claustrophobic, with nothing more to give or receive – that's when I turn again to celibacy as the only viable means of resuscitation. And once I have drunk deep from the well of celibate solitude, and have reclaimed my self, then I again begin to yearn for intimacy.

Because then again I have a self to give.

CONTENTS

The Rosary

The Five Joyful Mysteries

- *The Annunciation*
- *The Visitation*
- *The Birth of Our Lord*
- *The Presentation in the Temple*
- *The Finding of Our Lord in the Temple*

The Five Sorrowful Mysteries

- *The Agony in the Garden*
- *The Scourging at the Pillar*
- *The Crowning with Thorns*
- *The Carrying of the Cross*
- *The Crucifixion of Our Lord*

The Five Glorious Mysteries

- *The Resurrection*
- *The Ascension into Heaven*
- *The Descent of the Holy Ghost upon the Apostles*
- *The Assumption of the Blessed Virgin Mary into Heaven*
- *The Coronation of the Blessed Virgin Mary in Heaven*

INTRODUCTION

THE JOYFUL MYSTERIES

*"The devotion of the Rosary contributes wonderfully
to the destruction of sin, the recovery of grace, and
the promotion of the glory of God."*

-Gregory XVI

When I was a kid we said the rosary every night at 6:45 sharp.
That was the time "The Rosary Hour" came on the radio, and, since
we'd been told many times that *"the family that prays together stays
together,"* we'd stop whatever we were doing, gather round the radio,
and kneel down to say the rosary. The rosary lasted exactly fifteen
minutes and consisted of five decades. (A "decade" consisted of ten
"Hail Mary's," with an "Our Father" and a "Glory Be" wedged in
between). The idea was to say the prayers fairly rapidly while you ran
a little movie in your head about some event in the life of Jesus. These
little movies were called "mysteries" and they were grouped into
three series of five. The Joyful Mysteries covered Jesus' childhood,
the Sorrowful Mysteries dealt with His adulthood, and the Glorious
Mysteries took place after His death.

Different mysteries were said on different days of the week. The
Joyful Mysteries were said on Mondays and Thursdays, the Sorrowful
on Tuesdays and Fridays, the Glorious on Wednesdays and Saturdays.
On Sunday, the mysteries varied, depending on the time of year. The
mysteries each had a distinct tone, and I was always glad when the
Joyful Mysteries came around, because it was a lot easier to think
about Jesus going to the temple as a kid than getting thorns shoved
into his head as an adult. The Glorious Mysteries were always hard to
visualize. They had too many words ending in "ion."

Now, if I had been a Muslim kid, the Glorious Mysteries might
have been a lot easier. According to the Islamic Ahmadiya tradition,
Jesus didn't really die on the cross. Instead, He went into a deep
trance, and then, when things calmed down, He slipped out of the
tomb and headed off through Afghanistan to Kashmir, looking for the

ten lost tribes of Israel. According to my friend Hassan, He brought only one of His apostles with him on the trip.

I asked Hassan if it was Peter that accompanied Jesus.

"Are you kidding?" he laughed. "Peter would have gotten into a fight the first time they stopped at a bar. No. It was Thomas – the doubter. He's the only one of those guys you could trust as a tour guide."

Now those Glorious Mysteries would have been a lot easier to visualize.

***

According to the Catholic rosary, one's childhood years are joyful, the adult years are sorrowful, and things only get glorious after you die. This may explain why my favorite western song as a kid was, "I wanna live fast, die young, and leave a beautiful memory." It seemed very Catholic to me.

I was fortunate that my childhood years, like those of Jesus, were quite joyful. But I've often wondered about all those other kids whose childhoods were full of pain. Maybe there's a different rosary for those kids, one where the Sorrowful Mysteries come first, and the Joyful Mysteries may, or may not, follow.

This book is about my own Joyful Mysteries, the period of childhood through age 25. The Sorrowful Mysteries have yet to be written, probably because I'm still processing some of the pain from my adult years. As far as the Glorious Mysteries go, if I follow Catholic tradition, I'll have to wait until I'm dead; however, if I go the Moslem route, glory could start with retirement.

I have to admit, I'm leaning toward Mecca on this one.

I.   The First Joyful Mystery: The Annunciation

"Let us contemplate, in this mystery, how the angel Gabriel saluted our Blessed Lady with the title 'Full of Grace', and declared unto her the Incarnation of Our Lord and Savior Jesus Christ."

The New Key Of Heaven
A Complete Prayerbook for Catholics
Regina Press, 1949

Our spirituality is largely determined by our childhood experience. If we experience love from our family, then God is love; if we experience abuse, then God is violent and warlike; if we are raised on rules, then God is a stern lawgiver. I was fortunate to grow up with two very loving parents, so my first impression – before my Grandmother moved in – was that God was a benevolent source of love. I bonded with Jesus at an early age – mainly, I think, because He too was the only child of a devoted older father and a loving mother. Lacking siblings, I would usually turn to Jesus for advice and comfort. (Good thing, because, when I was seven, my grandmother moved in with us, hauling with her a much more severe version of God than I had experienced previously.)

My Mother was 38 years old when I was born, my Dad, 55. Their paths had crossed one summer in Billings, Montana, when a hairdresser friend insisted that my mother should meet her Uncle Joe, who was visiting from California. My mother had been an unattached schoolteacher for 20 years and had been set up with a lot of "Uncle Joes," so she tried to wrangle out of the invitation. But this Uncle Joe was persistent. He eventually showed up at her door, and when they looked at each other it was all over. A year later, they were married and she joined him in San Francisco, where I was born, a scant two years later, in 1941.

My Dad had been born in 1886, in Winona, Minnesota, the second youngest of ten children. His own father died when he was 12, so right after high school he took a job as a mail sorter on the Chicago & Northwestern Railroad to help support his mother and younger sister.

He eventually moved to California in the early 1900s, got into the timber business in Plumas County, and eventually married the daughter of a Susanville lumber baron in 1922. At some point, he contracted TB and spent some time in a sanatorium. His marriage didn't work out, perhaps partly due to his wife's alcoholism, and they were separated for several years before her death in 1937. I don't really know much about my Dad's early life. One of my great regrets is that I failed to get more details of his life before a stroke wiped out his ability to speak. I was seventeen when that happened, and I realized, too late, that I had been so caught up in my own life that I had neglected to find out about my father's. My mother, being a proper lace-curtain Irish girl from North Dakota, had thought it improper to probe into her husband's former life, so much of his early years still remain a mystery.

Ullainee

My mother's maiden name was Ullainee Kennedy. "Ullainee" is not a common name. It's not even a rare name. It's a name that, to my knowledge, has existed only twice in the history of the human race. Its first incarnation was on the moist poetic pages of a certain Father John Ryan, a priest-poet from the Deep South, who wrote bellicose, yet sentimental, Dixie-Catholic verses in the 1850s. One of his longest, and most lugubrious, poems is entitled "Their Story Runneth Thus." It is the tale of two lovers (they happen also to be cousins) who decide, early in their chaste infatuation, that they will offer their love to God and part company – he to the seminary, she to the convent. They give each other secret love-names. Hers is Ullainee, his, Merlin.

Many years later, after he has left the seminary, Merlin is wandering around a graveyard, where he finds a rose bush covering a gravestone with the name "Ullainee" on it. Realizing there is a convent nearby, he knocks at the door and asks the mother superior about the gravestone. She gets a tear in her eye, says, "Ne'er so fair a flower ever bloomed," and proceeds to tell him about Ullainee's entry into the convent and her subsequent winning of the hearts of all the nuns. Finally she takes him to the chapel and shows him a painting by Ullainee that hangs there. In the painting, Christ is on the cross and

2

just below, on the ground, are two crosses woven in red and white roses. The cross of white roses has "Ullainee" woven into it in red rosebuds; the cross of red roses has "Merlin" woven in white rosebuds.

Father Ryan was my grandmother's favorite poet (as well as her favorite philosopher, theologian, and war historian). Perhaps this explains why she named her firstborn child after a dead nun and saddled her second child (my uncle) with "Merlin," a name he hated with a passion and promptly changed to "Jim" as soon as he reached the age of reason.

My mother never entered Fr. Ryan's convent, but she did become a schoolteacher, which in those days was tantamount to becoming a nun, since schoolteachers were expected to model propriety at all times. However, if you were an intelligent and lively 17-year-old girl from a small North Dakota town in 1920, becoming a schoolteacher was one of the few avenues of escape. Otherwise you were doomed to stay put and marry one of the three or four boys in your class who made it to graduation.

My mother's first teaching assignment (at age 18) was a one-room schoolhouse in a small farming community several miles out of Hebron, North Dakota. Hebron lies about 100 miles due west of Bismark and, still today, is a typical farming community of about 800 people, with the railroad tracks paralleling the main street through the center of town. Hebron's claim to fame is a brick factory, located on the East edge of town, which has supplied brick to North Dakota for almost 100 years. There are two church steeples, one on the north side of the tracks (Protestant), and the other on the south side (Catholic). This is just as it was in 1920, when my grandfather worked in Urban's Mercantile on Main Street and my mother taught school nine miles out of town and boarded with a Hungarian couple who spoke very little English.

"They were the only Catholics in that area," she explained to me almost 80 years later.

***

My mother stopped teaching twenty years later, when I was born, but as soon as I entered first grade, she went back to it. She was

3

known for her strict, but fair, discipline, and this reputation did not come spuriously. She never ventured out on the playground without her big brass police whistle around her neck. That way, she said, kids could never pretend they didn't hear her when she caught them doing something wrong.

Over the course of the years, she developed her own unique theories about schoolyard discipline. Her basic principle was *All problems originate in the bathroom.* It was this hypothesis that caused her to notice, one day during recess, a suspiciously large number of fourth grade boys going in and out of the bathroom. One group would come out, round up their friends, and then they would all go back in together. This kept up, until the entire fourth grade boys' class was in the bathroom. My mother stalked across the playground, ready for battle, then threw the door open and blasted her police whistle into the cavernous space.

"All right, I want everyone out of here right now!" she demanded.

She heard timorous whispers from the other room. "It's Mrs. McAllister!"

Then a stream of frightened fourth-graders filed past her. She remained at the door listening, using her wily schoolteacher instincts to ferret out the real trouble-makers. Sure enough, she heard it – a muffled sound from the next room. Someone was still hiding in the stalls.

She blasted her whistle again. This time the reverberation in the now almost-empty space was deafening.

"I said everyone out, and I mean EVERYONE OUT RIGHT NOW!!"

There was a slight pause, and then three painters, red-faced and still clutching their brushes and paint-cans, obediently shuffled past her.

No one messed with Mrs. McAllister.

"Mac"

Everyone called my dad "Mac," which I always thought was his first name, until my mother explained to me that his real name was Joseph, just like Jesus' father. My dad was a typical Irishman. He had a mischievous wit and loved to make up extemporaneous stories, just

4

plausible enough to be true, but also rather far-fetched. About the time we were ready to swallow his hook, he would arch his right eyebrow and a wry little smile would begin to show at the corner of his mouth. This was the signal that we had again been sucked into one of his tall tales.

In the 50s, my dad worked in San Francisco for a small trucking firm called General Transfer. Their office was right next to the Ferry Building at the base of Market Street, and was a typically male affair, the grit of the loading docks evident on the undusted desks and counters of the three-man office. Near as I can tell, my dad did a lot of the paperwork for the company and also served as a sales rep for some of the customers. One of his clients, and also a good friend, was a Chinese businessman named Tommy, who always colluded with my dad to provide me with a box of contraband firecrackers on the fourth of July.

During the Depression, my dad had lost everything he owned, so he was a great believer in stockpiling essentials. Our basement was jammed with cases of industrial toilet paper, paper towels, dented cans of fruit cocktail, and whatever else had fallen off the truck. The toilet paper was the overlapping sheet variety, which fit into our rectangular "Blake, Moffitt and Towne" metal dispenser. This was the standard type of toilet paper used in those post-war days, and the first time I saw a <u>roll</u> of toilet paper in the bathroom of one of our new upscale neighbors I was fascinated by its luxurious inefficiency.

Although it was her doctor, rather than the angel Gabriel, who announced to my mother that she was pregnant, nevertheless, the news had miraculous overtones. She was 38 at the time, my Dad 55, and neither of them had imagined they would be able to conceive a child together. Assuming there is consciousness in the womb, I'm sure I picked up fetal hints that my birth had some sort of mythic significance to my parents.

II.   The Second Joyful Mystery: The Visitation

"Let us contemplate in this mystery, how the Blessed Virgin Mary, understanding from the angel that her cousin St. Elizabeth had conceived, went with haste into the mountains of Judea to visit, bearing her Divine Son within her womb, and remained with her three months."

The New Key Of Heaven
A Complete Prayerbook for Catholics
Regina Press, 1949

Mayme

My dad's folks had died many years before I was born, so I never knew them, but my mom's parents were still living in Montana. They came out to visit several times, and eventually, when I was about seven, they came to live with us in Kentfield. My grandmother turned out to be the most influential person in my young life, channeling to me a steady, though very restricted, capillary stream of what I would later recognize as the infinite and unconditional love of Jesus. It was she who formalized my introduction to God the Father/Judge, and who initiated me into her own floating salon of angels and saints, all of whom she employed as advocates before the bench of that stern Lawgiver.

She was the oldest of eight children, six boys and two girls, and had attended a boarding school operated by Benedictine nuns in Minnesota. These were no-nonsense women with their hearts set on their heavenly goal and their eyes scanning the horizon for any deviation from God's laws. The girls under their care were precisely trained in the manners, etiquette, and discipline which characterized "proper" young Catholic women of the late 1800s. A nun sat at the head of each table in the dining hall and watched closely to ensure the girls sat upright, held their silverware correctly, and chewed their food the required one hundred times before swallowing. (In deference to my grandmother, I have experimented with this chewing protocol many times, and have found that even the toughest meat invariably disappears completely after about 32 chews. This suggests to me that about two thirds of the meals at St. Ben's consisted solely in what the Bible would call the "gnashing of teeth.") My grandmother must have flourished under this Benedictine brand of training, because I still have the gold pin she was awarded by the nuns in her senior year. On the back is engraved, *"St. Benedict's Academy, June 20, '89,"* on the front *"Mary Moran, Order and Neatness."*

Though the nuns called her "Mary," her real name was Mayme, a moniker that does more justice to the ferocity of her religious fervor. Why she never became a nun was a total mystery to anyone who ever knew her. It wasn't just her prudish behavior that bespoke celibacy. It was also her world-view, which combined the Manichaean idea that the body is intrinsically evil with the Irish Catholic notion that the world is, at best, a forlorn prelude to the afterlife. Since the body is evil, any form of physical pleasure is to be avoided, and any kind of physical suffering is to be welcomed as fuel for salvation. Drinking was absolutely unacceptable to my Grandmother – possibly because of her experiences with several pub-crawling brothers. (Joe, the youngest, and her favorite, was a promising young minor league pitcher when he got drunk in a bar one night, stumbled out into a blizzard, and passed out half way home, losing the index finger on his pitching hand to frostbite.) As a consequence, when Mayme married my grandfather, Peter Kennedy, she made him promise that liquor would never touch his lips. He took the vow willingly, not realizing that liquor wasn't the only thing that wouldn't touch his lips, once the Irish Catholic sphincter closed round their marriage.

***

Despite (or perhaps because of) her severe and intrepid religiosity, I grew very close to Mayme. In the absence of siblings, she became my closest friend and confidant, and I spent hours in her room, listening intently to stories of the saints, praying the rosary with her, and rubbing her arthritic arms with BenGay. Through her, I got my first exposure to the conspiracy theory of history, that dramatic view of the world which pits the forces of evil, led by wily Satan, against the forces of good, represented by the Catholic Church and its dashing commander in chief, Michael the Archangel. Satan never fights fair, always resorts to trickery and deception, and plants landmines of sin throughout our earthly environment. If we die with serious (mortal) sins on our soul we go straight to Hell and we're done for. If we die with less serious (venial) sins on our soul, we go to Purgatory and have a chance.

***

414. Q. What is Purgatory? A. Purgatory is a state in which those suffer for a time who die guilty of venial sins, or without having satisfied for the punishment due to their sins.
415. Q. Can the faithful on earth help the souls in Purgatory? A. The faithful on earth can help the souls in Purgatory by their prayers, fasts, alms-deeds; by indulgences, and by having Masses said for them.

– Baltimore Catechism

***

Mayme explained in some detail how the politics and economics of Purgatory worked, how through prayers and acts of self-denial, you could tap into the Treasury of Grace that had been established by Jesus and the saints. The "poor souls" in Purgatory had each been sentenced to a specific period of suffering, whatever length of time it took to "purge" the remaining sins from their souls. You could actually shorten their sentences by offering prayers or performing other pious acts on their behalf. Any poor souls you helped would, in turn, help you if you landed in Purgatory, since, by then, they would be in Heaven and would be able to intercede with God on your behalf. Purgatory was a place of intense suffering, similar in caloric ferocity to Hell, but without the ultimate pain of Hell, which came from the dual realization 1) that you were never going to get out and 2) that the pain would never diminish. I remember struggling to grasp this image – hellfire enveloping my body, roasting me, but my flesh never charring to the point of numbness. Eternal, undiminished pain. Another challenging mystery to ponder in my youth.

The "poor-souls" (always pronounced as one word by my grandmother – "persols") were undergoing this same unmitigated pain, but they were not trapped into the ultimate despair of knowing it would go on forever. Each poor-soul had been sentenced to a specific term of suffering – 100 days, 50 years, 10 centuries, etc – and each had to serve out that term, unless people like my grandmother and me gained "indulgences" and signed them over to that specific poor-soul. Indulgences were amnesty credits that could be applied either to one's own future sentence in Purgatory or to the sentences of those already there. My grandmother emphasized to me that it was better to offer indulgences up for others, rather than selfishly hoarding them in my own spiritual vault. (God didn't like selfish people, even if they were Catholics.) She and I spent much of our time liberating poor-souls from Purgatory. She had a large collection of holy cards with short prayers on the back. At the end of each prayer would be printed, "100 days indulgence," "20 years indulgence," or some other denomination. She had one or two prized cards, which carried a "plenary indulgence," meaning that all one's sins were forgiven and one could go straight to Heaven. I used to think of these holy cards like baseball cards, and a "plenary indulgence" card was the Topps equivalent of a 1950 Ted Williams. I even remember sniffing my grandmother's collection of holy cards to see if they too smelled like stale bubble gum.

Indulgences

839. Q. What is an Indulgence? A. An Indulgence is the remission in whole or in part of the temporal punishment due to sin.
840. Q. What does the word "indulgence" mean? A. The word "indulgence" means a favor or concession. An indulgence obtains by a very slight penance the remission of penalties that would otherwise be severe.

Baltimore Catechism

Our strategy was to score at least two plenary indulgences a day for the poor-souls. That meant that we sprang two people from Purgatory that day and hence had two more advocates in Heaven. But we were careful not to take advantage of the situation. We would only use the high denomination holy cards for one of the plenary indulgences, lest God think we were chiselers. For the other plenary indulgence, we would say the "poor-soul's rosary." This was said on a sawed-off version of the regular rosary, which my grandmother had obtained from some obscure religious order that evidently had political connections to the Vatican's Office of Weights and Measures. The poor-soul's rosary had only four decades instead of the usual five, and, instead of having to say a "Hail Mary" on each bead, you simply said "Jesus, have mercy." You could whip off a whole rosary in about three and a half minutes if you stayed focused, thereby cutting someone loose from maybe a million-year sentence in Purgatory. (Another of our strategies was always to offer our plenary indulgences for the poor-souls who had the longest sentences.)

I found out later in the seminary that these same indulgences had caused some unfortunate problems in the fifteenth century. It seems the Church had come up with the idea of trading plenary indulgences for contributions to the building campaign for St. Peter's Basilica. At the time, it seemed to be a great deal for everybody. The Church got a lot more donations than they would have otherwise, and the rich got a chance to buy themselves and their loved ones a fresh start. For a few gold coins, they could buy an automatic absolution, and, as long as their money held out, they wouldn't even have to stop sinning. They could just re-donate for a new plenary indulgence every time they needed one. It was brilliant consumer strategy – a religious precursor to the ATM machine.

Things went fine until an ascetic monk named Martin Luther started causing trouble. For some reason, he didn't think that it was right to "sell" indulgences, and he started making all sorts of noise about it. Rome's designated fundraiser, a Dominican named Johann Tetzel, tried to persuade him to change his mind, but Luther stubbornly refused to stop criticizing the church, not just for indulgences but for other abuses as well. Eventually, he and a bunch of other malcontents broke with the Roman Church and started the Protestant Reformation. And all over a few silly indulgences.

Much later, I learned another interesting thing about indulgences. The Catholic Church created plenary indulgences during the crusades, as a way to counter the military benefits package that the Moslems were offering their soldiers. Any Moslem soldier who died in a holy war, or "jihad," was promised an immediate passage to Paradise, where, senses enhanced and orgasms extended, they would get to loll around with beautiful virgins for the rest of eternity.

The Vatican, with its Manichaean bias against sexual pleasure, couldn't include the virgins in its benefits package, but did promise Christian soldiers a plenary indulgence if they died in battle, thereby guaranteeing them immediate entry into Heaven with the equivalent of a Purple Heart. This fit in well with the Vatican's public relations strategy of changing Jesus' image from crucified pacifist to Commander in Chief of the Christian ground forces.

Luckily, eight years old, at my grandmother's knee, I was blissfully ignorant of all these distasteful political facts, so indulgences seemed an incredible form of magic, giving me awesome powers to help others, merely by saying a few designated prayers.

My grandmother taught me several other creative ways to achieve plenary indulgences, many of them relating to specific days (saints' feast days, first Fridays, Easter, etc.) or to certain repetitions of prayers (e.g., nine days in a row – a "novena", three times a day for a month, once a week for a year, etc.). You could also earn indulgences by offering up your sufferings to God or by engaging in acts of self-denial. I remember complaining once to my grandmother that this latter approach to indulgences didn't seem as reliable as the prayer cards, in that you could never be sure just how many days or years indulgence you were gaining. She explained that this was where faith came in, that you just had to let God keep the books for you and trust that He would always be very fair. This seemed reasonable to me, but I still preferred the guaranteed returns printed on the back of the holy cards.

My grandmother gained a lot of indulgences by offering up her suffering on behalf of the poor-souls. Her shoulders constantly ached from acute arthritis, and I would regularly rub them with BenGay, though we both knew that this would only slightly diminish, not remove, the pain. To this day, when I smell the unmistakable odor of BenGay, I think of poor souls floating upward from a pungent Purgatory.

"The Flesh"

Self-denial was a concept that featured prominently in my Manichaean grandmother's worldview. Not only did self-denial strengthen the Spartan souls of spiritual warriors, but it also protected them from the poisonous effects of *"the flesh."* I didn't realize how pervasive the world of the flesh was until one hot summer day when I was nine years old. The temperature was about 100 in the shade, and I had taken off my shirt to play in the back yard. When I came back in the house, I stopped, as always, at my grandmother's room to say hello. She was sitting in her rocking chair, saying her poor-soul's rosary. When I came in, she looked up at me and creased her brow.

"Hmpf!" she said, and raised her head slightly as she turned her face away from me toward the wall.

I was frightened. I had seen her do this to other people, many times, but she had never done it to me. "What's wrong, Grandma?" I asked.

"Hmpf! Well I'm surprised," she said in a quiet, somber tone.

"What is it, Grandma?" I blurted, growing more panicky by the second.

"I'm surprised and I'm disappointed," she said, still not looking directly at me.

"Disappointed?" I whispered.

"I didn't think you were that weak."

"What do you mean, Grandma?" My eyes were starting to burn with insistent tears.

She slowly turned her face back toward me. "I'm surprised and disappointed, because I didn't think you were so weak that you couldn't keep that shirt on and offer the suffering up for the poor-souls. I just didn't think you were that weak."

Her words stung me and shocked me. I, her beloved friend, had displeased her and I was now being judged, along with all those other laggards, as wanting in zeal. I was frightened, because I suddenly realized, on a deep unconscious level, that I could lose my grandmother's love; that, for her, moral strictures came before love and, if violated, could destroy love. I found out later that this was exactly what had happened to my grandfather, that for a brief, real or imagined, infidelity, he had been excluded from her heart forever, doomed to be tolerated as her lawful husband, but never respected or loved by her again.

Needless to say, I retrieved my shirt immediately and put it back on with all the dedication of a Sir Gawain donning his armor. My grandmother had again reached my soul, cinching me into yet another of her delicately stitched, but inextricable, religious corsets. It was years before I could again allow myself to welcome the sun's warm rays upon my shoulders.

As I look back on this event, even as I feel the sensory suture of that moment, I can't bring myself to get angry with my grandmother. She was merely handing on to me what had been passed down to her – all in the spirit of love, such tough love as was allowed to exist in that strict Irish Catholic culture. The fact that she reinforced my strength, even as she poisoned the wells of pleasure for me, says that she herself had only warrior strength to give, and that she was unaware that pleasure could ever be unlocked from guilt. I appreciate the strength and discipline she bequeathed me, but it has taken me years to exorcise the subtle feelings of guilt that still struggle to infect even my simplest pleasures. My grandmother didn't create this pathology by herself. It was part of the Irish Catholic program deeply embedded in her psyche from birth. Far from resting on the gentle words of Jesus, this program was based on the Good vs. Evil split originally taught by Zoroaster and later developed by Paul, Mani, and Augustine. By the time my grandmother received it from the Benedictine nuns of Minnesota, it had become a basic operating system, invisible to the majority of its users, but controlling their thoughts and behavior nonetheless.

In Persia, around 600 B.C., Zoroaster taught that there was one God, *Ahura Mazda*, who was the good and loving creator of all. God had two sons to whom he granted free will. One of the sons (*Spenta Mainyu*) chose Good and Truth, the other (*Angra Mainyu*) chose Evil and Falsehood. Thus began the dualistic battle between Good and Evil, Light and Darkness. However, it's important to note that Zoroaster never taught that matter, or creation, was evil. He never pitted the spirit against the flesh, and, in fact, he considered asceticism to be as much of a sin as over-indulgence.

13

Eight centuries later, another Persian named Mani appeared, claiming to be the fulfillment, not only of Zoroaster, but of Jesus and Buddha as well. He taught a radical dualism, in which God, the Father of Greatness, is opposed by *Ahriman*, the Prince of Darkness. In Mani's view, *Yahweh*, the God of the Old Testament, is really another name for *Ahriman*, the evil creator of matter. The human body is thus intrinsically evil, a dark prison confining the light particles of man's soul. This is a deeper, more fractious, dualism than that of Zoroaster, and it necessitates a strict, almost violent, asceticism in order to release the soul from its earthly prison. (It also sows the seeds of a radical anti-Semitism, portraying *Yahweh*, Israel's Creator-God, as the Prince of Darkness.)

Paul definitely foreshadows this Manichaean attitude in his frequent swipes at the "lusts of the flesh," and his portrayal of women as venal temptresses. His flesh vs. spirit dichotomy set the stage for centuries of Catholic guilt and, with it, a flourishing confessional industry within the church.

It was Augustine, however, who took the Manichaean binary code and turned it into the equivalent of a "Catholic Operating System," a program so basic and so pervasive that it has invisibly orchestrated the lives, thoughts, and emotions of millions of Catholics during the last 16 centuries. Augustine was a practicing Manichaean in his youth, even though he found himself unable to follow their strict rules of chastity and celibacy during his libertine days. He eventually immersed himself in the writings of Paul, converted to Christianity, and rejected the teachings of Mani. He did manage, however, to drag into Christian theology some pretty heavy Manichaean baggage, especially his doctrine of Original Sin, which declared that moral guilt is passed from generation to generation directly through the act of intercourse. This locked future generations of Catholics into a sexual Catch-22 from which even the esteemed sacrament of marriage couldn't grant them release. Celibacy alone seemed to offer an escape and soon became the Church's lifestyle of choice, a tragic example of "throwing the baby out with the bath water."

The essential element of this system is its dualism – Good vs. Evil; Light vs. Darkness; Christ vs. Satan; Spirit vs. Flesh; Church vs. World; love vs. sex. Once this either/or dichotomy was established, salvation became rooted in schizophrenia. Whatever a person was doing, there was something else more valuable that he or she should be doing. Even if he felt he was pleasing God, that was probably a self-delusion, indicative of the deadly sin of pride. If he felt he was displeasing God, he was probably right, and that meant he needed to be doing something else. It was a no-win situation, one designed to leave people off balance all the time.

We The Righteous

The one positive aspect of this moral schizophrenia was that a Catholic got to project his or her guilt on to other people. Since my grandmother felt that every human instinct was, if not actually sinful, at least something to be overcome by self-denial or abstinence, there was ample room for criticizing the lax behavior of others. Hers was tough love par excellence, and it was the same love she directed at herself. I often think that when Jesus said, "Love others as you love yourself," He didn't mean it in the exhortative form we usually hear it, but in the indicative: "In fact, you actually love others the same way you love yourself." Given my grandmother's commitment to self-flagellation, it's no wonder she felt perfectly justified in relegating others to Hell.

Exclusivity

Q. 166 Are all obliged to belong to the Catholic Church in order to be saved?
A. All are obliged to belong to the Catholic Church in order to be saved.

Q. 167 What do we mean when we say, "Outside the Church there is no salvation?
A. When we say, "Outside the Church there is no salvation," we mean that Christ made the Catholic Church a necessary means of salvation and commanded all to enter it, so that a person must be connected to the Church in some way to be saved.

15

Q 168 How can persons who are not members of the Catholic Church be saved?
A. Persons who are not members of the Catholic Church can be saved if, through no fault of their own, they do not know that the Catholic Church is the true Church, but they love God and do his will, for in this way they are connected with the Church by desire."

Baltimore Catechism

***

Our next door neighbor, Henry Peck, was such a sweet guy, and did so many nice things for my grandmother, that she found a way to excuse him for being Jewish, and to grant him tenuous salvation, through the "baptism of desire." What that meant was that, if Henry were in his right mind – namely, if he really understood the laws of salvation and was capable of making a rational choice – he would no doubt choose to be baptized a Catholic. It was just the unfortunate circumstances of his birth as a Jew and his upbringing in New York City that had blinded him to the truth thus far, but a merciful God would excuse him for this, since he was living a good Christian life already.

Henry's wife, Liz, was a different matter however. She had no saving graces in my grandmother's eyes. She smoked, drank, played cards, cussed, wore shorts, gardened on Sundays, and chewed gum. The fact that she was a loyal neighbor, had a good sense of humor, and loved her dog didn't matter. My grandmother had no use for her. Unfortunately, Liz's garden was right outside my grandmother's window, and Liz spent most of her weekends tending her vegetable patch.

One day I came into my grandmother's room and found her standing at her window looking out at Liz, who was whistling happily as she pulled the weeds around her tomato plants. My grandmother turned to me with that offended look usually worn by medieval inquisitors and television evangelists, and shook her head. Then, very slowly and solemnly, she pronounced the ultimate judgment:

"A whistling woman...
and a crowing hen
bring the old Devil
right out of his den."

I remember getting a sinking feeling in my stomach, as I realized that this was at least strike nine for Liz and that, even though I was quite fond of her, I would have to accept the fact that she was doomed to Hell.

It was a real shame.

I eventually got into the habit of consulting my grandmother about the status of everyone's soul. When new people moved into the neighborhood, I would immediately go to her and inquire about their ranking on the scorecard of salvation. She would grade them all, reserving some of her harshest judgments for those whose names indicated they should be Catholics but who "weren't practicing their faith." I reveled in this categorization of others, because it made me feel superior, armed as I was with her inquisitorial righteousness. I found a great exhilaration in pigeonholing so many diverse people into such simplistic categories. It was also a bonding experience with my grandmother, since, in the process of judging others, she and I felt righteously united against an Enemy who had corrupted just about everyone else on earth. Even my parents did not escape our censorious judgments, for they drank alcohol, and hence were among "the weak." In retrospect, I see my grandmother as a very manipulative person, who systematically programmed me toward her own intolerant worldview. This, however, she did without guile, even out of love. What others would see as programming, my grandmother saw only as the time-tested pedagogy of a benevolent mentor.

Her pedagogy included a very effective interrogation technique, which she would use on me whenever she felt I might be telling her a lie.

"Stick out your tongue," she'd say. "If you're fibbing, there'll be a black mark running down the middle of it."

The few times I did try to tell her a "fib," she immediately detected the black line. At first I figured she somehow knew I was lying, and that she was making up the black line bit to teach me a lesson. But then one time I went and looked into the mirror myself

17

and, sure enough, there it was – an ugly black line running the full length of my pink tongue. You didn't mess with my grandma.

Peter

My grandfather, Peter Kennedy, knew only too well that you didn't mess with my grandma. He spent most of his time in the basement or out in the back yard, not because he didn't love my grandmother (he did, dearly), but because every time he got near her, she'd snarl at him like an old dog protecting her bone. He would meekly acquiesce, and move out of the danger zone, usually down to the basement, where he kept his gardening tools, as well as his stash of outlawed smoking materials, which he kept hidden in an old Folger's coffee can. This was his world, where he could be himself, protected from my grandmother by the basement steps, which her arthritis prevented her from descending. On the underside of those same steps, my grandfather kept a record of the first rainfall of each year, the first frost, and the date of each year's spring planting. Today, fifty years later, those stairs still bear his penciled graffiti, the only markings of his turf he ever felt free to make. He was a thin, wiry man with high cheekbones that gave him a Native American appearance. That was fitting, because he had spent enough time with the Sioux in North Dakota to earn the nickname, "Hiamuga," which meant "Iron Tooth." (He was the first person the Sioux had ever met with fillings in his teeth.)

Peter had grown up in the rolling, green farm country of Wabasha township, along the Mississippi river, sixty miles south of St. Paul. This area looks so much like Ireland that it's no surprise that Irish immigrants like the Kennedys chose to farm there. As a boy, my grandfather delivered groceries in a horse-drawn wagon, and was instructed by his employer to hand his cargo over without resistance to the brash young Indians who frequently waylaid his wagon. He went on to pursue a career in retail sales, and, eventually, owned his own trading post in North Dakota, where he learned to speak Sioux from his customers, often accepting their invitations to reservation pow-wows, where they taught him some of their dances. In exchange, he carefully caught the large tarantulas frequently found in the banana bunches delivered to the post, and put them on display for his Sioux customers, who were mesmerized by these strange prehistoric insects.

Peter's passion was gardening, and he turned our back yard into an Eden of vegetables. I loved my grandfather, but during my childhood I never really appreciated him. In my youthful judgment, his gentle love for mother earth seemed an inadequate substitute for my grandmother's martial commitment to an all-powerful sky father. But now, years later, I see Peter standing there, in his verdant little shrine, hoe in hand, pleated pants held up by worn suspenders, shirt rolled up to the elbow, exposing tanned, veined forearms, his stained, soft-brimmed hat cocked on his head, pipe clamped resolutely between loose dentures – and I recognize him as the simple and unassuming St. Francis that he was. Without knowing or speaking it, he had tapped deep into the pagan roots of our native Irish Catholicism. Forty years later I would understand and appreciate his legacy. Forty years later, I would realize that my grandparents' visitation had introduced me both to the Heavenly Father and to His bride, the Earthly Mother.

III. The Third Joyful Mystery: The Birth of Our Lord

Let us contemplate, in this mystery, how the Blessed Virgin Mary, when the time of her delivery was come, brought forth our Redeemer, Jesus Christ, at midnight, and laid Him in a manger, because there was no room for Him in the inns at Bethlehem.

The New Key Of Heaven
A Complete Prayerbook for Catholics
Regina Press, 1949

I was born at St. Joseph's Hospital in San Francisco, but I grew up across the bay, in a small neighborhood nestled in the protective shadow of Mt. Tamalpais. In the original 1907 real estate brochure, the area was originally christened "Kent Park," and boasted such modern amenities as "electrical lights, paved streets, and a grammar school within walking distance." Thirty-four years later, when my parents moved there, Kent Park had changed its name to "Kentfield," houses were selling for about $3000, and the Golden Gate bridge had just been built, making it possible for my father to drive to work in San Francisco without having to take a ferry across the bay.

There were about twenty kids in our neighborhood, and over half of them were Catholic, especially those who lived on our street, Inman Avenue. Almost all us Catholic kids were bussed to St Anselm's Grammar school, about 2 miles away. Catholicism was our common culture, even though it was filtered through the different ethnic lenses of German, Irish and Italian. My best friends were "Jim Boy" and Tony. Jim's folks were quiet, strict Germans from Indiana, Tony's were vivacious Italians from San Francisco, mine were wry Irish from North Dakota and Minnesota. Both Jim and Tony had older siblings, always a veiled threat during any of our frequent fights, and a luxury which I, as an only child, sorely missed. It wasn't just protection I wanted from siblings. It was companions, co-conspirators. I also wanted an escape from the stigma of being an "only child."

In retrospect, I realize that, because I <u>was</u> an only child, my need for relationships was much more intense than that of my siblinged peers, which caused me to burrow more frenetically into their lives and force friendships out of them that they might otherwise have avoided.

When that didn't work, I talked to Jesus.

The "Catholic" Label

For us kids, "Catholic" was a brand name. If people were Catholics, it meant they were okay, even if they were mean or weird. Just being Catholic gave them some sort of immunity. Other people you could write off, but Catholics you had to try to love, because they were "brethren." On that level, Catholicism was a compassionate force, encouraging tolerance where otherwise there might have been cruel ostracism. Such tolerance, however, didn't usually extend beyond the boundaries of the Church. We were wary of outsiders, because we knew that, as Catholics, we were under siege. Every day at school the nuns would have us pray for Cardinal Mindszenty, who was being tortured in a Hungarian prison cell just for practicing his religion. Then we'd pray for the overthrow of "Godless Communism." We didn't really know who communists were, but we were told that they were evil and tricky and that they hated Catholics. We knew that a lot of communists were Jews, and that some were Protestants. The Masons were mostly communists. And the owner of Jack's Drug Store in San Anselmo was definitely a communist. Otherwise, why would he be selling those nasty magazines with pictures of women in swimsuits? We were surrounded by communists. According to the nuns, anybody who wasn't a practicing Catholic could very well be a communist.

Our neighborhood provided an important counterbalance to the parochialism we learned from school and parish. Although almost half the residents of our neighborhood were nominally Catholic, everyone was, first and foremost, a <u>neighbor</u>. Perhaps this was due to the fact that no one had any kind of inheritance rights to the area. Everyone was relatively new to Marin County. No one's family had lived here for generations and, since we were all newcomers, we were not inclined to pull rank with each other, especially on the basis of religion. Ghetto-Catholicism flourished in large cities, where Catholic parishes became cultural enclaves, providing their members with every social, political and economic amenity. In our suburban neighborhood, the church didn't have that kind of pervasive power. Our next door neighbor was Henry Peck, a Jew from New York City, who quickly became my dad's best friend. Henry was a lovable bumbler in many respects, and gave his wife Liz lots of material on which to hone her caustic humor, but Henry was also the most charitable man I had ever met, reaching out to everyone in the neighborhood at one time or another. Though I didn't realize it at the time, Henry played a crucial role in my spiritual development and later, in the seminary, his image would inspire me as I began to question the arrogant self-righteousness of those who claimed that only baptized Christians could enter the kingdom of heaven. Had my neighborhood not been such a supportive and diverse community, I might not have been so troubled when I began to perceive the terrible discrepancy between the ideals of Jesus and the cynical righteousness of the organized Church. Had I grown up across the bay, in a large San Francisco parish, perhaps I would have been sufficiently reinforced in my Catholic parochialism that I would not have reacted so vehemently when I saw non-Catholics judged and devalued. I might have been a better candidate for the hierarchy.

During the 40s, Kentfield was a quiet little community, with older houses, many originally built as vacation homes, dotting its oak-covered hills. The only stores were at Kentfield Corners, a tiny business area across from Marin Junior College. "The Corners" were an easy quarter mile walk from my house and we'd often go down there to buy comic books or ice cream. Caesar's Soda Fountain was on the corner, a drugstore next door, Meuller's Hardware down the street, and two small groceries, one owned by Harry Mendleson, a Jew, and the other by Tim Egan, a Catholic. Next to Mendleson's was a barbershop and next to that was Berthenier's gas station. Kentfield Elementary School was down at the other end of College Avenue and across from that was the junior college. That was pretty much it, except for a tiny post office and the volunteer fire department whose whistle would always blow at twelve noon.

Blackberries grew everywhere, especially along the creek, and there were at least as many vacant lots as there were houses. These lots served as our baseball fields, battlegrounds for mudball fights, and sites of our various fort-building projects. When a new wave of developers appeared in the early 50s, and began covering our lots with their surveyors' stakes, we went into battle mode. We would wait until the stakes were all in place, then sneak out at night and pull them all out. The builders, however, kept on coming, and nothing we did seemed to slow them down. Finally, in a desperate guerilla move, I dumped a can of dirt down the vertical exhaust pipe of a tractor that was poised to begin scraping our ballfield the next day. A week or so later, my Dad sat me down and said, "I want you to just listen to me. Don't say anything."

I could tell something bad was coming, so I sat there trying to look as innocent as possible.

"Evidently someone poured some dirt down the smokestack of that tractor up on the corner, and it pretty well ruined the engine – to the tune of about $450. Someone said they saw a kid up on the tractor last week, and they thought it might be you, but they weren't sure."

I started to say something, but my Dad put his hand up to stop me. "I don't want you to say anything," he said. I just want you to know what happened, and how much it would cost if they knew for sure who was responsible. Since they don't know for sure, there's probably nothing they can do about it. But I thought you better know what's going on."

That was all he said. And we kept the unspoken secret between us, just as if we were undercover saboteurs who had just taken out a Nazi tank.

My Dad didn't like developers any more than I did.

Saint Anselm's

All the Catholic kids in our neighborhood were bussed to St. Anselm's grammar school in San Anselmo, about two miles away. The school was a three-sided mission-style structure, whose rough stucco walls embraced a large cement playground with a flagpole in the middle of it. An arcade ran along the inside of the building and provided the only access to its eight classrooms. Low green benches lined the arcade and it was here that we sat and ate our lunches, waiting anxiously for the sound of the wooden clacker that would signal our permission to go out and play. In the middle of the building's longest side, there was a small complex of rooms which housed the infirmary, the music room, and a tiny office for the principal. (Since the principal also taught the eighth grade, she didn't have time or need for a very large office.) At the extreme ends of the building were the boys' and girls' bathrooms, properly separated by as much space as possible. Behind the boys' bathroom was a small cafeteria where hot lunches were served. A small window in the front of the cafeteria opened out to the playground, and here students would line up to buy ice cream bars or Hostess fruit pies. A full lunch cost 40 cents, which my mother provided me daily, but I usually just bought an ice cream sandwich at the window and pocketed the other 30 cents. That was risky, because Johnny Bocabella and his gang of hoods would regularly go around asking us if we had any lunch money, and if we said yes, they'd grab it. It was my first experience of taxation, and I learned to lie (and justify it) accordingly.

***

> *"I pledge allegiance to the cross of Christ*
> *and to the faith for which it stands…"*
>
> *-Beginning of the Salute to the Cross*

Every morning, when the bell rang, the entire school would line up, grade by grade, on the playground to solemnly recite the "Salute to the Flag" and the "Salute to the Cross," followed by the singing of "America the Beautiful." Before we could begin, each nun inspected her class' line to make sure it was perfectly straight, two by two, one arm's length between each student. Total silence prevailed until each class was in perfect battle array. Then two eighth grade boys would march out, one holding the flag, the other the cross. The first would elevate the flag and shout, "Salute to the Flag!" and we, with right hands in military salute, would singsong, "I pledge allegiance…to the flag…of the United States of America…" Then the second student would extend his right arm, holding the cross aloft, and shout "Salute – to the Cross!" and we would shift our right hands over our hearts and belt out, "I pledge allegiance…to the cross of Christ…and to the faith…for which it stands…"

After that, we'd all sing "America the Beautiful," or, if Sister Superior was in an especially militaristic mood, and wanted to rile up the Protestant seminary students who lived across the street, we'd get to sing "An Army of Youth." That was always my favorite, because it was our denominational fight song.

> *"An Army of youth, flying the standard of truth*
> *We are fighting for Christ Our Lord*
> *Heads lifted high, Catholic Action our cry*
> *And the cross our only sword!*
> *On earth's battlefield, ne'er a vantage we'll yield*
> *As dauntlessly on we swing*
> *Comrades true dare and do*
> *'Neath the Queen's white and blue*
> *for our flag!*
> *for our faith!*
> *for Christ the King!!"*

This was our youthful battle hymn, and it filled us with paradoxical images of heroic warfare and saintly submission. We knew that our battle with the world would ultimately be won, but not by earthly conquest. Only through the selfless sacrifice of martyrdom.

In those days of the late '40s and early '50s, all the teachers were nuns. Though they ranged in age from about 21 to 75, they all looked the same to us, black crepe robes hiding their bodies and stiff white linen framing their faces. They were designedly mysterious, and we knew better than to get too close. My first experience of mystery came shortly after I started first grade at St. Anselm's. The lunch bell had sounded, and we had dutifully put our books away and filed into the cloakroom to get our lunch pails. Once I reached the classroom door I bolted out into the arcade, hoping to catch up with my friends. Suddenly I was enveloped in darkness. I had run into something, but I didn't know where I was, only that things were hitting me on the head – sharp metal things, smooth wooden things, things on strings. Then I felt blows as someone tried to beat me away. I felt like I was being attacked inside a dark hardware store.

I had run right into Sister Conradine and become entangled in the multiple layers of black crepe that made up her habit. In those days,

25

every nun had an arsenal of weaponry hanging inside her habit – scissors, clackers, keys, rosary beads. It was deeper than I had ever imagined penetrating the mystery of nun-ness.

Luckily, Sister Conradine was one of the few nuns who had a sense of humor. After her initial panic, she calmed down, extricated me from her skirts, and told me NEVER to run on the arcade again. I saw a glint of laughter in her eye, and I knew that I would live to see another day as a St. Anselm's student.

The Male Mystique

"As regards the individual nature, woman is defective and misbegotten, for the active power of the male seed tends to the production of a perfect likeness in the masculine sex; while the production of a woman comes from defect in the active power."

– Thomas Aquinas
Summa Theologica, Q92, Art. 1

It didn't take long for Catholic kids in the '50s to figure out that ours was a church in which men ruled and women served. The altar rail stood as a symbol of that distinction, and women were never seen inside the sanctuary, except at odd hours when they were allowed to sneak in and perform housekeeping duties – like changing the altar linens, arranging flowers, or scraping up spilled candle wax. Altar-girls were unheard of in the 50s. On any given Sunday, there might be four generations of men parading around the altar in various robes, but the women, all wearing some kind of Paul-mandated headgear, were relegated to the pews. The message was clear: official religion was man's work.

In second grade, we got our first crack at this male hierarchy. Those of us who had evinced enough self-control that there was a chance we could stand still for half an hour without going into some sort of spasm were chosen to be trained as "torchbearers" for Friday night Benediction. The nuns made a big deal out of this first selection process. Anyone who was interested in becoming a torchbearer had to officially submit his name to his teacher, knowing that he would only be picked if she thought he was worthy to serve at God's altar. By second grade, none of us thought we were worthy of anything, so it was a pretty scary crap-shoot.

The day finally came when our teacher read off the names of that year's torchbearer draft. Those of us whose names she called were immediately slotted into an elite fraternity. Not everyone's name was on the list. This of course made those of us who were on it feel very special. We were God's elite troops.

Now I realize that the only reason that Johnny Bocabella, our class' standout athlete, wasn't "chosen" as a torchbearer was that he never submitted his name. The nuns would have picked him right away, but his Dad probably advised him against it, knowing that Johnny's calling was to swing a bat, not to carry one around with a candle on the end of it. (I'm really glad I only figured this out later in life, since it would have put a serious dent in my elite torchbearer veneer.)

We torchbearers immediately became a fraternity. It's like we had been initiated into the first degree of a prestigious secret society. The next step would be" altar-boy," and that, in turn, might lead, through various steps, to "priesthood." After that, God only knew – Bishop, Cardinal, maybe even Pope.

(No – we shouldn't say that. We had no right to exalt ourselves, even in our imagination…But we HAD taken the first step…And after that it was up to God…So it WAS a possibility.)

The job of the torchbearer was to kneel in front of the altar as devout, candle-bearing witnesses, as the priest "exposed" Jesus, the Light of the World, to the congregation. We would blend our light with the Christ-light, as the priest held aloft the consecrated host, encapsulated in a gold-spired "monstrance" (fr. "*monstrare*", to show, highlight, demonstrate). He would lift the monstrance high, then sweep down, then up, then over, in the sign of the cross; and the congregation would bless themselves in the same cruciform pattern.

The "torches" that we "bore" were five-foot long wooden poles with candles mounted on the top. These were kept behind the large marble altar, out of sight of the congregation, inserted in holes which had been drilled into a long wooden shelf.

As torchbearers, we had to wear cassocks and surplices, so part of our training consisted in learning how to select the right size of these mystical garments. The cassocks were all kept in a tall cabinet, and

27

there must have been at least thirty of them, in various sizes. On that magical first day of training, we were instructed to try on several of them, until we found one that fit, and then we were told to find some identifying mark on the label that would enable us to find that specific cassock again. Usually there were six torchbearers, chosen according to height, the first pair being the shortest and the last the tallest. We were all in the same grade, so there wasn't a huge height difference between us. That meant that, on any given Friday night or Sunday afternoon, there might be another guy your same height who would go for your favorite cassock if he got there first. So you better get there early if you wanted to be sure you got the cassock that fit.

You also needed to check for candle wax. The last kid who wore it might have tilted his candle and sloshed a bunch of wax on it. You didn't want to walk out there in front of all those people with a big chunk of wax hanging off the front of your cassock.

Or missing buttons. That was another thing. You didn't want to parade out there looking like your fly was open.

Over the black cassock, you wore a white surplice, which you also had to check carefully. It, too, might have candle wax on it, or it might have gotten ripped at the collar when the last kid was taking it off. That's why you always wanted to get there early, so you'd have time to check out your wardrobe. Plus, if you got there early, you might get to hang out with the older altar-boys and young priests who made up an exclusive and intriguing inner circle within this all-male hierarchy.

When it was time for Benediction to begin, we torchbearers would line up, two abreast, and then process out to the middle of the sanctuary where we would genuflect together, two by two, and then go to either side, just in front of the altar rail. Eventually, there would be three of us kneeling on each side. We didn't have anything to do during the first part of Benediction, except kneel there and look pious. Shortly before the Blessed Sacrament was taken out of the tabernacle to be "exposed" to the congregation, we would get our signal. We would all stand up together and proceed around either side of the altar to the back, where our torches were kept. The altars were huge in those days, symbolizing the Church Universal and Triumphant, so they gave us plenty of protection. We could easily all fit behind the altar, out of sight of the congregation. One of the older guys would come with us and light the candles. We would carefully pull them up from their slots and line up, still out of sight. Then came the tricky part – coordinating our re-entrance so that we appeared simultaneously from each side of the altar. If our timing was off, even by a little bit, the effect would be spoiled, with one side lurching out first and then screeching to an embarrassed halt when they noticed their counterparts on the other side had failed to show.

Once we got back to our places in front of the altar rail, we stood with our backs to the congregation, waiting for the signal to kneel. This was perhaps the trickiest maneuver of the whole evening, since we had to keep our candles upright in one hand while we grabbed the back of our cassocks with the other hand and lifted them up enough so that our back foot wouldn't get caught on the hem when we extended it backwards to kneel. (That was one other thing we learned to check when picking our cassocks – whether the stitching in our back hem was loose. Many torchbearers learned the hard way, pitching over backwards like a taut bow when their heel caught a loose hem during a kneel.)

We stayed kneeling throughout the rest of Benediction, sustaining a reverent position while the incense billowed up in our face and the hymns of the congregation wafted overhead. This is where our Spartan training came in, enabling us to keep our backs straight and our minds focused, despite the frankincense-induced nausea and dizziness that often overwhelmed us. If we did begin to waver, all we had to do was remember that at least three of the nuns were behind us, watching our every move. That was like a dose of smelling salts.

Being a torchbearer was like becoming an apprentice in the clerical union. Your elders watched your moves and assessed your attitude, and, if you passed muster, they started preparing you for the next step: altar boy. If you went on to excel as an altar boy, they would usually start suggesting to you that you might have a vocation to the priesthood, and that you might want to think about entering the seminary. If you entered the seminary and excelled there, your bishop might decide to send you to Rome for your last four years of theology. That meant you were in line to become a bishop someday.

But it all started with being a torchbearer. You had to be able to handle fire, wax, and hems.

29

Soul Wash

"Not that which goeth into the mouth defileth a man;
But that which cometh out of the mouth, this defileth a man."

Matthew 15;20

For a basically good, God-fearing kid, I got in a fair amount of trouble with the nuns. Though I was raised to be obedient and respectful of my elders, I began to realize in the third grade that I might not be able to achieve sanctity in that particular arena. Our teacher was Sr. Mary Coleman, a grumpy old nun who first kindled in me what would later become a bonfire of resentment against authority figures. I don't remember much about her class except that it wasn't any fun and that she didn't seem to like us very much. This was in marked contrast to the nuns we had had in first and second grade, whom I remember with warmth. My only clear memory of third grade is the day I muttered "You old goat!" under my breath, so quietly that I was sure no one – least of all Sr. Coleman – would hear it. But her ears were more sensitive than her heart, and the next thing I knew she was yanking me down the arcade towards the boys' bathroom saying she was going to wash my mouth out with soap. When we arrived at the green wooden door, she crashed through it without hesitation and hauled me into the washroom. The familiar trough was there, with the spring-loaded faucets and – Oh God! It hit both of us about the same time! – the powdered soap containers with the little lever underneath, which you had to jostle up and down to get the soap out. Up to that time, I think we had both been visualizing scented Pamolive or buoyant Ivory bars, but here we were, face to face with those corroded soap dispensers. That didn't slow her down at all. She marched me over and jiggled herself a handful of the coarse Boraxo. Then she said, "Open your mouth, Boy!"

I did and she stuffed it full of granular bits of soap. Then she scooped her hand under the water faucet and got a palmful. "Open up, Boy!" she demanded.

I could feel a few drops of water slap against my lips. "Now chew it," she said.

30

I was torn. Part of me wanted to spit the soap into her face and run out. The other part didn't want to give her that satisfaction. I wanted to show her – per my grandmother – that I could handle anything, that I was indeed the ultimate Christian warrior. I imagined myself as a young Christian martyr, being tortured by a cruel Roman soldier. I would not give in. I would not deny my faith.

I looked her in the eye and chewed the soap, slowly and methodically, feeling the Spartan power surge through my body. She couldn't crack me. I was stronger than she; and, unknown to her, God, the righteous Judge, was on <u>my</u> side.

I was adopting the basic Irish Catholic warrior strategy, taught me by my grandmother: Find a just cause, take a stand, and then find someone willing to martyr you for your beliefs. Even though I couldn't claim that my original cause was totally just (calling Sister Mary Coleman an "old goat"), I could certainly claim the higher moral ground once she rolled out the Boraxo. The more discomfort I could endure, the more I felt I was emerging as a victor, even in this battle against one of the "holy nuns," whose childish temper tantrums we had been brainwashed into accepting as divinely inspired.

Catholic Basics

Naturally, my early spirituality revolved around Jesus. Though I never quite understood all the talk about him being our Savior, and dying for our sins, I was thoroughly inspired by what he said and did. I loved the story about him getting left behind in the temple when he was twelve and how he amazed all the elders because he already knew so much about religion. And how he stuck up for the woman caught in adultery and made all the guys who wanted to stone her back down. And how he was so nice to the poor people, but really came down hard on the rich hypocrites. And how he turned over the moneychangers' tables and chased them out of the temple. And especially how he loved his friends (including me) so much that the bad guys couldn't scare him out of it, even when they tortured him and killed him. He was a very cool guy and I decided I wanted to be just like him.

Now, you have to understand, all the time I was learning about Jesus, I assumed he was a Catholic, and this, of course, made it much

31

easier to relate to him, us being members of the same religion and all. That's basically what we were learning from the nuns at St. Anselm's, that Jesus was the Son of God and, naturally, a Catholic, and that he had thrown the Jews out of the church because they were moneygrubbers, and that he was sad that the protestants didn't get what he was saying, mainly because they were so horny and disobedient and undisciplined, but that he loved them anyway, even though they didn't deserve it. Eventually the Jews (who were really mad about the money tables) hooked up with the Romans (who were really future protestants) and killed him.

That was my basic grammar school theology expressed in the same cold war terms that would eventually be used in the sacrament of Confirmation when, at age 13, we would officially become "warriors of Christ," ready to do battle with all of Jesus' enemies. We had been told that, during the confirmation ceremony, the bishop would give each of us a light punch to the jaw, which was supposed to jar us into realizing that life was a battle and that we better be ready to fight. I loved this kind of imagery. I was ready. We got to choose our own special "Confirmation name" when the time came and I wanted one that sounded tough and no-nonsense. My first choice was Lance, but that wasn't acceptable because there was no Saint Lance. So I picked Mark, another one-syllable, right-to-the point name.

The Brotherhood

One of my first adventures as a Christian warrior came in the fifth grade. One of our classmates, Johnny Bocabella, was a legend in Marin County, because, even as a kid, he was a great athlete. He could throw a football further than kids twice his age and hit a baseball twice as far. He was tall and muscular, and he later went on to be a major league baseball player. Unfortunately for us, in the fifth grade, he was also a bully.

He could do no wrong with the nuns, probably because the only time they got to watch television was when Notre Dame was playing, and they thought Johnny might someday play for the Fighting Irish and be their claim to fame. They always appointed Johnny as one of the team captains in our class, and he always picked all hoods on his team, including Danny Quinn who was even bigger and tougher than he was. The other captain was Piero Sandri, a big good-natured kid who was my best friend. Piero would always pick all the less aggressive guys on his team, and we'd usually get beaten by Bocabella's team. That was okay though, because we felt we were on the side of righteousness, fighting the good fight. Bocabella picked on just about everybody in the class, except the hoodlums in his clique – and Piero. I only remember him fighting with Piero once, and it was pretty much a draw. But the rest of us had all gotten used to him messing with us. It was part of life.

We were in the fifth grade when Davy Crocket hit the Disney Hour and ran once a week for a couple of months. We all started wearing coonskin hats and carrying Davy Crocket lunchboxes and singing "*Daavy, Daavy Crocket, the king of the wild frontier*" on the school bus. We were caught up in heroic idealism, especially when Davy and his Indian friend drew their knives across their wrists, pressed them together, and became blood brothers.

One kid in our class, Pete Howell, was really inspired by the blood brother thing, maybe because his dad was in a union or something. One afternoon Pete passed a note around to a bunch of us "good guys" telling us there would be a secret meeting after school on the porch of the old gymnasium. This was the only safe space at St Anselm's, where you could be pretty sure the nuns wouldn't find you.

About six of us showed up. Piero wasn't there, because he always got a ride home right after school. I would have felt a lot better if he had been there. Pete launched right into his presentation.

"Look at this," he said, and held up a small twig. He held it out for a moment and then dramatically snapped it in two.

"That's us when we're by ourselves. Bocabella can do whatever he wants to us." He snapped another twig in two and paused to check out our reactions. We were all nodding glumly. "But now look," he said, and pulled out a small bundle of twigs tied together with a string. "Try breaking this!" He passed it to the kid on his left, who tried unsuccessfully to break it and then passed it on. We all tried our best, but no one could break the twigs.

"See?" he said. "You can't break them when they're together. And that's what we need to do with Bocabella." He held the bundle of twigs aloft. "We need to form a brotherhood, and whenever Bocabella comes after one of us, we all band together like this (holding up the twigs) and rush him in a body."

This was pretty exciting stuff for young warriors of Christ, already pumped up by Davy Crockett; and it got even more exciting when he pulled out an official-looking document for us to sign, pledging our undying loyalty to the anti-Bocabella Brotherhood. He even had a pen with red ink so that it looked like we were signing it in blood. (We talked about pricking our fingers, but we figured it would be too hard to read and, besides, it was probably sinful to shed your own blood, even for a good cause like this.) We all signed the pledge and then formed a circle and put all our hands together like we used to do before CYO basketball games.

We walked back down the stairs feeling a new sense of power and purpose. Then, just as we rounded the corner of the auditorium, one of the guys said, "Look! There he is!"

Sure enough. There was Bocabella, with his back to us, sitting on Billy Allen. That's what he always did. He'd get you down on your back, pin your shoulders with his knees, and then sit on your stomach, bouncing up and down while he rythmically slapped your face, first on one side, then on the other. We all knew what Billy was feeling.

The Brotherhood was outraged. "Let's get him!" someone shouted. "All together!" someone else yelled, and we charged. I got there first and promptly planted my smallish fist into Bocabella's massive back. Then I moved aside to let the others mount their attack.

But no one was there.

I looked back and saw them all standing back where the charge had been sounded. Bocabella stopped slapping Billy and looked around at me. He had a look of mild disbelief on his face when he said, "McAllister??!!" in that cynical, sing-song voice he always used for such occasions. At that point he jumped off Billy and started after me. I had about ten yards on him and made it about a quarter of the way across the schoolyard before he caught me. He still had the look of disbelief on his face when he administered the mandatory punch to my shoulder. But it wasn't the usual, bone-shattering punch he usually threw. It was kind of a half-hearted punch, delivered, it seemed to me, with a certain amount of hesitation.

My friends had all disappeared. Billy Allen had run toward home. There was just Johnny Bocabella and me, all alone on a deserted playground. He could have knocked me cold and nobody would have seen him. But he didn't. He just looked around, and then looked at me, and then shook his head, with just a hint of a smile, and walked off.

We never became friends, Bocabella and I.

But we did share a secret.

And he never sat on me again.

The Outsider

Throughout grammar school, sports were a major social touchstone. Everyone was encouraged to play whatever sport was in season, but the teams always ended up being pretty much the same – Bocabella and his band of thugs on one side and Piero and his band of white hats on the other.

There were, of course, some kids who managed to avoid sports altogether, despite the nuns' admonitions and threats. Perhaps the most accomplished outsider in our class was Wendell Joost. Wendell had arrived in the fourth grade, part of a new group of students whose parents had just moved from San Francisco into an upscale new subdivision called "Greenbrae." Wendell prided himself on being a seedy character who loved to antagonize authority figures. As if his name wasn't stigma enough, Wendell had orange hair, freckles, and a habit of chewing his tongue. For some reason, this latter habit infuriated the nuns, and we got used to our lessons suddenly coming to a screeching halt, when the nun, driven to the edge of a nervous breakdown, would scream, "Wendell Joost, stop chewing on that tongue!!" Wendell would never reply. He'd just sit there and look at her with those inscrutable madman's eyes, until she would give up and go on to something else.

During recess, Wendell would wander around by himself, looking at the ground, periodically picking something up and putting it in his pocket. Later in the year we discovered that he had been collecting a rare type of popsicle stick that had little half moons cut out on either side so that the top looked like a spade – or, if you had Wendell's imagination, a helmet. In a couple of months, he had picked up about two hundred of these sticks and painted faces under the helmets, along with a variety of military coats signifying different ranks.

35

Periodically, someone would whisper, "Look at Joost" and we'd look over to see him with his hinged desktop slightly elevated, his arms inside, and rows of little soldiers marching around inside the perimeter. Of course he was chewing his tongue the whole time and acting as though he didn't realize that half the class was surreptitiously watching him.

Wendell was probably the only real genius in our class. His imagination knew no bounds and his sense of morality followed suit. We could never trust him, but he came up with such fascinating ideas that he always sucked us in, even though we knew better. One week he started a bank at his house where we could deposit our play money and take out loans. When he realized we weren't taking out enough loans, he started a gambling casino in his basement to ensure that we would need to borrow more money from him; then he started a neighborhood newspaper; then he invented a tiny roller coaster that could be carried around like a skateboard; then he put up a phone line between his house and a friend's, using some very thin phone wire, which his dad, a Navy quartermaster, had gotten for him. I strung a phone line between my house and Jim Pulskamp's house, but the wire I used was regular lamp cord wire, which was heavy and expensive (3 cents a foot down at Meuller's Hardware). I wanted to string an additional line to another friend's house, so I asked Wendell how much his wire had cost and if he could get some for me. He told me he'd get me three hundred feet for a penny a foot. I was excited. That was a third of what I had paid for the electrical cord, and it would be much easier to string. I gave him three dollars and he said he'd have the wire for me in a couple of days. A week went by, and when I asked him where the wire was, and he said his dad hadn't been able to get it yet, but he was still working on it. Another week went by and still no wire. Finally I told Wendell I wanted my money back if he couldn't deliver the wire by the end of the week. Friday afternoon he showed up at my house with a couple of tangled rolls of rotting old wire he'd picked up at the army surplus store. I blew up. I told him that wasn't what I ordered, and I wanted my money back. He refused to give it back, saying that we had only agreed on three hundred feet of wire and that's what he had brought me. I told him that he knew darned well that I wanted the same kind of wire he had used at his house, but he just shook his head and walked off, leaving me with a tangled ball of what looked like World War II field wire. I tried to string it, but it was so brittle that it kept breaking, plus I discovered that it had already been broken and spliced about every ten feet anyway. When I hooked a phone and battery to either end, just as I suspected, there was no signal.

Three dollars was a lot of money in those days, and I was really angry. So I thought about it for a long time and came up with what I thought was a fair solution: I went up to Greenbrae, followed Wendell's phone line along the fence, and cut it every ten feet, the average space between splices and breaks in the wire he sold me. That, I felt, was the only way to deal with Wendell.

But I should have known that Wendell never played fair. A couple of days later he called my parents and plaintively reported to them that I had destroyed his property and that he wanted me to pay for the damage and apologize. My parents, being the moralistic Irish Catholics they were, sat me down and asked if I had done what he said I did.

I said, "Yes, but..." and tried to explain what led up to my actions, but they weren't about to let me off the hook. Neither of my parents liked or trusted Wendell, but if I had destroyed his property, I had to pay him back. I also had to apologize.

My dad drove me up Wendell's house, doing his best to keep his real feelings about Wendell at bay. We knocked on the door, and Wendell answered it with a smug look on his face. My dad and I went in, sat down, and I reluctantly handed Wendell three dollars and said, "Sorry, Wendell." He gave me his best Uriah Heap smile and chewed his tongue.

We all knew Wendell was destined for bizarre things, and as he got older, he never disappointed us. His next project was an electric chair, a big throne-like object constructed out of two-by-fours and wired to a couple of huge train transformers. Several of us were there the afternoon he strapped Johnny Schembs into it and started diabolically turning up the dials on the transformers. None of us thought it would work, especially Johnny, who was the dare-devil of the group. We all figured that, if it <u>did</u> work, we'd see sparks and smoke fly out of it when Wendell turned up the transformers. When that didn't happen, we all laughed and began to make fun of him. By the time Johnny started hollering that his wrists were burning, it was too late. We got the straps off as fast as we could, but he already had some pretty nasty burns. Wendell was starting to emerge as our own Doctor Frankenstein.

Perhaps inspired by the questionable success of his electric chair, Wendell next built himself a coffin, painted it a shiny black, and attached gold handles to it. Later, in high school, he read <u>The Loved One</u> by Evelyn Waugh and was so inspired by it that he decided to start a pet mortuary. He and his friend Stanley Kohler bought an old hearse, fixed it up and started advertising burial services for family pets. Before long they were buying children's caskets and using them to bury German shepherds and French poodles. They offered full funeral packages, complete with eulogies and the wealthy matrons of Marin ate it up.

Wendell later became a licensed mortician and, at one point, managed to contract tuberculosis from a corpse. I was home from the seminary for the summer and heard he was in the hospital, so I went to visit him. We hadn't seen each other for several years and, for the first time since I had known him, he actually seemed genuinely happy to see me. He claimed that his illness was due to his employer's negligence, and that he was going to sue. I believe he did, and I believe he won.

The last time I ever saw Wendell was at a party in the Haight Ashbury in 1967. We talked for a bit and I asked what he was doing.

"Would you believe that I'm a member of the John Birch Society?" he asked.

"I'd believe anything about you, Wendell," I replied.

He pulled out a badge and stuck it in my face. "And would you believe I'm doing it under cover for the FBI?"

Shortly thereafter, Wendell supposedly got involved with Anton LaVey and the Church of Satan. Legend has it that Wendell provided them with their first altar, a gravestone which he stole from an old cemetery.

Turns out the nuns' distrust of Wendell was well-founded.

The Sin of Sex
The Sexiness of Sin

"Sensual pleasure can never be without sin."

St. Gregory the Great (My namesake)

The word "sex" was seldom uttered by Catholics in the 50s. Instead, we had code words for sex, words such as "the flesh" or "impurity" or "carnal pleasure." As we got older, the words got longer and harder to pronounce – "lasciviousness," "fornication," "adultery." Though we didn't really understand any of them, they all conjured up images of hellfire and charred, writhing naked bodies. That was enough.

Going to hell had always been a source of anxiety for me, but it became a major preoccupation after Father Leonard told me in confession that something called "masturbation" was a mortal sin. That was the first time I had ever heard the term, and it sounded like something out of a horror movie. When I realized it described something I had been innocently doing for some time, I was terrified. How could something that felt so good have such a horrible name? Masturbation, I realized later, was but one of the many sexual icebergs which grew up from Catholicism's pervasive subcontinent of Original Sin.

Father Leonard was the second pastor we had at our new parish, St. Sebastians. Since we didn't have a church, we used the chapel at Marin Catholic High School, and I was one of the few altar boys in the parish. Each Friday night or Saturday afternoon, I would go to confession in one of the small, closet-like cubicles in the back of the chapel. Invariably, after he'd finished giving me absolution, Father Leonard would lean over and whisper through the grate, "Uh, Greg, do you suppose you could serve the 8:30 Mass tomorrow?" He never even pretended not to know who I was, and it never bothered me, since my sins were pretty inconsequential and predictable week to week – like getting mad at my mother, or using "swear words" such as "damn" or "hell." He must have decided that my guilt needed a little enhancement that day he started quizzing me about rubbing my penis and getting pleasure from it. I was surprised to know that anyone else was even aware of penis rubbing. I figured it was something I had discovered on my own. When he told me it was a mortal sin, and that I'd go to hell if I kept it up, I was shocked. How could I have come so close to eternal damnation and not even have known about it? My grandmother had talked a lot about hell and about sin, but "penis" and "sex" were words that had never crossed her lips.

My folks hadn't discussed sex with me before this either, and it would be another year before my dad would get up enough courage to sit down with me and candidly confront the issue. When it finally happened, I could tell he wasn't comfortable talking about it, and that he'd probably been put up to it by my mother. He limited his remarks to something like this:

"Uh, you may find that once in a while...you'll be having a dream...and that you will, ah, wake up and...uh, feel fluid coming out of your penis. That's called a 'nocturnal emission' and, uh, well, it's not a sin, even though it feels good. So don't worry about it."

That was the extent of my sex education, administered by a loving father who was no doubt trying to pass down to me the one legal loophole to pleasure that he had discovered as an Irish Catholic.

Death

"Remember that thou art dust and unto dust thou shalt return."

Ash Wednesday Liturgy

My grandmother died just before Christmas when I was in seventh grade. This was a traumatic event for me, even though I knew that she was ready and willing to go, and even though I wasn't worried at all about her getting right into Heaven, what with all the poor-souls she had saved from Purgatory. I also knew she was very relieved to be free of what she had always called "this vale of tears."

But I was still upset. She had been my closest companion for the last five years, and, now that she had left me behind, life seemed very strange and empty. I was in a black hole. She had so oriented me to the afterlife, that every earthly moment seemed empty and insubstantial. Nothing lasted. Nothing was worth anything. During a

Boy Scout softball game, I stood out in center field, looking down at my mitt as I snapped the fingers of my right hand.

"Gone...gone...gone," I said with each snap. "Nothing lasts. Every moment disappears as soon as you pay attention to it."

I struggled with this feeling of fleeting emptiness for at least a year, and it haunts me to this day, often casting life into a futile evanescence. My grandmother taught me not to fear death, but she was unable to teach me how to embrace life.

The feeling that life was meaningless and empty, except as a preparation for the world to come, haunted me, and I found myself growing more and more separated from my peers as I strove to achieve the kind of perfection I knew my grandmother and God expected. During this time Jesus receded into the background and God the Father – the judging God of my Grandmother – moved in, sternly watching as I entered the dangerous rapids of puberty.

Sex was all around me. My eighth grade classmates were going to mixed parties, despite the prohibitions of the nuns. Friends in the neighborhood were starting to smoke, and pass around dirty pictures, which I found alluring and therefore ran from. Puberty was frightening. A few years earlier, I had realized that I wasn't cut out for "growing up." I wanted to stay nine years old, because I liked the innocence and security of it. I liked the fact that I could still be mischievous without being taken seriously, something that would change after I became a teenager. I liked the fact that even God didn't take me seriously at this age; that meant I couldn't really anger Him. But later...? That summer of my ninth year I stood across the street from my house, my foot up on the rail of the bridge which covered the creek. I stared into the slow-moving water, thinking, "I never want to get any older than I am right now. It won't be any fun. People will start taking me too seriously." This was two years before my grandmother died. I was looking into the future, to the time when I would, indeed, become much too old and take myself much too seriously.

When my grandmother died, I was more convinced than ever that she had been right: life was truly fleeting, the material world was an illusion, and the only things worth doing were those that would bring one to Heaven. My grandmother's core admonition to me had been: "Greggie, I don't care if you never make a cent; just be a saint." I, of course, took her quite literally, and committed myself to the cultivation of virtue and the avoidance of material success.

As long as she was alive, her powerful presence gave credence to her worldview, but once she died, that worldview began to seem rather dour and oppressive, though I still felt bound by its strictures. As puberty set in, things got worse, and I began to feel despair, as though I was on the brink of violating my pact with my grandmother and plunging headlong into Hell. Under her tutelage I had begun to see myself as one of the elect, one of those courageous few who were willing to live by the letter of the law. Now "the few" had suddenly become reduced to "the one."

Rites of Passage

Eighth grade was a rite of passage in many ways. It was the year we were to receive the sacrament of Confirmation, Catholicism's pale equivalent of the Bar Mitzvah, which signified our passage into adulthood, and, more importantly, our initiation as "Soldiers of Christ."

Late in the summer, I heard that Piero had moved to San Francisco, where his dad taught at the university, and that he wouldn't be returning to St. Anselm's for eighth grade. I was devastated. He was my best friend and the captain of our team. How would I ever make it through the year?

I also heard that two of my other friends weren't coming back either. Arnie Kunst had moved to Sacramento, and Phil Beyman was transferring to the public school in Kentfield. Phil and I had been traffic boy partners the year before, and he had talked at length about how he wanted to get away from the nuns and transfer to public school, but I never thought his mother would let him do it. But all of a sudden he was gone.

To make things worse, just before we returned to school in the fall, we heard that Sr. Noella, the school principal and eighth grade teacher, had suddenly become seriously ill and died, just before the start of school. She was well liked, both as a teacher and as a principal, and we were disappointed and saddened by her death. We took our grief out on her replacement, an elderly nun who had been prematurely snatched from a skin cancer operation and pressed suddenly into service as our teacher, the bandages still on her face. We nicknamed her "Scabby," in a typical show of adolescent empathy. Thus began one of the worst years of our grammar school lives. Scabby had very little sense of humor and her frequent outbursts of anger only egged us on to make her life as miserable as possible. When she came in after recess one day and found the wilted carrot that Danny Taylor, at my urging, had tossed onto her well-molded seat cushion, she was outraged. Somehow the carrot symbolized to her an obscene scatological insult, and she went berserk, interrogating the entire class one by one to discover the perpetrator of the foul deed. Danny didn't confess and none of us squealed on him. The stalemate continued all afternoon and, when the final bell rang, there were still no admissions. That didn't stop Scabby. It was a Friday, and she knew everyone wanted to get home, especially the degenerate types that would have done such a thing. So she picked out her least favorite students, about 10 in all, mainly boys, though a few girls as well, and told them they would have to stay all weekend until someone confessed. The rest of us thanked our lucky stars and bolted out of there.

The standoff continued for three more hours, according to reports. Then, at around six o'clock, Bob Murnane, who had been emerging as a moral force in our class ever since his announcement that he was thinking about entering the seminary, stood up and boldly confessed. Scabby was satisfied. She had won the day. The forces of evil had succumbed to her stern hand. She let everyone go home.

On Monday morning, she announced solemnly: "Robert Murnane has confessed to putting the carrot on my chair."

Murnane leapt out of his chair. "I didn't do it, Sister. I only confessed so that we could go home. It wasn't fair making everyone stay like that. You forced me to confess."

Now Scabby was on the defensive. Parents had called the school when their kids were late getting home on Friday and she knew she was on shaky ground. In what was as close to an apology as nuns could allow themselves, she changed the subject and told us to take out our Arithmetic books.

"Pachukes"

That was the year of pegger pants and black wing tip shoes, with horseshoe taps on the heels and white paint on the welts. It was also the year of the "DA" (duck's ass) hairstyle with the little fishhook dangling over the forehead. The official colors were pink and charcoal, and you had to wear your MacGregor windbreaker with the collar up. The belts were skinny pink suede with black on the edges. Very cool.

The nuns tried to outlaw the whole style, but fashion prevailed over fear, and even straight arrows like myself came to school decked out in pink and black. The whole thing had a certain sexual aura to it, as disobedience always did in Catholic schools. I got my first pair of horseshoe taps at the shoe repair store in San Anselmo. As I crashed out of the store and down the sidewalk, I felt like John Wayne walking into a shootout. What a rush!

Even with my horseshoe taps, I never made it to "cool." I didn't have what it took to become a member of the hip elite, probably because I had already committed myself to be a saint. Sanctity implies a certain vulnerability and cool guys aren't supposed to be vulnerable. I, on the other hand, was very vulnerable, a skinny kid prone to getting a lot of colds and sore throats; a perfect candidate for sanctity.

In the eighth grade I got a case of strep throat that was so painful I was unable to swallow. The doctor hospitalized me immediately and suggested to my parents that we try one of the new "miracle drugs" which had recently come on the market. My mother heard him say "miracle" and probably assumed it was a Catholic drug. I was given a massive dose of something called "Teramycin" and woke up the next morning without a trace of a sore throat. The miracle had happened. Or so I thought.

Confirmation – facing death

The most important event of the year for us eighth graders was Confirmation, which always happened in May. This was a big deal, because it was the only sacrament administered to us by a <u>bishop,</u>

and, in order to prove our worthiness, we had to be able to answer any catechism question he asked us. There was no way to know what questions he'd pick, or which kids he'd call on, so we all had to memorize everything. The presence of the bishop at confirmation made this a high stakes event for the nuns as well, and they let it be known that they weren't going to tolerate any foolishness from us. Half the class was made up of public school kids, and a lot of them hadn't had the brainwashing we Catholic school kids had, so it was a bit of a dicey operation for the nuns. You could tell they felt like they were in some foreign country trying to educate the natives.

Each parish had a separate confirmation ceremony, so the kids from St. Sebastian's parish were bussed every Friday afternoon to Marin Catholic High School, where we had our confirmation class in the chapel. One Friday in April, as our bus pulled into the parking lot, we saw a large group of high school students crowding around an ambulance, which was just beginning to pull away. There was a tangible aura of shock and grief over the crowd and someone came over and told us in hushed tones that a classmate of ours, Russell Thayer, had been hit by a car driven by one of the high school seniors and that they thought he was dead. He and a friend had evidently hitchhiked over to watch a baseball game. I felt a sickness in the pit of my stomach as I thought of Russell, sitting in our classroom at St. Anselm's an hour earlier, and now being hauled off to the mortuary…dead. He had always been a popular kid, a little wild, a good athlete, not much of a student (which, of course, made him that much more cool), and not really part of my group of friends. But he had invited me to his birthday party in the third grade, before a more rigid social structure split us onto opposing teams, so I had always felt an unspoken bond with him.

I had already been viewing life through the gray lens of death, ever since my grandmother died the year before, but this was a whole different experience. I had never worried about my grandmother or Sister Noella getting into heaven. They were shoo-ins. But I wasn't sure about Russell. Given his wild streak, he could have done something bad during the week, figuring he'd confess it on Saturday. And here it was, Friday afternoon, and he was suddenly snatched away, maybe with a mortal sin still on his soul. Part of me knew that the tragedy of his death should occasion heartfelt grief in me, rather

45

than moralistic speculations about the state of his soul; and I envied the genuine emotions felt and expressed by my female classmates; but I couldn't escape my grandmother's mindset, so I prayed what now, in retrospect, seem very condescending prayers for Russell's delivery from evil.

Russell's luck had been bad from the start. In second grade, at our First Holy Communion, we had all lined up in our white suits and dresses, ready to process into church, and then noticed that Russell was missing from the line. The story soon reached us that Russell's mother was in the hospital, and that his father, distracted by the chore of getting three young children ready for church, had failed to keep close enough watch on Russell, who had forgotten and taken a sip of water, thus disqualifying him from receiving his First Holy Communion that morning. (In those days, Catholics had to abstain from both food and water from midnight if they wanted to receive communion). What, in more humane times, would have occasioned a simple dispensation by an understanding pastor became a tragic flaw which branded Russell for life.

Russell's death further weakened the already-tenuous connection I had with "the world." As I looked around me, I found it very strange that people could go blithely about their day-to-day lives, seemingly oblivious to the ever-present threat of death and judgment.

How not to succeed in high school

A year later, in 1954, I entered Marin Catholic High School, still trying to reconcile my dead grandmother's moral rigidity with the Elvis revolution going on around me. I was placed in the college prep track, which meant a hefty curriculum of Latin and Algebra, and I embarked on an active social program. I enthusiastically joined the ham radio club and the school newspaper, and I tried out for the freshman basketball team, where my athletic fantasies were rapidly downshifted to the status of third string forward.

Shortly after school started, on the eve of the big football game with Drake High, I came down with my annual Fall cold, complete with sore throat, sniffles, etc. This time, however, there was something else. Bright red dots started to appear on my chest. I didn't think much about them, but showed them to my mother anyway. She immediately called the doctor and the next thing I knew I was in the hospital for a week, subjected to two bone marrow tests to determine the cause of my "thrombocytopenic purpura." My platelet count had fallen precipitously, so my blood wasn't coagulating properly, resulting in internal bleeding with telltale red dots or "purpura." When the tests came out inconclusively, my disease was labeled "Idiopathic thrombocytopenic purpura," meaning that the doctors couldn't figure out what caused it. Years later I was told by a technician in a blood bank that thrombocytopenic purpura was one of the proven side-effects of Teramycin (my "miracle drug"), but at the time, my doctors didn't even consider it. I was out of school for eight weeks, and had to go to the hospital every morning for blood tests. My activities were severely restricted, lest I bump into something and erupt in a plasma volcano. Then the doctors put me on Cortisone, and I suddenly blimped into a chubby-cheeked doughboy.

I had never been much of a student during grammar school, always preferring sports and mischief to studying, but now I had no choice. When the doctor finally let me go back to school, he gave me strict orders:

"No sports of any kind. Absolutely no fighting. And be careful not to bump into any desks, because you could bleed to death."

Egghead

I waddled back to high school seeing myself as a fat wimp, unsuited for survival on the earth plane. My self-confidence was destroyed, or at least severely damaged. With all my other options cut off, I started actually studying for the first time in my life. After a while, to my surprise, I found that the discipline and focus of studying appealed to my Spartan psyche. Later that year, I even got elected class president. That came as a real shock, since I still considered myself a loser, due to my blood disease. I was terribly shy around girls and coped with dances by becoming the school's sound technician, so that I could play the records rather than dance to them. Sex was still a mysterious thing to me, terrifying in its undefined pervasiveness, a dangerous mystery from which my grandmother's values had excluded me. Everyone seemed to know more about it than I did.

In my sophomore year, I began to make friends with some of my instructors, who of course encouraged me to engage in more academic pursuits. Father Cornelius Burns, a scholarly young priest whose childhood polio had left him with a limp that might well have precipitated his academic orientation, became my mentor. He was a committed teacher of Latin and English, and his enthusiasm for learning infected me. At his urging, I entered and won an essay contest sponsored by the Optometrists' Association of California, and was flown to Los Angeles, along with him and my parents, to receive the award.

He distilled classical learning for me, and gave me a passion for figuring out the roots of words and their often-unpredictable evolutions. He also bequeathed me a couple of proverbs, which I've come to appreciate more the older I get:

"The weakest ink is stronger than the strongest memory."

I now write down the title of every book and movie suggestion I get from friends, even when the hubris of drink tells me that there is no way I can possibly forget them.

"Repetitio est mater studiorum" I remember this one well, perhaps because he repeated it so many times. ("Repetition is the mother of studies"). In our Catholic world of eternal essences, repetition seemed to bring insight and salvation. It seemed an efficient tool for programming a stable future. In those days, when life seemed more predictable, and principles more immutable, I followed this proverb devotedly.

Later, however, after I had plunged precipitously into the existential chaos of the 60s, repetition lost its appeal and I preferred to crash heedlessly into new adventures rather than savoring the lessons of the past. I knew Father Burns would never have approved of this reckless approach to life and learning, and did my best to forget his admonitions, but his proverb remained graven into my soul and my memory.

***

Part of me really longed to be more of a clutch player in the game of life, but the other part was still striving toward the detached sainthood to which I had dedicated myself at my grandmother's knee.

In the absence of much real experience of normal teenage life, I was left with only my fears and moralistic judgments. Even these, however, were no longer the sure and righteous judgments of my grandmother, but had become the meek and tentative judgments of a plump wimp struggling to salvage some vestige of his former identity as a spiritual warrior. I spent a lot of time talking to Jesus during that time, trying to figure out what was going on in my life. Since there was nothing I could do about my illness, I decided to follow my grandmother's advice and "offer it up" to God. I found consolation in that conscious acceptance of the will of God. Pretty soon the "will of God" included everything over which I had no control – most of my life, actually.

Vocation

Q. What name is given to this divine call and how can we discover this call?
A. This divine call is named a vocation to the priestly or religious life. We can discover it in our constant inclination to such a life from the pure and holy motive of serving God better in it, together with our fitness for it, or, at least, our ability to prepare for it, also in our true piety and mastery over our sinful passions and unlawful desires.

– Baltimore Catechism

Near the end of my sophomore year, there was an announcement on the loudspeaker that the entrance exam for the seminary would be given the next weekend. Anyone who was interested needed to sign up within the next two days. Over the years, the idea of becoming a priest had periodically crossed my mind, but it never went beyond a vague fantasy, never got to the point of my actually wanting to do anything about it. I went to bed that night, vaguely aware that the test was going to be given and that there was a sign-up procedure for it, but not really giving it any serious thought. Shortly after drifting off to sleep, I got a sudden, strong message that I should take the test. I don't remember whether it was a voice, or an impulse, or a dream. All I know is that it fit the general description of a "vocation," a calling from God. And it seemed to come from Jesus rather than from some

49

more generic Godhead. It was enough for me, a feeling of connection with a deep center within myself. I got up, walked into the living room, where my folks were still up reading, and announced to them that I had decided to take the test for the seminary.

My mother, ever the controlled schoolteacher, was surprised, and quite obviously pleased, but kept a shackle on any overt enthusiasm. My dad, on the other hand, got very excited. He had been a longtime member of the Serra Club, a Catholic men's group dedicated to encouraging vocations to the priesthood, so, for him, my potential decision to enter the seminary was a real coup. He was ready to start calling his friends. I warned them both that I wasn't making any decisions beyond taking the test, not to get their hopes up, and definitely not to start telling their friends. They both agreed, but I knew my dad was never going to be able to contain himself.

I'm sure part of the appeal in taking the test was that I knew it would bond me closer to some of the priests who were my favorite teachers. They would begin to see me as a potential colleague, a member of their fraternity. That was important to me, since I had basically substituted academics for a social life.

I wasn't really thinking much about how my classmates at Marin Catholic would react. I guess I assumed no one would notice or care, since I had never thought of myself as worth noticing. What I found, to my surprise, was that there was a real mystique about someone going to the seminary. In those days, Catholics took the notion of a vocation very seriously, and if someone was called to the priesthood, that was a very special thing. I was surprised at the response I got from the other students. Girls who had never previously spoken to me went out of their way to wish me well. Guys that I had always seen as tough, and wild, and cynical about religion suddenly became very serious and sincere when they told me they thought I would make a good priest. It was as though they appreciated me for doing it on their behalf. All of a sudden, I had become a different person in their eyes, and I was communicating with a deeper part of them. I liked the feeling. It imbued celibacy and priesthood with a heroic dimension.

The seminary test was given at Sacred Heart High School in San Francisco on a Saturday morning. I don't remember much about it, except being worried that I would score too low in Latin and have to repeat my sophomore year. Latin was the most important subject in the seminary of the '50s, and though I had taken Latin for two years at Marin Catholic, everyone knew that seminarians were smarter than regular high school students and besides, they specialized in Latin.

The Little City of God

"There are two cities, the City of God and the city of the World; and these two cities are made by two loves: the earthly City by love of oneself even to contempt of God; the heavenly City by love of God even to contempt of oneself."

– St. Augustine

The results from the test came back a few weeks later and I was informed that I had done well enough on the test, not only to be accepted into the seminary, but to be placed in the "A" group in my class. (True to the Catholic principle of unabashed hierarchy, the seminary divided students into two groups, based on their test scores.) The test, I found out later, had not been the sole criterion for entry into the seminary. A thorough behind-the-scenes investigation had occurred, involving my pastor, my teachers, and, I assume, the entire archdiocesan gossip network. My family was evidently found to be reputable, no divorces or other moral blotches on their record, my personal character was deemed acceptable, my mental health seemingly intact. I received an official letter of acceptance from Fr. Campbell, the President of St. Joseph's College, the minor seminary. Enclosed was a small booklet entitled "The Little City of God," written by the Very Reverend Lyman A. Fenn, former president of St. Joseph's and then a professor of Moral Theology at St. Patrick's Major Seminary. I opened it and read:

"St Joseph's College is the little 'City of God,' complete in itself, standing isolated against the 'City of the World,' having within its limits and independent of 'that other city,' all the means and possibilities to equip young citizens for their future warfare against the 'City of Confusion.'"

I loved it. This was right down my alley. Spiritual warfare, in the Augustinian mode. Let me at 'em! Further on, in the section on the training of young seminarians, I read:

"Constant self-surrender which leads to abiding self-control, is the keynote of his character building; not the modern self-improvement or progress."

Though I didn't realize it at the time, this repudiation of progress by Fr. Fenn would later pitch the two of us into mortal combat during the ideological wars of the 60s. However, in 1957, to an idealistic 16 year old Irish Catholic warrior, the idea of a strict, authoritarian medieval boot camp was an appealing concept.

#174

My new identity arrived next – a batch of laundry numbers that were to be sewn on every item of clothing I planned to bring to the seminary. My number was 174 and my mother and Mrs. Pulskamp spent what seemed like the entire summer sewing numbers on my underwear, handkerchiefs, shirts, and socks. Along with the laundry numbers, came a list of items which we were required to bring with us to St. Joseph's: shoe shine kit, dust mop, broom, waste basket, drinking glass, spoon, rug, and dresser. I went about collecting these items as if they were hallowed ceremonial objects.

The instructions said that nothing was to be hung on the walls of students' rooms, so I didn't have to worry about packing any pennants or photographs. And I really didn't have to buy any new clothes either. Seminarians were expected to wear a tie and either a sweater or jacket to all classes, meals, and prayers, and all our clothes were to be "conservative in color and design." Consequently, every male I knew took the opportunity to unload on me any dull and ugly item of clothing that he hadn't worn for the past thirty years. (Sadly, but predictably, my cheerless wardrobe resonated perfectly with the somber fashions of my classmates.)

As the summer wore on, I began to find that my persona was gradually changing. Instead of the self I had always been, a new self was being thrust upon me by my friends and acquaintances. I was suddenly a priest. They began to protect me from "worldly" things, assuming I was now a "man of the cloth." They would suddenly crease their brows when I walked up, and feign deep conversation. I was gradually being turned into an alien, a person apart. Since I had always considered myself a bit of an outsider anyway, the only person

I knew who was personally committed to sanctity as a career goal, this reaction didn't totally surprise me, though I found worrisome the new respect people were showing me. What if I didn't stay in the seminary? What if it turned out that God wasn't really calling me to the priesthood? What then? All these people – especially my father – would really be disappointed. And my grandmother, what was she thinking about all this, as she peered down from her heavenly rocking chair? She was probably pleased, but she was also watching my attitude, making sure my motives were pure and that I wasn't falling prey to the sin of pride.

I worked at the high school that summer, watering plants, re-coding locker combinations, and varnishing desks. I was paid $1 an hour, $40 a week. I liked the job, enjoyed the challenge of proving myself a "good hand," and felt that I was finally emerging from the wimp status imposed on me by the previous year's mysterious blood disease.

I was also getting more and more excited about the seminary. I had talked to a few friends who had already gone to St. Joseph's, and had heard favorable reports about it. The seminarians sounded like a fun group, mischievous as well as studious. There was also a well-organized sports system in which everyone was expected to participate. Students were drafted on one of four teams when they first entered, and they remained on that team for the duration of their stay in the seminary. This would be my first opportunity to play sports since my illness, and, since I would be away from home, my parents wouldn't have to know or worry about it. The idea of a sports program in which everyone participated really appealed to me. That way sports could become what they had been in my childhood – a joyful way to bond with others through play, rather than an elitist competitive system that excluded 90% of the student body. As the departure date neared, my excitement grew, but it paled in the face of my dad's exuberance. He couldn't restrain himself from trumpeting to everyone that his son, his only son, was going into the seminary.

I better make this good, I thought.

IV.   The Fourth Joyful Mystery:
The Presentation in the Temple

Let us contemplate, in this mystery, how the Blessed Virgin Mary, in the day of her purification, presented the Child Jesus in the temple, where holy Simeon, giving thanks to God, with great devotion received Him into his arms.

<u>The New Key of Heaven</u>
A Complete Prayerbook for Catholics
Regina Press, 1949

Finally, the day arrived and we packed up the green '53 Chevy with my dresser, mop, rug, clothes, drinking glass, shoeshine kit – everything checked off from the list we had received at the beginning of the summer. My dad drove and my mother and grandfather sat in the back seat, flanked by the boxes, mop, and broom that hadn't fit in the trunk. We drove across the Golden Gate Bridge, then south through San Francisco until we reached the peninsula. We took El Camino Real south, all the way through Mountain View, until we reached Grant road, where we turned west through miles of rich orchard country with acres and acres of fruit trees. Father Fenn had described the area in <u>The Little City of God</u>, and had managed to imbue even its minor geographic features with an aura of moral superiority:

"The Preparatory Seminary is situated five miles southwest of Mountain View in a sheltered depression of the first rises of the Monte Bello ridge bounding the western edge of the Santa Clara Valley. Westerly behind the campus rise the solemn heights of Black Mountain, sheltering the valley from the winds of the Pacific. Before it, seen through a gap in the low easterly hills, is an expanse of rich fruitfulness stretching seven miles to the lower reaches of the Bay and across the Valley to the quiet and majestic Coastals. The climate is equable. Sea and mountain air, and hot dry sunlight, are

tempered one by the other and the shelter of the surrounding hills deflects winds and fog to great heights."

We drove through the acres of fruit trees before turning on a quiet road marked "St. Joseph's Avenue" which narrowed into a stand of eucalyptus trees and then turned into a long lane, bordered on both sides by hedges. Eventually we reached a large grassy circle with palm trees. We followed the arrow to the right until we reached the top of the circle where the seminary building stood. It was a four-story edifice with an elegant bell tower extending two stories above the roofline. As Father Fenn had written, the building had "a certain severity of outline, unavoidable in an architecture designedly stout." This was no frat house.

A Step at a Time

We were met in front of the building by an older seminarian – a "Poet" or "Rhet," I later learned – who looked up my name, read off my room number and pointed up to the third floor. He told us we could use the elevator in the front hall for the transportation of the dresser, but that we would have to use the stairs for everything else. He hastened to add that the elevator was off limits, except today, and that we would need to park around the other side of the building and use the door over there.

"No one is allowed to bring anything through the front door."

Fine. We could handle stairs. My dad was a youthful 71, my grandfather a nimble 87. We had stairs at home. No problem. We drove around the building, parked, and wrestled the dresser up a short flight of stairs to an outside door, then down a long corridor to the elevator, up to the third floor, then down another corridor and around the corner to my assigned room. The door stood open, revealing a room about 9 x 12, with a washbasin and mirrored medicine chest next to the door, a small closet next to that, a twin bed, and a window. I went to the window and discovered that the room looked out to the front of the building, where our guide was busy giving directions to another family. Luckily the staircase was closer to my room than the elevator was, so that made things a little easier than they might have been, but after about three trips my grandfather was huffing and puffing, so my mother told him to sit down in my room and we'd do the rest. A lot of other guys were moving in, and many of them had little sisters and brothers who were yelling and running up and down the corridors. As I looked around, I didn't see anyone whose folks were as old as mine, and that made me feel somewhat vulnerable and a bit more protective of my little band of oldsters. Even in this old world place, we represented an older world yet.

Once we got everything in the room, my mother made the bed for me and made sure everything was sorted out in my closet and medicine chest. By now, I was getting anxious for them to leave, because I knew I needed to start focusing on my new surroundings and, as long as they were there, I wouldn't be able to do it. Finally we went down to the car and said our goodbyes. I could tell this was a lot tougher on them than it was on me, even though I was feeling a little choked up myself, realizing how much I loved these three people who made up my small family. We hugged and kissed and they all said they would be praying for me, and to write when I could, and that they would write, and not to forget to eat well, etc. Finally I watched them drive off in the Chevy, back to the world that, until now, had been mine. Then I turned around and climbed the stairs to my new world, realizing that three flights <u>was</u> a lot of stairs.

First Impressions

As I approached my room, I noticed someone moving stuff into the room next door. He saw me, smiled, and introduced himself as Dick Ormsby. He had a resonant voice that had a welcome warmth to it and he said he'd be happy to show me around once he got his stuff put away. He'd already been in the seminary for two years, having entered right out of the eighth grade, at age 14, like most of my other classmates. They were called "orig's" (originals), I learned later, and I was, consequently, a "non-orig" – a term that implied second-class citizenship in the seminary of that day.

Dick spent the next half hour filling me in on seminary trivia and terminology – professors' nicknames and foibles, the personalities of our classmates, highpoints of the daily schedule, etc. I had heard a lot of this lore before, from other guys who had spent time in the seminary, but it was good to get a recap, since it was going to take me a while to assimilate everything.

Suddenly I heard a sound floating down the corridor, a rich tenor voice, singing in a British accent.

"All I want is a room somewhere, far away from the cold night air."

Dick started laughing. "That's Bob Carroll. He's gone to every movie and play ever made, and he knows all the songs. He saw 'My Fair Lady' this summer."

Bob rounded the corner, a light-complected redhead with a sharp beak and dancing blue eyes. He reminded me of a bird. I shook hands with him, not realizing that I was meeting someone who would prove to be one of the most fascinating human beings I would ever experience.

Dick and I walked around "the House", meeting all sorts of guys, some of whom seemed excited to be back, others who expressed regret at having to leave summer vacation behind. Some were very friendly, others merely polite, and a few seemed cynical, almost mean. I began to realize that the seminary was not much different from any other school.

By 5:30 the last of the parents had driven off, and Dick told me it was time to get ready for our first official function, supper. We made our way to the central courtyard where everyone was gathering in preparation for the Angelus bell. On the way we checked the bulletin board where the dining room seating assignments were posted. As luck would have it, Dick and I were assigned to the same table.

About 200 seminarians, all wearing ties and jackets, were milling around the courtyard, exchanging greetings, shaking hands, and asking each other about their summer vacations. I began to detect a social hierarchy in the group and to notice that much of it revolved around sports. The upper echelon seemed mainly populated by jocks, or at least by those who could engage in jock-like banter. Jibes were being thrown good-naturedly from one group to another and gradually certain individuals began to emerge as the focus of attention. I was still under Dick's wing, and most of the guys we met didn't seem to rank very high on the jock scale. But then we ran into a group of guys who looked like the local mafia. Their leader was a guy built like a linebacker who was wearing a fancy sports jacket and white bucks. Dick seemed a little less sure of himself as he introduced me to him.

"Greg, this is Mike McLaughlin, another classmate of ours."

McLaughlin reached out his hand and gave me a rather half-hearted handshake, all the while looking over my shoulder, playing the crowd. Then, speaking out of the corner of his mouth in a low, almost conspiratorial tone, eyes still darting around behind me, he said, "What parish ya from?"

"St. Sebastian's. In Kentfield."

"Marin, eh? I used to play ball with a guy from Marin." He gave me the name of some guy I'd vaguely heard of, but had never met.

"I've heard his name, but I don't know him."

He and his sidekicks were already moving on, heading toward another more boisterous group as I feebly said, "Nice to meetcha."

"Mac's the assistant captain of the Trojans," Dick said. "He's a jock."

"Is he always that rude," I asked.

"No. Just when he's in a group. When he's by himself, he can be a pretty nice guy." (Lucky for me, because by the grace of the Phoenecian alphabet and our Irish heritage, McA and McL ended up sitting next to each other for the next six years.)

At exactly 5:57 the Angelus bell sounded and suddenly the courtyard cacophony went strangely silent. Many students closed their eyes and moved their lips in silent prayer. Others continued looking around, shooting furtive smiles at friends. Then, as soon as the bell finished its toll, everyone began walking rapidly, silently, toward the "refectory," i.e., dining hall. It was very strange having everyone go silent and then suddenly start moving like that, and I was glad Dick had prepped me for it, so that I wasn't left standing there in a daze.

Fine Dining

We entered the refectory and everyone stood at his assigned chair, still in silence. I noticed there was a raised platform to one side of the room and there, atop their three-foot Mt. Olympus, stood the faculty around their table. When everyone was in place, Fr. Campbell, the rector, said something in Latin and the entire community barked something back in a single voice. I had no idea what they were saying and again experienced the old fears about my inadequacies in Latin. I later realized that their proficiency in responding came more from repetition than from cognition.

The prayer finished, everyone sat down, still in silence, and I noticed an older student ascending some stairs to a pulpit set high at one end of the refectory. Very methodically he opened the Bible and began reading from the New Testament, pronouncing each word very distinctly and carefully. This seemed to be serious business, and he wasn't about to sacrifice enunciation for expression. The reading ended in the same pained precision it had started, and, after a moment of silence, the rector's voice came again: "Tu autem, Domine, miserere nobis."

From the assembled students came, "Deo Gratias!" and everyone started talking at once. There were nine students at each table, all sitting in strict hierarchical fashion, from the "tablehead" down to the lowly "pilers," the youngest students, who were responsible for scraping the leftovers into a large pan at the end of each table. The tableheads were all in their senior year of high school – known as "fourth high" in seminary jargon – and it was their duty to keep order on the table. This job was made easier by a strict set of rules and customs that controlled behavior in the dining room. For instance, no one was allowed to stand up without the tablehead's permission, and then only at the risk of being reprimanded by the presiding faculty.

Each seat at the table was assigned a function. To the tablehead's immediate right sat his "right-hand man," to his left, the "left-hand man." These two were usually from "third high" and the former had the important duty of cutting the meat into nine equal pieces, the latter of similarly doling out the dessert, which was called "mystery," due to its often unfathomable ingredients. Just below them were the "butter cutters" whose job, on alternate days, was to carefully inscribe nine equal sections in the as-yet-undefined slab of butter which graced each table. Though the job title was "butter-cutter," the substance itself was never referred to as "butter," but rather as "grease."

Next to the bottom of the table sat the "milk-pourers" who had perhaps the easiest job, namely pouring the milk into nine squat glasses and passing them around the table. Milk was a staple, and you could usually get more of it by merely holding the milk pitcher in the air until one of the waiters came by and brought it into the kitchen for a refill. Actually, seconds could be requested for anything, though you were a lot less likely to get seconds on meat or mystery than on boiled potatoes or milk. This is where the skills of your right and left-hand men came in, since the faster the meat or dessert was subdivided and dispersed, the faster the empty plate could be held up, and the better your chance of securing seconds. Depending on the eating habits and appetite of the tablehead, meals sometimes resembled a track and field event much more than a gourmet dining experience.

At the bottom of the table sat the "pilers." These were always first high kids, who, I soon discovered, were also called "Sixth Latiners," due to the fact that they were still facing six years of Latin. Their job was to pile up all the dishes, after scraping the leftovers into a flat pan, and then to sort the dirty silverware in another pan. It was a messy job, but it was considered a good test of character for 14 year olds freshly ripped from their mothers' bosoms.

We got a full description of all these roles and responsibilities at that first supper. Because I was entering in third high, I was assigned the rather exalted position of left-hand man. This put me under a lot of pressure at dessert time, because one slip of the knife and the whole table would start howling, even though only the left-hand piler would really suffer the consequences of my inequity, since he would be left with the last, presumably the smallest, piece. Luckily, the butter-cutter to my left was also new to the seminary that year, so my inexperience was paled by his own and by that of four "Sixth Latiners" who were also on our table. The tablehead was a guy named Rich Mangini, an easy-going, pious sort of guy who was fun to be around, though he could definitely get his Italian dander up if someone challenged his authority. The ultimate weapon of the tablehead was to "stand up" on one of his charges. No one was allowed to stand up without permission, so if your tablehead "stood up on you" that meant he was calling the wrath of the faculty down on both of you, and you better be ready to defend yourself against his accusations. It was something that rarely happened, but, when it did, it would fill the room with whispers of ominous speculation.

That first meal ended with the ring of a bell and then another blurp of Latin from Fr. Campbell, followed by a hearty "Amen" from the student body. Everyone started talking again as they walked out of the refectory toward the chapel and I noticed again a certain hierarchy developing as certain students seemed to magnetically draw groups around them. Everyone went into the chapel for a token "visit" to the Blessed Sacrament, some staying but a moment, others engaging in what appeared to be a more intense spiritual conversation. After that, for about 20 minutes, we were allowed to walk around the grounds talking until the seven o'clock bell summoned us back to the chapel for the recitation of the rosary. Boisterous groups would randomly form during these short "recreation" periods and phalanxes of six or seven people would often pass each other and trade barbs like rival armies. Gradually, I came to realize that, often enough, these groups were rival armies, consisting of members of opposing sports teams locked in a year-long battle for the pennant.

The Draft

There were four teams in all – Bears, Indians, Ramblers, and Trojans. I knew that at the end of that first week in the seminary I would be picked by one of those teams, and that that team would determine a major part of my seminary identity. No one ever switched teams. You were a Bear or a Rambler for life. Your team comprised your basic social circle, and your performance on your team largely determined your status in the community at large. It also determined a good deal of your status with some of the faculty. All the members of the faculty had previously gone through seminary sport systems themselves and had acquitted themselves either well or poorly as athletes. Their own athletic prowess usually determined how much importance they felt sports should hold in the assessment of a priestly vocation.

I suppose the seminary was like any adolescent society, but here it was even more intense. There weren't any girls to turn our heads, any cars to race, any family events to distract us. The only outlet for all that pent-up adolescent adrenaline was sports.

61

The Training of His Mind

"The student for the diocesan priesthood receives a scholastic training which in length, in thoroughness, in intensity and continuity is equalled by no other profession."

The Little City of God
By Lyman A. Fenn, SS., DD.

During that first week, many things grabbed my attention. I had been placed in the "A" group of my class, due I guessed to my rather facile ability to do well on placement tests, rather than to any genuine knowledge or skill. I spent every new class period attempting to figure out just where I stood in this rather awesome intellectual hierarchy. This was not misplaced humility on my part, as my class included more than its share of intellectual luminaries. The first time I heard Tom Sheehan translate Latin, I was in awe. He leapt into the passage like a frog into a warm lily pond. While the rest of us struggled over esoteric grammatical constructions and idioms, Tom swam through them effortlessly and joyously. I had never seen anyone enjoy learning that much. He approached all the other subjects the same way, chewing into history and literature and trigonometry with his insatiable intellect and inspiring the rest of us to attempt the same. There were other intellectual standouts in our class as well. Eddie Gaffney, the son of a longtime San Francisco congressman, combined a Renaissance brain with an Irish politician's wit. Bob Carroll was a literary genius and cultural savant, whose refined social graces masked a sarcasm that could wound and cripple anyone foolish enough to challenge him on matters belletristic. Alex Potter had a rebel's eclectic intellect which never quite bought the whole seminary system, but never openly rejected it either. Mike Murray, another "non-original," who had arrived a year earlier than I, had a quick, pragmatic mind that he dutifully applied to his assignments, but mainly reserved for his real passion – the sports page. Maurice Maybury was only an average student when it came to liberal arts, but a prodigal genius in math and science. There were others in the class, too, whom I watched with awe that first week: Conrad Gruber, Al

Larkin, Bob Murnane, Bill Finnegan, Pat Browne. They all seemed to be out of my league.

The most daunting class for me that first semester was Fr. Jack Olivier's Latin class. Jack was a bright, well-groomed Frenchman with a sarcastic wit and a fierce anal streak when it came to Latin and music (he was also the choir director). His class was hard, but often sparkly and entertaining. He was one of the most respected teachers we had, and I struggled to please him. Periodically, he would give us a Latin phrase to translate and discuss, and three of these have lodged in my brain ever since, assuming new depths of meaning in successive stages of my life. The first was *"Nemo dat quod non habet,"* which, simply translated, meant "No one gives what s/he does not have." As I recall, Jack explained that it was a theological concept, referring to the "Gifts of the Spirit," or something like that. It made little sense at the time, but it's made a lot more sense since then, as a rationale for my frequent bouts with unrequited love.

Another of Jack's sayings was *"Quidquid recipitur, recipitur per modem recipientis."* This one was more complicated and harder to memorize, but it seemed to contain a basic truth. "Whatever is received, is received through the mode (or capacity) of the receiver." This quote, Jack explained, had to do with Grace, and how not everyone receives the fullness of God's Grace, but only as much as they can handle. This seemed self-evident at the time, but, like the first, has assumed a much deeper significance since then. Together, these two sayings seem to form a complementary koan of love's mystery: You may be in love with someone, (have the love to give), but that person may not have the capacity to receive it (or vice-versa). Once you frame love in those terms, rejection seems easier to handle.

The third Latin saying that I will always thank Jack for is *"De gustibus non est disputandum"* (In matters of taste, there should be no argument). This fed my nascent libertarian spirit in the seminary, and has proven invaluable since then. Some years ago, I even taught it to my 8 year old son, hoping to give him an alternative perspective on conflict. Within the week, he used it on his mother after she attempted to convince him that Taco Bell's green chile was better than their red.

"Mom, de gustibus non est disputandum!"

"Whaaaatt??!!"

The Training of His Character

"The spirit that enforces the rule is not the coercive one of the barrack-room. Its prompt and exact observance is directed always towards forming in the boy the dispositions of Christ. His liberty being respected, he is urged to recognize the Divine Will in all that is required of him."

The Little City of God
By Lyman A. Fenn, SS., DD.

If the academics were demanding, they didn't hold a candle to the spiritual disciplines. On any given day, we were expected to pray at least 30 different times, and that didn't even include Mass, meditation, spiritual reading, confession, etc. I had always considered myself a pious person, but this was overwhelming.

The social milieu was also very different from anything I had ever experienced. All these guys were being trained to be "other Christs," so no matter what their mental state on any given day, they really TRIED to be friendly. This was shocking to me after my previous high school experience, because, even though Marin Catholic was a fairly friendly and intimate place as far as high schools went, you didn't have everybody saying hello to you like they did in the seminary. I reveled in that at first, until I detected a mechanical quality to the greetings and eventually began to prefer the rare explosions of genuine anger to these predictable smiles of programmed charity.

Physical Training

"The competition at St. Joseph's is very keen.
An intensive training precedes each sports season.
Boys who do not make the squads in any particular sport are just as anxious for their teams to win as the players themselves, and constitute an active rooting section on the sidelines."

The Little City of God
By Lyman A. Fenn, SS., DD.

In that first week, everything was new and fresh and challenging, especially the <u>big</u> thing that was going on behind the scenes, invisible to us newcomers. The team captains and their scouts were meeting regularly to decide whom they would pick in that year's draft. Every day, during the "long recreation," those of us who had just arrived at the seminary were expected to suit up in our athletic garb ("BOs" in seminary jargon) and participate in various games, while clipboard-bearing senior jocks walked around making judgments about our futures.

As much of a challenge as the seminary's entrance exam had been, this was more intense. I had longed to return to sports for two years, ever since my blood disease had turned me into a flabby egghead, and this was my chance. It wasn't that I was a great athlete, waiting to excel. It was that I missed, more than anything, the male ritual of self-definition that happens in team sports. I missed being part of the game. I missed the self-discovery that happens on court and field, and the bonds that develop on teams. Though playing sports wasn't my only reason for coming to the seminary, it was the thing about my vocation for which I was most grateful, for now I had an excuse, nay a mandate, to return to sports. Despite my parents' understandable concerns about my getting injured and bleeding to death, they had to realize that sports were an integral part of seminary life and training, and that, if God was calling me to the priesthood, He was also calling me back to sports. Admittedly, I was a bit nervous about the purpura myself, but I trusted that everything would be okay, and I was very excited.

My enthusiasm was dampened a bit one afternoon that first week, when, after hitting a pretty good line drive to right center, I was approached by my classmate and alphabetical next-door-neighbor, Mike McLaughlin. Mike was an outstanding athlete, slated to be next year's choice for Trojan captain, and he was scouting the new recruits. He sidled up to me with his clipboard and spoke out of the side of his mouth as though we were engaging in an illegal drug deal.

"Ever play any ball at Marin Catholic, Mac?" he asked in muted tones.

"No," I blurted nervously. "I got a blood disease in my freshman year and wasn't able to play."

He lifted his eyebrows, looked at me over his glasses, and curled the edge of his mouth.

"…Disease?"

Then he nodded sagely, made a quick mark on his clipboard and shuffled off, scribbling something else as he went.

During the next few days, I tried to identify the entire student body in terms of what team they were on. I started with my own class, seeing everyone in terms of green (Ramblers), blue (Bears), red (Trojans) or Yellow (Indians). I learned that the Indians had been a recent addition. Previous to the seminary's population explosion in the 50s, there had been only three teams; consequently, the Indians didn't go back generation to generation in the seminary like the other three teams. That was certainly true in our class. Almost all the captains-in-waiting had come from royal jock families: Mike McLaughlin, Denny O'Brien, and Danny Fitzgerald all had older brothers who had excelled in sports. Only Mike McNamara, next year's Indian captain, had no lineage. For one thing, he had no brothers who had been in the seminary (which may have been the reason he ended up on the Indians in the first place). I began to think of the Indians as the orphan team.

As I sat in Latin class, I tried to correlate the "A Group" students by their teams. Sheehan, Gruber, Larkin, Moorman, and Murnane were all Ramblers; Gaffney, Matosich, Duggan, and Murray were Bears; Potter, Perry, Ormsby, Carroll and Browne were Indians. There weren't very many Trojans in our class to start with, and the only two I could identify in the "A" group were Bill Finnegan and Larry Singleton. Bill was a cool, cynical guy who always seemed to be drinking cough syrup, and whose claim to fame was getting kicked in the ass one day by Fr. Taylor, who snuck up behind him when he thought he heard Bill doing an imitation of him outside the swimming pool. Singleton's memorable moment was when he was asked to translate "carpe diem" in Latin class, and he rendered it, "Grab the day."

I'm not sure why I was so curious about everyone's team affiliation. It certainly didn't determine their intelligence, or their personality, or even their athletic ability. And it was ridiculous to think that anyone had chosen the team they were on, even though they often acted as though they had. In retrospect, it was a lot like being born a Catholic or a Jew. It determined your social circle, which, I suppose, was plenty.

As the week wore on, everyone was speculating about the draft. The Indians had first pick because they had finished in last place the previous year. Everyone figured they'd pick Jack Conneely, a first high kid whose reputation as an athlete in his grammar school CYO league had preceded him. He was a cocky, tough little guy who immediately emerged as a leader by being the first in his class to charge the "fourth high stairs." This was a yearly ritual that took place during the week-long retreat at the beginning of the year. There were two sets of stairs on the high school side, one near the junior study hall, the other near the senior. The latter was the domain of the third and fourth year students, and they would typically gather on the stairs during the short recreations after meals. The extended silences of the retreat tended to build up the adrenaline level to a point where it had to find some release during these recreational windows, so it became a game to see which of the first high students were daring enough to rush the stairs and attempt to fight their way to the top. Usually the biggest guys were prodded by their classmates into doing it, and I remember one kid named Voight who reluctantly assumed the role of their Goliath for the first few days. But the guy who kept coming back, day after day, accomplices or not, was Jack Conneely. He'd wait until we were distracted by mail call or something else and then dart toward the stairs like a crazed kamikaze, thrashing his way up the stairs until the sheer mass of bodies congealed and pushed him back down. He had an instinct for competition, and this included challenging the jock pecking order. He won respect eventually, but his cocky attitude caused him to get a lot of "jake shampoos" (head inserted into a flushing toilet) in those early days.

One evening, during the retreat, I was standing on the stairs with other members of the third and fourth high classes, waiting for Conneely and his cohorts to charge. Instead, they threw an orange at us, which landed at my feet. I picked it up and, anxious to prove my bravado, threw it back at the large crowd of sixth latiners who had gathered down the road. As the orange arched its way toward them, the crowd parted, leaving only the visiting retreat master to receive the full impact of the orange on one of his polished black oxfords.

Somehow, this event has always stood out in my mind as a precursor to my relationship with organized religion.

When the draft came, the Indians did end up picking Conneely first – with some trepidation, as I remember, because he seemed awfully brash and hard to control. Everyone was afraid he might get thrown out, and then they would have wasted their first pick. Later I found out that I was also picked by the Indians, though much further down the line. I really hadn't had any inkling about which team would pick me, and was happy to have been picked at all. Once I had received the official mantel of "Indian," I had an automatic bond with one fourth of the student body. Even if we had nothing else in common and might never otherwise have had anything to do with each other, the serendipitous sharing of "Indian" gave us an instant bond.

Friendships

The first benefit of my new team came in the person of Pat Browne, who befriended me shortly after I became a fellow Indian. Pat was a tall good-looking kid who was a pretty fair athlete and a member of the jock elite. He was the first of the jock crowd that I really got to know, other than Mike McLaughlin, my alphabetical neighbor, and Mac wasn't about to bond with someone like me who wasn't a Trojan and who might end up on medical waivers. Pat was a funny, caustic guy, and a master of the one-line put-down. He was also one of the most straight-forward guys I ever met. You always knew where you stood with Pat and, if he liked you, you felt special – mainly because he spent most of his time categorizing the rest of the world as "assholes," "kiss-asses" or "wimps." He was an amazing combination of cynicism and vulnerability and was the first guy I knew who was as committed to pursuing friendships as I was. This might be explained by the fact that he, too, was an only child of older parents. His folks were native Irish and his dad worked for the railroad in nearby Sunnyvale. Pat eventually became a member of the Sulpicians, the French order whose specialty was teaching in seminaries, including St. Joseph's.

Pat would emerge after a meal, tap me on the arm and say, "Let's take a walk." Usually he had some story to tell me or some rumor to share, and I was pleased to be his confidante. However, even though we became good friends, we were both careful about what we revealed to each other, because we never knew what would later come out of our mouths in the heat of a bull session, when a circle of us would be standing around "cutting each other down." This, like sports, was an adolescent male ritual and sometimes could get pretty bloody without anyone really intending it. Our respect for personal boundaries was not that well honed at 16 years old. We were much more vulnerable than we let on, and consequently could strike back in ways that were much more hurtful than we were aware or intended. If sports and studies were essential to seminary life, the ability to fight back in one of these bull sessions was equally important. Pat was my role model in this craft. He would stand there on the edge of the circle, head cocked to one side, hands plunged deep into the pockets of his green, leather-sleeved "car coat," biding his time. The barbs would be thrown back and forth, from this side to that, and he would laugh along, waiting for his opening. Then he'd lay his one-liner in, stay long enough to get the laugh, and then deftly move out of the line of fire again. He had a good, swift delivery, and no one was very anxious to take him on. When I joined the group, he directed a lot of his lines my way, perhaps by way of initiating me into the process. After a while, I got pretty good at it myself, but first I had to pay my dues by being the butt of a lot of his jokes.

The one guy who could give it back to Pat was Al Potter. "Potts" was also an Indian, and was a big irreverent kind of guy who knew all Pat's idiosyncrasies on the basketball court, baseball diamond and soccer field. They always played on the same team and it wasn't uncommon for one of our basketball games to come to a complete halt while the two of them stood there swearing at each other for not passing the ball or because one of them had missed a shot. Al was real bright, and he decided early on that he probably wasn't going to become a priest, but that he wanted to stay in the seminary long enough to get a good education. This decision elevated him, in our eyes, to the status of a detached outsider, a role that was both mysterious and somewhat frightening to those of us who had not yet allowed ourselves to think such thoughts. The seminary faculty usually expelled anyone they perceived as not having a vocation to the priesthood, lest that person weaken the obedient consensus of the

69

brethren, so it was a tribute to Al's courage that he shared his plans with his classmates, and a tribute to his popularity that we protected his secret.

Amicitia Inimica

Many seminary friendships were based more on loyalty to a shared institution than on deep personal bonds. I suppose this is generally the case in "total institutions" whose members are kept in a pre-individualized state, dependent upon the approval of superiors for their self identity, but the seminary added another element – the mysterious ban on "particular friendships." The Latin term was "amicitia inimica," translated as "hateful friendships," and it made any one-on-one intimacy a subversive act. We were told always to be in groups of three or more, never just with one other person. Some guys were fortunate and came into the seminary accompanied by former friends from grammar school or had older siblings already in the seminary. These felt empowered to simply ignore the "amicitia inimica" taboo, and their friendships often gave them a healthy immunity from the more rigid and dehumanizing aspects of seminary culture.

Those of us who came in alone, however, without siblings or outside friends, often embraced the seminary rules much more uncritically, and sought to attain that "priestly detachment" which guaranteed that no friendship would ever get deep enough to jeopardize our commitment to the institution. Generally that was the way it worked in the seminary of the 50s. When someone decided to leave, his peers would feel vaguely deserted or rejected, because their former friend had broken his bond with the very institution that had created and defined their relationship. The person leaving would remember his own judgments about people who left, and would feel similarly judged by, and alienated from, those who remained. In many cases, friendships would die, only to be reborn years later, after both parties had gone through individualizing experiences outside the structure of the institution.

But I'm ahead of my story. In those first months of seminary life, I bonded with everyone – classmates, teammates, tablemates – taking advantage of any common bond the seminary structure provided. It was an exciting adventure, finding my place in this community of like-minded peers. Community life was very intense, since the seminary walls and rules functioned much like a garbage compactor, driving us inward and walling us off from any contact with the "outside" world.

Escapes

"Twice a month, on Thursdays, the Senior Division students may go on walks in the afternoon to nearby stores. Junior Division students may go once a month and must be accompanied by a faculty member. All must sign out for these walks and must report back by 4:15 P.M."

St. Joseph's College: Summary of the Rule

We were not allowed to leave the grounds, except for a semi-monthly "walk" into a nearby town, and then only in large groups. The walks happened on Thursdays, our weekly day off, and the rules were very clear: *"When out on these walks, students may not hail automobiles or accept rides, nor go to shows; nor into stores forbidden by the faculty. Nor are they to buy, or even pick up and read, magazines on display in the stores."*

You can imagine what the residents of Mountain View thought when they looked out their windows and saw groups of 15 to 20 teenage boys wandering along suburban roads, furiously smoking as many cigarettes as possible, then descending on Loyola Corners, a small shopping strip, where they furtively ducked in and out of stores, trying to avoid being seen by their superiors or their more scrupulous classmates. One of the favorite off-limits places was the local café, which had a jukebox. Eating in such restaurants was forbidden, especially places where you could listen to "Blue Suede Shoes" while you munched on your hamburger. I was shocked to realize that many of my own classmates regularly "franged" in this manner (Latin, "frangere," "to break," as in "break the rule.")

It strikes me as strange that, even though we were not allowed to eat hamburgers or buy Time Magazine, we <u>were</u> allowed, and almost encouraged, to smoke. This is probably due to the fact that a large proportion of the faculty were addicted to nicotine, and that smoking

71

still had the Marlboro man image which coincided so neatly with that of the Christian warrior. Once you reached the third year of high school, you were allowed to smoke on your bi-monthly "walk," and this became a badge of coolness and maturity. Since I didn't enter the seminary until third high, I didn't fully appreciate the initiatory aspect of this smoking ritual until that first Thursday when I signed up with a group of classmates to go on a "walk." The first thing I noticed was that many of my classmates came down from their rooms in their flashiest (though still acceptably "conservative") shirts and pants, and many had combed their hair differently, coming dangerously close to the forbidden "faddish haircuts," as though they were going to a dance or something. There was an air of intense excitement as they gathered around the door of Father Canfield's room. One by one, he doled out the cartons and packs of by-now-stale cigarettes, which had been entrusted to him at the beginning of the year. "Cat" Canfield was the dean of discipline and was responsible for stockpiling all the smokers' tobacco products between walks.

The transportation of one's cigarettes seemed to be a matter of great stylistic concern. Some guys tucked them into shirt pockets, others inserted them under shirt sleeves so as to create a fashionable square over the bicep, and others tucked an individual cigarette over the ear, so as to have it readily available once they stepped off school property. A few of the real macho types stuck cigars in their shirt pockets in addition to their cigarettes, just in case they needed a nicotine supercharge. As a non-smoker, I was awed by the ceremonial artistry of it all.

Since we were in third high, we weren't required to have a faculty member accompany us on our walks. We merely had to organize a group of ten or more and sign out. The kids in first and second high, on the other hand, had to cajole a faculty member into accompanying them. Usually the jocks were the first to get organized, and they usually tried to get "Sarge" Strain to accompany them. Sarge had a stiff "cool guy" mystique about him and many of the jocks had chosen him as their confessor. Since one's confessor was bound by the vow of secrecy, he was forbidden from revealing anything about his penitents during faculty meetings. This meant that, if Sarge should stumble into the Loyola Cafe and see some of his penitents wolfing down hamburgers, while reading Time magazine and listening to

Elvis on the jukebox, it would be between Sarge and them, not something he could bring back to a faculty meeting. Plus, Sarge was pretty loose about such things, having learned somewhere along the line that "boys will be boys."

In addition to Sarge, there were one or two young faculty members, fresh out of the seminary themselves, who were pretty good about overlooking infractions of the rule, but many of the older faculty weren't so understanding. If you were the last group to get organized, you might get stuck with Mike Sheehan or Johnny O'Neill. In that case, it was safest to go with Johnny O, because, even though he was rigid in his enforcement of the rule, he was so absent-minded that he probably wouldn't even notice that you were eating a hamburger and, if he did, he would probably forget your name before he got back to the seminary.

Johnny O's absent-mindedness was legendary. One Thursday he drove into town to get something at the drugstore and, on his way out of the store, encountered another faculty member who also had driven into town. Thinking that Johnny O had walked in with a group of students and might be too tired to walk back, the other priest offered him a ride. Johnny O gratefully accepted, totally forgetting that he had driven into town himself. It was a week later, after the faculty bursar noticed a house car missing and started questioning the faculty about its whereabouts, that the mists cleared enough for Johnny O to remember that he had left it in the drugstore parking lot.

Rules, Rules, Rules

"The citizens of the City lead a busy life whose every detail, prayer and study, work and play, is embraced by the ever present rule."

Lyman A. Fenn, SS., DD.
The Little City of God

"His will, once wayward, wavering and irresolute, has become more direct in purpose, more instant to commands, more ready to the whispered promptings of grace...Twenty thousand hours of virile discipline have chastened,

73

strengthened and subdued him into some beginning of a warrior of Christ."

William J. Sheehy, SS., M.A.
"A Junior Seminarian"

Besides being restricted in our physical contact with the "outside world," we were not allowed to read the daily newspaper, have our own radios, or turn on the television set in the recreation hall without the explicit permission of the Rev. President (which he usually reserved for such events as Papal elections, space launchings, or 49er games). The only books we were allowed to read were those which had been approved and stamped by the Rev. Librarian, and we were allowed to read only Catholic magazines, although even some of those were suspect. All our mail was read before we received it (or at least slit open to give that impression) and all our outgoing mail had to be placed in the seminary mail box unsealed. We were even required to use self-sealing envelopes, so that the faculty could read our out-going mail without having to lick the envelopes when they were finished. We were restricted in our correspondence to *"parents, near relatives, priests, guardians and former teachers."* The seminary oral tradition was replete with stories about guys who had been thrown out for writing to girls, even to female cousins. In retrospect, I often wonder if many of these stories weren't planted by the faculty to deepen their hold on our youthful psyches.

As repressive and ridiculous as these rules seem to me now, at the time I found them invigorating and challenging to my Spartan spirit. I remember telling my parents, with a certain pride, that they had to be careful what they wrote to me, lest it be offensive to the faculty censors. It gave me the same prideful rush I am sure the young CIA agent feels, when he tells his family that his activities are so crucial to national security that he can never again be a normal member of the family, but now is fated to be above and beyond them in all things relating to his mission. Heady stuff, for the true believer.

Visiting Sunday

Our only other significant contact with the outside world came once a month on Visiting Sunday, the third Sunday of the month. As usual, the parameters of such an event were precisely defined:

- *"Visitors may call to see the students only on the third Sunday of the month from 12:30 to 4:15 P.M. Visitors are restricted to parents and near relatives.*
- *Visitors may be entertained in the parlor, on the front roads or lawn, on the flat ground on either side of the service road, and on the college campus* (i.e., the playing field).
- *Visitors may not be taken into parts of the house other than the first floor of the administration wing. Visitors are not to use the pool or basketball courts or recreation rooms. Nor are they to use the area to the west of the house either for parking or for entertainment.*
- *To receive visitors at any other time, the students need explicit permission."*

-St. Joseph's College: Summary of the Rule

As usual, the tone of the rule left no question about the seminary's attitude toward sentimental family ties. (I'm sure that many a mother of a tearful 14 year old seminarian had to muster all her blind Catholic loyalties in order to suppress her maternal instincts enough to relinquish her child to the cold nurturance of these rule-bound seminary "Fathers.") Most families brought picnic tables on visiting Sunday and set up extravagant feasts on the front lawn or further down, under the huge eucalyptus trees that lined the service road. Just like in church, people had their favorite spots, which they claimed every month.

At 12:30 sharp, we would emerge through the elegant front doors, dressed in our black suits and ties, and peer into the assembled crowd to make out the face of our parents or siblings. Younger brothers and sisters would cry out, and all sorts of greetings would take place, from exuberant Italian hugs to repressed Irish handshakes to hearty German shoulder slaps.

I looked out at the crowd that first visiting Sunday, located my folks and walked with them over to the space they had picked out. They had brought a picnic lunch, highlighted with a pumpkin pie sent by Mrs. Pulskamp, our neighbor up the street who was my best friend Jim's mother. She had advised my folks about the visiting Sunday routine, having experienced it ten years earlier when her oldest son, Bill, had spent a year in the seminary. Bill had gone into the seminary right out of the eighth grade, before he had any idea of what life was all about, and he had rebelled against the discipline. She had learned her lesson, and had instructed Jim that he wouldn't enter the seminary until after high school, so that he would have a better chance of "making it." (Jim did wait until after high school, and he did "make it." He's now a monsignor and the Chancellor of his diocese. His mother knew what she was doing.)

On that first visiting Sunday I regaled my parents with all the seminary lore I had soaked up in the preceding weeks. I was bursting with enthusiasm, and they happily soaked up everything I had to say. Although I'm sure they missed me terribly, they never mentioned it, and I, self-styled Spartan Christian warrior that I was, never perceived that my absence might be a cause for pain and sadness. This was God's work, after all, and human emotions were irrelevant to God's work.

Though I loved my parents deeply and felt sad to see them leave that first visiting Sunday, I didn't feel as sad as many of my classmates from large families who had to leave sisters and brothers. Rather than depriving me of siblings, the seminary had provided me with whatever near-siblings I would ever have.

Our schedule was different on Visiting Sunday than on a regular Sunday, in that Compline was substituted for Vespers. On regular Sundays, we had a long recreation period from about 1 P.M. to 3:50 P.M. and then suited up in our cassocks and surplices for Vespers at 4 P.M. On visiting Sunday, we took leave of our parents at 4:15 and went to chapel for Compline at 4:30. I always preferred Compline to Vespers, because it only had three psalms, compared to Vespers' five. However, there was an ominous note to Compline, since it was the last hour of the day and was designed to prepare one for the dangers of the night. With images of visiting relatives and friends still fresh in our minds, we were reminded by the cantor: *"Fratres, sobrii estote, et vigilate" ("Brothers, be sober and watchful"*). That woke us out of our reverie. And then he went on: *"for thy enemy the Devil, as a raging lion, goeth about seeking whom he may devour."* Here it was again – that warning about enemies, coming right on the heels of our latest encounter with "the World," in the form of our loved ones. Had we been tempted that afternoon? Had we given the Devil any encouragement? Had we embraced any worldly values during those three short hours?

"I confess to Almighty God…that I have sinned exceedingly in thought, word and deed: through my fault, through my fault, through my most grievous fault."

We must have done something sinful during that afternoon, something to compromise our spiritual commitments, something to displease God and bring his wrath down on us. And if we dared to say, "No, I did nothing wrong," that assertion itself would be sinful, for pride would have wormed its way into our soul again.

By the time we finished Compline and reached supper, any memories of our afternoon would have been dusted for fingerprints of sin and sanitized appropriately. Visiting Sunday suppers, superfluous as they were after us gorging ourselves on maternal meals all afternoon, usually consisted of some kind of low-end menu from the back pages of the nuns' meal manual. Something like fried baloney and mashed potatoes. This had the desired effect of wrenching us away from the pleasures of the world and plopping us back into the disciplined routine of seminary life.

Confession

Every Friday night, we would go to confession. Our confessor would post a list of times, usually at 3 to 5 minute intervals, for us to show up at his room and confess our sins for that week. Since confession was considered an essential part of our spiritual life, and since we had to confess <u>something</u> in order to be absolved, we had to get very good at identifying and remembering anything resembling a sin. Like most of my classmates, I suspect, my list of sins was boringly repetitive week after week: "Uncharitable, 6 times" (usually during one of our bull sessions); "Disrespectful of elders, 4 times" (making fun of the faculty, usually for some sort of psychotic behavior on their part); "Selfish, 5 times" (taking a little more than my share of the potatoes at dinner); "Angry, 7 times" (usually during ball games). I had pretty much totally repressed sex after Father Leonard told me in the eighth grade that masturbation was a mortal sin, so I wasn't able to bring my confessor much excitement on that level. Nor did I break the rule significantly enough to give him anything to keep quiet about in faculty meetings. I was what you would call a boring penitent. Luckily most of my confessors were boring types themselves who wouldn't have known how to handle a real sin if I could have mustered one.

New students were assigned confessors and then, later on, they could switch to a different confessor if they chose. I was assigned Fr. Perkowsky, a new member of the faculty who taught Greek. "Perky" was a gentle type of guy, very sincere, and a conscientious confessor. He was a good fit for me, and I stayed with him the entire year. When he was transferred to another seminary the next year, I spent a couple of weeks sampling different confessors until I could make up my mind about a new one. I also looked at which types of guys had chosen which confessor, since that would give me a good idea of the confessor's personality and spiritual approach. As I mentioned, the jock smokers seemed to prefer "Sarge" Strain. The guys from old seminary lineages seemed to choose "Pop" Rock. Easy going middle-of-the-roaders gravitated towards Fr. Cronin, or "Crobo," the math and physics teacher.

After sampling a few of these more popular confessors, I decided to go with "Charlie" Dillon, the seminary vice president renowned for his fierce eccentricity as a chemistry teacher and his almost scientific precision as a confessor. His other penitents were Spartan types like myself who were looking for a confessor more like George Patton than Tom Dooley. Charlie was also known as "Chuck," but the nickname that really did him justice was "Zeus." He was correctly perceived by the student body as the power behind the throne, the hurler of thunderbolts. The president of the seminary was "Beansy" Campbell, a round little priest who looked like he had stepped right off the soup can label. The only weapon in Beansy's arsenal was the invocation of precedent, as in his constant refrain, "We don't want to set a precedent." When that approach failed to work, and a bigger gun was needed, Charlie Dillon was rolled in. Charlie always spoke in regal pronouncements, right arm raised sceptre-like, with hooked forefinger driving logical propositions into our pulpy brains like so many nails. His jaws were permanently clenched back at the wisdom teeth, which gave his voice nowhere to go except through his nose and bared front teeth. These nasal pronouncements brought the certitude of the scientific method to every situation, reducing to logical fallacy any deviation from seminary law or custom. No one, student or faculty member, had the intellectual tools or moral courage to challenge his arguments, so he reigned supreme, our resident Zeus.

Naturally, with my grandmother as my earliest spiritual mentor, I was inexorably drawn to this type of confessor. Why choose comfort or consolation when you can choose rigor, severity, and absolutism? In retrospect, I see that the only way for me to exorcise my Jansenist ghosts of authority, self-denial and discipline was to confront them head-on in their most intense personification.

Charlie Dillon was one of the most severely objective people I ever met. What he may have lacked in warmth, he made up for in fairness, impartiality and intellectual challenge. As his penitent, I knew I was just another student, subject to the same laws of his universe as any other. He never failed to challenge me when he thought I was wrong, even though, as the years and my questioning instincts progressed, such challenges were more and more difficult for both of us. Charlie was a furnace in which I refined a lot of my own dross. When I visited him almost twenty years later, in a parish house in Seattle, I found him approachable and refreshingly open to hearing – and of course arguing with – my by-then-radical ideas about the seminary and the church.

"The Bone" – Seminary Version

Since we were being trained to be preachers, a lot of emphasis was placed on voice development and public speaking. Our speech teacher was "Doc" Connor, a rather eccentric priest whose single-minded mission in life was the promotion of the "sphenoid," a wedge-shaped bone housing a sinus cavity at the base of the cranium behind the nose, which, when activated by sound waves, would amplify and modulate the human voice to a degree otherwise impossible. We called Fr. Connor "Doc," only after noticing that he called everyone else "Doc." It seemed to be the only name he knew. His constant refrain, in class and out, was, "All right, Doc, put it in the bone." The "bone" was his beloved sphenoid. His approach, though somewhat bizarre and certainly the butt of a lot of jokes, was remarkably effective. It started with learning how to breathe from the diaphram rather than from the upper chest. Then the voice was directed up to the sphenoid sinus, rather than merely depending on the vocal cords in the throat for resonance. He illustrated the process by drawing a cane on the board and showing the flow of air coming up from the lungs, passing through the sphenoid bone (behind and slightly higher than the nose), and then exiting down through the nostrils. To achieve this, we were subjected to a constant series of exercises in which we filled our lungs with air, careful to expand only our rib cage, not our chest, and then let the air pass slowly through our newly-animated sphenoids while chanting "Eee, Oooh, Aaah, Oooh, Uuuum."

Doc Connor had discovered this method after almost losing his voice as a young priest. Faced with sacerdotal expulsion if he couldn't regain his power of speech, he located a speech therapist by the name of Doctor Schuller who had lost his own voice as a young man and only regained it when he discovered how to excite his own bone. According to Doc Connor, Schuller would sit for hours bouncing his sphenoid-enhanced Ooohs and Aaahs off a distant mountain in Southern California. He emerged from his 40 days in the desert as "The Master," the title by which Doc always referred to him, and the only known instance when he didn't call somebody "Doc."

Once we were sufficiently adept at projecting our voices by "putting it in the bone," we had to start working on pronunciation. Doc's recurring mantra was "Draw out your words, Doc. Draw out your words." It would take him about ten seconds per word to say this, so intent was he that the medium be the message. All this was in preparation for us to ascend the pulpit in the refectory as the "reader" for that meal. This was a huge ordeal for each of us, for it meant being the target of Doc's criticism in front of all our peers, as well as the faculty. We had to read the prayers before and after the meal, as well as whatever book was being read during silent meals. When it was our turn to read, we prayed that there would be no visitors that day, so we could get our turn over with. If there was a visitor and we were granted a talking meal, we had to keep returning, reading the pre and post-meal selections, until we were able to read through an entire silent meal. That meant getting nervous all over again at every meal. Such indigestion could go on for days if there happened to be a spate of visitors.

Reading during silent meals was often a painful experience, not only for the reader, but for the rest of the student body as well, since they had to suffer along with him. Periodically, the bell on the faculty table would sound, interrupting the reader, and Doc Connor would slowly finish chewing his last bite and drawl, "All right Doc, slow it down. You're going too fast. Try it again, Doc." The reader, red-faced, would back up to the beginning of the paragraph and start again, drawing out his words in painful exaggeration. Just about the time he began to settle down, the bell would ring again, this time for some faulty pronunciation. Doc, like most of the faculty, could be cruel at times in his critiques. Usually this happened when he began to take the reader's mistakes personally, as though he felt the rest of the faculty were judging him for not adequately training us. We would instinctively feel this happening, and a wave of anger would roll over the refectory at each sound of the bell.

Silent meals were often a cause for resentment anyway, since the books to which we were subjected had often been chosen merely for their absence of "worldly" content, not for any literary merit or relevance. The first book I remember being read in the refectory was "Little Britches" and it went on for months. Though at first somewhat shocked by hearing my classmates refer to it as "Little Bitches," I soon got their point.

Meal Mischief

Often these silent meals would breed a restlessness that could only be relieved through mischief. Shortly after my arrival I was introduced to the ritual of "drain-piping." The tables in the refectory had white tableclothes, but these in turn were covered with clear plastic to prevent stains and make cleanup easier. Often, during the meal, a conspiracy would be hatched at the top of the table and everyone along one side, with the exception of the poor kid who was the piler at the bottom of the table, would subtly raise the plastic tablecloth in front of them to create a trough. The person at the top of the table would then pour ice water into the trough and quickly replace the water pitcher on the table so that, by the time the piler felt his crotch inundated with freezing water, there would be no evidence of where it came from. This was a dangerous trick to play, because, if the piler was a nervous type, he might let out a howl and jump up, thus attracting faculty attention and "getting a bell." That would mean he would have to see the prefect of discipline after the meal and, depending on his sense of fraternal loyalty, might squeal on the rest of the table. But if the book being read was bad enough, it was worth the risk just to get a little diversion.

Another refectory sport was the "table game." Here the table head would assign different pranks to each member of the table and, if anyone failed to perform his assignment, he would be docked his mystery for a week. In fourth high, when I became a table head, I devised a table game in which one of the butter-cutters had to bring to the table the axle from the cart which the waiters used to transport the water pitchers. At the next meal he presented me with the axle and we all watched expectantly as the waiter began pushing the cart full of heavy glass water pitchers down the center aisle between tables. Almost immediately, the front wheel on the cart broke loose, causing the cart to list suddenly to the right, gouging its corner into the floor, and sending the water pitchers flying off the side like lemmings from a cliff. The waiter turned bright red and rushed around to salvage the remaining pitchers while the reader paused to take in the scene and the rest of us laughed hysterically. Another blow delivered to the silent meal.

The "Trustees"

Much like in the prison system, the seminary hierarchy was not confined to the faculty, but extended down to students, who, if they showed leadership abilities, were awarded "house jobs." These were positions of responsibility and authority, which implied that the recipient had found favor in the eyes of the faculty. Jobs such as librarian, sacristan, master of ceremonies, keyboy, infirmarian and bellboy were highly coveted. The job of keyboy was perhaps the most strategic – and the most subject to abuse. The keyboy held the keys to almost every room in the house, and was responsible for making sure that everything was locked and unlocked at the proper time. Normally, the faculty chose the most reliable and mature candidate they could find for this job, but, in our class, they inexplicably chose John Cunningham, the class's equivalent to G. Gordon Liddy. John parlayed his keyboy job into a position of great power and influence, using his keys to obtain copies of tests, raid the faculty refrigerator and provide his friends access to any room in the house. Unlike his Watergate counterpart, he never got convicted, though he had a few close calls, like the time Dr. Mumford woke up from a nap to find Cunningham and McLaughlin in his study, looking for a copy of the upcoming biology test. John quickly covered himself, holding up his clipboard and apologizing for interrupting the doctor's nap, but explaining that they were there taking wall dimensions, since the maintenance crew was going to be painting his room soon.

"I see," replied the ever-gullible Doctor. "Thanks very much."

"Rocky"

To me, one of the mysteries of education is how you can spend so much time in a class and remember so little about what you supposedly learned. Often the only persistent memories are the eccentricities of the teacher. This is certainly true of my fourth high religion course. I vaguely remember a textbook with a green and purple cover. And I remember lots of tests with one word answers. But mainly I remember "Rocky" Russell, our instructor. He was fresh out of an Eastern seminary and had just completed his Sulpician novitiate when he arrived at St. Joseph's. He was a well-scrubbed, big-chested guy who prided himself on his appearance and style. He was one of the first true clerical narcissists I ever met, though I now realize it is a common hazard of the trade. In his dealings with us in religion class, he constantly held himself up as an example of manly virtue, and it is indicative of his effectiveness as an educator that I remember only one thing he ever taught us. One afternoon he launched into a lengthy diatribe about male etiquette and capped it off by telling us that, if we wanted to become true "manly" gentlemen, we should always shave our armpits and use deodorant. I dutifully followed his advice that night, and spent a very uncomfortable next month learning why such an activity was really stupid, unless you planned to shave your armpits with the same regularity you shaved your face.

His treatment of the younger students was so autocratic and abrasive that he soon became the most hated member of the faculty, mocked by all for his pretentious way of speaking as well as his dramatic posturing on the tennis court. His unpopularity reached a dramatic climax one afternoon when a light bulb, mysteriously hurled from a fourth floor window, exploded at his feet just as he was dramatically sweeping into the backswing of a tie-breaking serve. We were shocked by the near violence of the event, the nearest thing to a Hitchcockian murder scene we had ever witnessed in the seminary. The assault had a huge impact on everyone, including the faculty evidently, for Rocky was quietly transferred to another seminary at the end of the year.

The "Sulps"

"The name Sulpician means nothing outside of clerical circles; for having no churches, no parish schools, giving no missions, not advertising, the Sulpicians scarcely come into contact with the laity of the Church. They themselves are diocesan priests who take no vows or promises but who band together under a sort of gentleman's agreement for the purpose of devoting their whole time and energy to the training of seminarians."

Lyman A. Fenn, SS., DD.
The Little City of God, 1937

Whereas Rocky inspired hatred and near-violence, the rest of the faculty inspired only good-natured mockery and mimicry. We knew we were stuck with them, despite their idiosyncrasies, and we held them in whatever respect we could muster from our cocky adolescent souls.

Actually these priests were only older renditions of ourselves. They, too, had entered the seminary as young boys and had spent twelve years confined in a medieval institution with few or no external reality checks. They had been elevated, in their own minds and in the minds of those around them, to the status of minor deities, earthly representatives of God on earth. They, too, had been told that their black cassocks symbolized their death to self and their oneness with Christ. They too had been programmed toward absolute obedience to their superiors *("A superior may err in commanding, but you can never err in obeying")*. Once ordained, they had chosen to become Sulpicians and remain within the walls of the seminary rather than going out to work in a parish, where some of their more blatant idiosyncrasies might have been revealed to them by a more reality-based and candid constituency. Within the seminary, surrounded only by malleable students and peers who had been similarly programmed to narcissistic clericalism, they were each free to sculpt their own brand of manic eccentricity. For us seminarians, it was like living in a Fellini movie, surrounded by colorful performers who never stepped out of character. We reveled in their antics, told endless stories about their performances, worked diligently at perfecting our own imitations of them.

Of course, even though we couldn't recognize it at the time, we brought our own eccentricities to the seminary, which no doubt provided the faculty the same kind of entertainment that they provided us. We were all males, after all, living in a community that had no balancing input from women. There were no wives or girl friends to call us on our foibles, so we were free to develop the kind of idiosyncrasies that only intimacy could truly challenge. The only women in our seminary lives were the nuns who worked behind the scenes, cooking our meals and washing our clothing for us. They functioned as servants and we were instructed not to communicate with them (which would have been difficult anyway, since they only spoke French).

So, we were left with each other, in a pressure cooker environment that bred incredible bonds, though not much true intimacy. Perhaps that's why these times were our "Joyful Mysteries" – we were enveloped in a celibate, pre-individualized innocence which enabled us to mistake our Little City of God for the real world. All our energies could be directed to the world within those walls. If we made fun of the faculty, we also felt a deep love for them, because we realized that, despite their oddities, they were genuinely committed to us. We were, after all, their only posterity, often their only family. They may not always have been good fathers, but they were committed to fatherhood. They were dedicated to forming us into that same priestly mold in which they and their clerical forebears had been formed. If we conformed to the mold, they treated us with respect and even with a cautious warmth; if we resisted the mold, they felt no compunction about destroying us. Such was the tradition of the Church in the late 50s and early 60s.

Tough Love

We knew that, at any time, a classmate could disappear, "thrown out" for some infraction of *The Rule*. He would suddenly be gone, his room mysteriously empty, and gradually the word would go around that he had been thrown out for some infraction of *The Rule*. The faculty prided themselves on being literalists in their enforcement of *The Rule*. Since *The Rule* was God's will, and since we all knew the dictates of *The Rule*, anyone who broke *The Rule* must be choosing to offend God and consequently wasn't worthy to be a priest. What in normal circumstances would have been considered laughably insignificant events became earth-shaking offenses when placed in the context of the seminary *Rule*. At this stage in my life, I questioned nothing about this inquisitorial approach to spiritual discipline. I followed all the rules and often felt surprise and shock when my classmates didn't do likewise.

The Prefect of Discipline at St. Joseph's was "Cat" Canfield, so named because of his unabashed commitment to sneaking around the corridors at night in soft-soled shoes spying on hapless students. He had perfected the technique of inserting his key into a locked door, turning it, and flinging the door open, all in a single motion and with a single sound. The first time he did it to me, luckily I was on my knees next to my bed saying my night prayers. His question, asked from the corner of his mouth, was always the same. "What are you doing, son?"

"Saying my night prayers, Father."

"Okay." Then he was gone, into the silence of the night.

One night I heard his key enter the door of my next door neighbor, Conrad Gruber. Conrad had just read a new book called <u>Christian</u>

<u>Yoga</u> written by a Catholic monk, and he had gotten mightily inspired by it – to the point of trying to master the various yoga techniques in his room every night after "lights out" (9:05 p.m.). Several times in the past week, I had heard him crash into my wall, in abortive attempts to master the three-point head stand. I assume he was still trying to master it the night that Cat threw open his door, because after I heard Cat's usual "What are you doing, son?", I kept hearing the word "yoga" come in their subsequent conversation, and whenever Cat said "yoga," it always had a ring of disbelief to it. Cat did have a rather bizarre sense of humor, and, evidently finding Conrad on his head in the dark struck him as funny enough to merit absolution, because Conrad escaped any kind of public humiliation, which was Cat's usual weapon.

One of the most stringent seminary rules was the one forbidding a student from entering another student's room. This rule also forbade a student from <u>permitting</u> another student to enter one's <u>own</u> room. The faculty defined "entering" a room as placing your foot down on the other side of the threshold. You could stand at another student's door (with permission, of course), and even reach into the room to get something, but you had to keep your feet either outside, or on top of, "the threshold." You could not step inside the threshold, even with one foot. The threshold was precisely defined as the four-inch wide riser which ran across the bottom of the door-jam. There was a lot of speculation about the genesis of this rule. Most of us were too naive to know anything about homosexuality, so we couldn't grasp the true phobic roots of the rule, but we opined that it had something to do with those mysterious "particular friendships" which the faculty kept warning us about.

One day we learned through whispered reports that a couple of guys two years ahead of us had been thrown out because one of them was in the other's room. I remember being horrified and immediately consigning the two of them to some sort of "deviant" file in my mind. I had no idea of what really happened, only that they had committed a sin that was serious enough to disqualify them from the priesthood. I was too naive to be able to visualize any specific acts that would justify my indictment of them, but still I reduced them to the status of moral lepers. Later we heard that one of them was standing at the other's door and, without thinking, stepped across the threshold to get something the other was handing to him. Unfortunately, the faculty prefect had just come out of his room and, witnessing this technical breech of the rule, went straight to the rector who summarily threw both of them out. It's a testament to the depth of my seminary brainwashing that, even today, my image of those two students is filtered through a scarlet gel, even though I am convinced they were totally innocent of any wrongdoing.

Another rule forbade us from reading anything that was not specifically approved by the Reverend Librarian. Since reverend librarians were always antiquarian classicists, and weren't likely to approve anything written after 1400 A.D., anything even close to a best-seller would automatically be disapproved, especially if it was a paperback. In fact, there was an unspoken prejudice against paperbacks in those days, as though the stiffness of a book's cover was a measure of its moral integrity. For a while, a daring guerilla band of paperback readers operated within the seminary. One guy would buy a paperback, remove the cover, read the first ten pages, tear them out, and pass them to the next reader. Eight or ten guys would be reading the same book in sequential, ten-page installments, the logic being that, if anyone was caught, he could probably stuff the ten pages in his mouth and swallow the evidence. The risk, of course, fell on the guy who bought and stored the book in the first place. We were all shocked when Phil DeAndrade was thrown out for possession of an unauthorized paperback. Cat Canfield, our CIA wannabe Dean of Discipline, had sneaked into Phil's room and tossed the place, eventually finding the paperback in Phil's closet, where he had ingeniously hung it under his suit pants on the rung of the hanger.

Phil disappeared in the usual manner, and Cat, far from being apologetic about invading someone's privacy like that, reveled in his victory. The rest of us lamented Phil's departure, but also reminded ourselves never to underestimate the omnipresence of the Cat and the binding force of *The Rule*. We may have found it strange that a grown man would choose to go out in soft-soled shoes every night, prowling the corridors and spying on students, but we never questioned his right to do it. The idea that <u>Phil's</u> rights might have been violated never occurred to us. In those days, we never thought in terms of rights, only in terms of our own duties and failures. This was the logical sequence of the Catholic program: 1. Original sin; 2. Personal guilt; 3. Salvation, through obedience to authority. In an institution like the seminary, where faith really meant obedience, we never questioned the exercise of authority. In fact, when Fr. O'Neill, in our Christian Apologetics class, dramatically pronounced that "the Inquisition was the best thing the heretic ever knew," we all nodded in the affirmative, perhaps feeling somewhat guilty for our own less-than-total endorsement of the stake as the ideal tool of persuasion.

If unauthorized books were seen as a threat to the integrity of our programming, you can imagine how the faculty viewed electronic media such as radio, television or film. Only on special occasions did we have "film nights," and then we were restricted to faculty-censored movies usually creamed right off the top of the "A" section of the Legion of Decency list. Some of these were palatable, others barely preferable to a couple of hours in study hall; but one of them – "The King of Kings" – was so corny and inane that it occasioned a near-riot among the student body and caused the faculty to issue a moratorium on all future movies that year.

We were allowed to watch television only on rare occasions such as the World Series or the coronation of a pope, or some other overtly Catholic event. We could listen to the radio only during our recreation periods, and then only to "classical or semi-classical" music. Like most visceral conservatives, the faculty feared and hated rock music, intuiting its power to shift our idling root chakras into high gear. Consequently, we were forbidden to listen to "modern" music of any kind.

The transistor had been invented in 1947, and by 1958 pocket-sized transistor radios with earphones were readily available. One had only to dangle a short length of wire out the window to access the wicked world of Elvis, but you had to be careful, because one of Cat's hobbies was electronics, and he could spot an illicit antenna a mile away.

I remember a bizarre incident in which a quiet guy about two years ahead of us was precipitously expelled for violating the radio rule. He was caught using the radio in the recreation room to tape the Indianapolis 500 on his Wolensak tape recorder. I remember being totally mystified when I heard about this. First of all, I couldn't imagine anyone in his right mind wanting to listen to four hours of whining car engines. But I also couldn't imagine how the Indianapolis

500 could possibly present a serious enough occasion of sin to merit expulsion. Nonetheless, in my easily-programmed naivete, I subconsciously began to associate car races – and the city of Indianapolis – with some sort of wicked behavior. A Penzoil Gomorrah.

The seminary succeeded in implanting a profound double standard in each of us. On the one hand, *The Rule* was the will of God, by which we were to prove ourselves worthy of the priesthood. On the other hand, we attributed a certain outlaw heroism to those who had the courage to break the gratuitous shackles which had been placed on our adolescent freedom. The challenge for each of us was to reconcile the liberating message of Jesus with the often-ridiculous rules which were imposed upon us in his name. That challenge was only faintly reflected in the adolescent rebellion of the 50s, but it would receive full papal sanction in the 60s when John XXIII began asking hard questions about the relationship of Spirit to Letter in the Church. Before John arrived on the scene, however, unquestioning obedience was the linchpin of seminary training, and the faculty felt it was their duty to enforce the rule as strictly as possible. They themselves had no reference points for questioning tradition. How could they? Anyone they'd ever heard of who had openly questioned tradition was now safely tucked away in the *Heretic* closet – except for Jesus (and of course they'd managed to forget that He'd gotten his start by questioning His own tradition). Luckily, the faculty's humanity would often override their inquisitorial instincts, and they would share our mirth over certain rule infractions. "Boys will be boys," after all, and any minor infraction could be forgiven – as long as the basic authority structure remained intact, as long as we admitted our guilt and acknowledged their control. That, after all, was the principle upon which the sacrament of Confession was based: As long as you admitted your guilt and acknowledged the Church's authority in your life, you could be forgiven – unless, of course, you were perceived as leading others astray or lessening their respect for the rule. In that case, it didn't matter. You had to be crushed like any other heretic.

Periodically there would be a "purge." Several students would be thrown out at one time, either because they all had been involved in a serious rule violation, or because they had begun to be perceived as some sort of collective threat to the stability of the institution. The faculty, at any time, could decide that a certain individual or group had a "bad attitude" and should be thrown out for the good of the whole. When such "purges" occurred, tremors of shock would run through the rest of the student body and anyone who had been even tangentially associated with the purgees would be put on notice that his own time might be coming unless he changed his ways. Such psychological reigns of terror were predictably effective in changing behavior, and were the crowning achievements of Cat Canfield's career. No doubt inspired by Joseph McCarthy's political witchhunts, Cat mounted extensive investigations aimed at exposing troublemakers. When a Christmas tree mysteriously appeared on the seminary roof one year, and a person-by-person interrogation failed to yield the prankster, Cat went into his gumshoe mode and eventually solved the crime by discovering a single pine needle adhering to a dirty sock in his prime suspect's laundry hamper.

Often, a student's "bad attitude" was accompanied by poor grades, and this provided Cat with another ritualistic opportunity to use the "purge" to instill fear in the student body. Every year, at the end of the first semester, just after the final grades had been tabulated, Cat would quietly enter the study hall and move silently to the back. We all knew why he was there, and we also knew he would be watching us to see if anyone was foolhardy enough to turn around and look at him, so we kept our eyes down on our desks. He had a list in his hand and, as he moved stealthily and silently through the hall, he quietly tapped first one, then another, student on the shoulder and whispered, "Father Campbell would like to see you." We all knew what this meant, that the students who walked out the door would never return, that their desks and rooms would be empty the next time we looked, that they had been thrown out "for grades." The fact that Cat surrounded this procedure with such ceremony and drama was testament to his innate talents of manipulation and control. He was the seminary's version of Goebels, the perfect embodiment of tough-love totalitarianism.

The first year I was there, my class (third high) sat in the front of the study hall, and fourth high sat behind us in the rear. About 10 minutes into the study period, Cat opened the door, nodded conspiratorially to the study hall prefect who was sitting at the elevated desk in front, then silently made his way to the back of the room. A deathly silence descended on the room. We held our breath, kept our eyes down, and waited. From far to the rear we heard a muted voice, then the scraping of a chair, then footsteps coming toward the front. We watched out of the corner of our eyes as one, then another, of the older classmen walked quickly, heads bowed, faces flushed, choking back tears, up the side aisle and out the door, on their way to the executioner.

Eventually, Cat reached our row, and we all went rigid, as he walked over behind Phil Maloney, tapped him on the shoulder, and whispered the death sentence in his ear. Phil was a warm-hearted, friendly sort of kid with a penchant for getting in trouble. He wasn't doing well in his studies, and he had told me earlier that day he was afraid he might get the kiss of death from Cat, but I didn't believe him. I thought he was being overly dramatic. I was new to all this and couldn't imagine them throwing a nice guy like Phil out of the seminary. Cat moved on, and Phil sat there for a minute, flushing bright red under his Irish freckles. Then he got up and sauntered awkwardly toward the front of the room. Unlike the others, he didn't just bow his head and go out the door. He turned around with his sweet Irish smile, shrugged his shoulders and gave us a wave. Then he left. I never saw him again, and had almost forgotten about him until a few months ago, when I read his obituary in The Catholic Worker. It seems Phil had devoted much of his life to serving the poor, had gotten his doctorate in Russian literature and had become a well-loved college professor in Montana. He died suddenly of a heart attack while meeting with a group of students at a local bar. May he rest in peace. He was a true priest, much more acceptable to Jesus than he'd been to the church hierarchy.

It's been 45 years since that day Phil was thrown out, and I'm sad to admit that only now am I beginning to appreciate the pain that Phil and others like him experienced at the hands of the seminary. I didn't feel much of anything at the time. I had been so deeply programmed as a Catholic warrior that I accepted the faculty's decision uncritically, and even harbored an unconscious judgment of Phil, which turned him into a stranger as soon as he walked out the door. In retrospect, I am amazed at my ability to cut a friend out of my life like that. What part of the Catholic "program" can explain that sort of reaction? If I were to identify the specific piece of "code," it would be that part of *The Rule* which banned "particular friendships." This prohibition was vague, yet ominous enough to poison the wells on any kind of intimacy, keeping all relationships at a cynical, good-ole-boys level, thereby insuring that our personal relationships would never become strong enough to threaten our institutional adhesion. This was the heart of celibacy, a position of armored self-sufficiency that enabled us to perform the manly act of emotional dissociation any time it was necessary. This programmed distrust of bonding may be the basis for the tragic loneliness which still afflicts members of the clergy and often leads them to inappropriate and desperate attempts to alleviate it.

When guys like Phil were thrown out, we were expected to accept it as God's will and forget about him. In fact, we were discouraged from communicating with anyone who left, especially if he had been "thrown out," lest he infect us with his "bad attitude." Those who had been thrown out were aware of this anathema, and knew that any attempt on their part to sustain seminary relationships would only confuse and jeopardize their friends who remained. Once in a while a guy who had been thrown out would dare to come back on Visiting Sunday to see his old friends, but this had to be done surreptitiously, lest the faculty see him and take it out on the friends he visited. He wore the equivalent of a scarlet letter in the eyes of those who remained, no matter how close they had been and how hard each tried to ignore or erase it. At a time when we were struggling with our own identities and needed desperately to discover trust through intimacy, we were bonded instead to a rigid set of rules imposed by a desensitized male hierarchy. This may have helped us cope with the loss of friends, but it also trained us to deny the reality and validity of pain. Once someone was gone, his memory would live on in stories about his exploits or foibles, but never in any heart-felt expressions of loss. That was beneath us. We were, after all, warriors.

That is not to say that all of us were armored warriors. There were some among us who were of a gentler, more feminine cast, and these suffered silently, knowing only that they did not resonate with the Spartan ideals outlined in Fr. Fenn's <u>Little City of God.</u> These found solace in music or literature or the arts or the liturgy, and only reluctantly allowed themselves to be dragged into macho activities such as the mandatory athletic program. They felt things the rest of us did not, and we, in those early days, were often so caught up in our narcissism that we ignored, or worse, made fun of them. Only later, when we began to emerge as individuals ourselves, did we begin to appreciate the depth and insights of these silent ones.

Infirmity

Resolutions of the Sick

To be used by him, or suggested to him, from time to time, as ejaculations:

- *I gratefully receive this sickness from the hand of my God.*
- *I shall constantly beg God's grace that, by His aid, I may soon be equally ready to die or live.*
- *I will be patient in my sufferings.*

The New Key to Heaven
A Complete Prayerbook for Catholics

Shortly before Easter in my senior year of high school ("fourth high"), just when I had begun to shed the stigma of my former illness, I ended up back in the hospital, this time with a ruptured appendix. I had awakened in the middle of the night feeling nauseous, with a severe pain in my abdomen. I hobbled down to the bathroom and threw up a few times, then returned to bed. The pain and nausea continued until morning, so I waited until everyone else had gone down to chapel for morning prayers and then stumbled, clutching my stomach, to the other side of the building and up the two flights of stairs to the infirmary. The nurse was an elderly woman whose dedication far outstripped her medical expertise. She immediately prescribed an enema, a remedy against which my mother had expressly (and wisely) warned me. I politely refused the enema and lay around in pain for the rest of the day, allowing her only to take my temperature which seemed to be escalating as the day progressed. When I wasn't any better by late afternoon, the Reverend Infirmarian came in and told me that I better call my parents and go home. This was his way of acknowledging that I was truly sick.

My dad and our neighbor, Mrs. Pulskamp, drove down to get me. It was dark by the time we got home, and the doctor didn't arrive at the house until about nine o-clock. He took one look at me and called the ambulance. My appendix had already burst and, by the time he could operate, peritonitis had set in. I came out of surgery in critical condition and remained there for the next three days (Good Friday through Easter Sunday). Given my previous blood condition, there was a chance I might not make it. I could read this in my mother's expression, as soon as I opened my eyes, and the thought that I might have to leave her and my dad behind made me very sad. Otherwise, I felt pretty dissociated from the whole situation. Death was no big deal. If it was God's will, I was ready to go. The "will to live" was not something I'd ever really cultivated, at least not on a conscious level. On the other hand, the acceptance of death was programmed deep in my soul.

Easter Sunday arrived and my condition suddenly improved. My parents were understandably ecstatic, feeling it was some kind of miracle. I accepted it as God's will, though, as I remember, I was also slightly disappointed at missing out on such a dramatic exit. Plus, it meant that I had to return to the world in the role of vulnerable wimp again, wandering around wearing a mandated corset to keep my stitches from breaking open.

College

St. Joseph's was a six-year institution, four years of high school, two of college. Unlike our contemporaries outside, we didn't graduate at the end of high-school, waiting instead until we completed the full six years. The transition from high school to college, however, did involve other rites of passage. All our classes were now held on the "college side" of the building, the new wing that had been added in 1956. We ate our meals in the college refectory, separated now from the howling sounds of Sixth Latiners. We were called "Poets" in our first year of college, "Rhets" in our second, supposedly because of our focus on Poetry as freshmen and on Rhetoric as sophomores. Perhaps the biggest change for a lot of us, though, was the fact that we no longer functioned as Bears, Indians, Trojans or Ramblers. The college side had recently adopted its own optional sports system, and new teams were created each season. This was a huge psychological shift for those of us who had identified with the same group of teammates throughout our high school years. All of a sudden, we were playing on the same team with those who had formerly been our bitterest rivals. Playing next to McLaughlin or Murray seemed strange and vaguely treasonous at first, but this sudden infusion of ecumenism soon evaporated our former social boundaries.

Another huge change that year was the influx of new classmates, as well as an exodus of old ones. When the dust settled, over a third of our class was new, 17 out of 44. Several of our classmates had quietly exited, some having secretly planned all along to get their high school diploma and then head for greener pastures. As we did every year, we scanned the bulletin board that first day to see the names of current classmates, wondering who the new ones were, but more interested in who was missing. I was sad, but not surprised, to see that Maurice Maybury's name was missing from the list. Everyone knew that Maurice was a math and physics genius and that he wasn't going to find much of an outlet for those talents in the ministry. Plus, he had confided to me the previous year that he had fallen in love over the summer. That surprised me at first because Maurice was such a shy guy, but he also had a sensitivity and vulnerability about him that might make love more possible for him than for most of the rest of us. Maurice had emerged as an eccentric genius the previous year, when he discovered that the huge Encyclopedia Brittanica at the front of our study hall had made a mistake in their entry on Einstein, misrepresenting one of his formulas. Maurice got so worked up about this, and got so little response from the rest of us (who had no idea what he was talking about), that he did the unthinkable: He made an appointment with Father Charles Dillon, the Vice President of the seminary and a widely-regarded expert on all matters scientific. Though we had not yet had Charlie for class, we were all scared to death of him. Nonetheless, Maurice marshaled all his Galileo-inspired courage, lugged the bulky volume up to Fr. Dillon's room, along with a notebook filled with his own mathematical calculations, and proceeded to take on Brittanica. We all waited to see what would happen, expecting to see Maurice shuffle dejectedly back to the study hall, another victim of Charlie's wrath. But he came back beaming and told us that Charlie had wholeheartedly agreed with him. We knew then that Maurice was a being apart, an extraterrestrial who had mistakenly landed in the seminary, a few miles off course from his intended target, Stanford Research Institute.

Maurice's real claim to fame came during his final year at St. Joseph's. One night, long after lights out, a cat started yowling down at the end of the corridor. One of the other students reported the next day that he himself had heard the cat, gotten up, and looked down the corridor. He saw the cat wandering around at the other end, yowling plaintively. Then he saw Maurice's door open, the cat walk in, and the door close.

The next morning, when we got to our first class, someone had written on the board "Congratulations, Maurice! Father of Five!" Maurice had taken pity on the cat and made a bed for her in the bottom drawer of his desk. He hadn't noticed her distended stomach when he let her in, and consequently was quite amazed to find five new-born kittens in his desk drawer when he woke up that morning. The story immediately made the rounds and was the cause of much mirth among the student body, especially because Maurice himself had so often reminded us of an ungainly Sylvester.

Maurice left the seminary at the end of that year, and we didn't see him again until our 25th reunion, in 1986. Sure enough, he had stayed with math and science and had worked on several well known NASA projects. Despite his achievements in science and technology, he was just as nervous and awkward as ever around his old classmates, possibly because no one would let him forget the cat story.

Charlie

None of us really understood why we were called "Poets" in our freshman year of college. True, we did take two semesters of Poetry, but the course which most captivated our attention and catalyzed our fear that year was the Chemistry course taught by the mythical Charlie "Zeus" Dillon. This was our first experience of Charlie, and the course, fittingly enough, changed the hierarchy on our academic Mt. Olympus. Classmates who had previously excelled at Latin, Greek, History, and English, didn't necessarily excel in Charlie's class. This was our first inkling that there might be different types of intelligence and different learning styles, and that science might comprise a domain of its own, separate from, and perhaps more demanding than, our usual verbal and writing skills. This was a frightening thought for me, because I wasn't one of those who bobbed easily to the surface in Charlie's course. I struggled to stay afloat. And when Ozzie Hoffman, the only person whom I had found irritating enough to actually punch during a basketball game, surfaced as the genius of the class, I was disgusted. The Church was right: science was not to be trusted…especially if guys like Ozzie could get it and I couldn't.

***

The course I liked best that year was Apologetics, where we learned how to defend the Faith against its enemies – heretics, atheists, and secular humanists. The course was taught by Johnny O'Neill, a typical fanatic Irishman, wedded uncritically to the Catholicism of his birth and the bellicosity of his genes. "Johnny O" was perhaps the most colorful member of the faculty, constantly stretching the fragile membrane which sheathed that always-imminent psychosis which was late '50s clericalism.

Apologetics was supposed to be a course in which we critically examined the ideas held by the opponents of Catholicism and learned how to refute them logically. What we really got was a facile and biased caricature of each of the world's great thinkers, and then a clever one-line put-down which, Johnny O assured us, would be all we would ever need to win any argument for God and the Church.

Somebody bring up Kant's theory of phenomenon and noumenon? All you have to say is, "That man had boxes in his head."

Someone say Luther was justified in opposing the church's policy of selling indulgences? All you have to say is, "That guy was just a horny monk who married a nun."

Johnny had all the answers and, like a Notre Dame coach, he doled them out to us from his dog-eared playbook. His was a heady, tough-guy Catholicism whose self-righteous canned cynicism was guaranteed to devastate any enemy. Several years later, in a coffeehouse on University Avenue in Palo Alto, I thought I had a cocky Stanford secular humanist on the ropes when I parried back to him one of Johnny O's lines:

"What you're saying is that the end justifies the means!!"

He looked at me for a minute and said, "Well, what else does?"

I knew what Johnny O would have done. He would have accused the kid of some esoteric heresy, warned him he was going to hell, stormed out in a fit of righteous anger and bragged about it when he got back to the seminary. But I wasn't able to do that. The kid had a point. Instead of responding, I just sat there and thought about it. In fact, I'm still thinking about it.

In that earlier, ingenuous time of my youth, Johnny O's certainty, despite its obvious eccentricities, struck a chord in my warrior soul. He was a fanatic, but so was I. We were solitary heroes, fighting the good fight in the midst of trivia and compromise. I felt that most of my classmates were just sliding along, playing both sides of the priest coin, not really living up to Jesus' demands. I alone could heed his call. I alone could deny myself the luxuries of comfort and compromise and face death. I alone was called to sacrifice. I was a real pain in the ass.

Father Figures

Only now can I step back and wonder whether my self-righteousness and need for certainty came from the fact that my dad had suffered a stroke, which wiped out his ability to speak and to register understanding. One day he was fine. The next day he was changed forever. It was the summer after my second year in the seminary that my mother got a call from my dad's partner at work, saying, "Something's happening to Mac. I think you better call the doctor." The next thing I knew my dad was in St. Joseph's hospital, getting tests for a stroke. At the time, I had no idea what a stroke was, but when my dad came back home, he was a different person. He had trouble walking, and he was slurring the few words he was able to speak. He was no longer the bright, funny guy my mother and I had always depended on. I thought, hoped, it might be temporary, that after a month or two he'd be back to his old self. Gradually, though, I realized that he wasn't going to recover, that he would never again be there for me in the way he had been previously.

I had lost my rock, and I needed another. Enter my grandmother's ghostly dogmatism, which once again trumped my dad's now-mute generosity of spirit, and impelled me to search, in vain, for his replacement among clerical authority figures.

I was unaware at the time how much my dad's absence affected me. His gentle humor had always been the solvent for the tin man morality I had inherited from my grandmother. Now, with him incapacitated, and my mother struggling valiantly to care for both him and my grandfather, all the while holding down a full-time job as a third grade teacher, I retreated to the rigor and security of seminary discipline.

My mother didn't drive, so, after my dad's stroke, she had to rely on friends for a ride on visiting Sundays. Luckily my boyhood friend and neighbor, Jim Pulskamp, entered the seminary as a college freshman, so his folks began bringing my mom, and sometimes my dad, with them. My dad would come and sit, wearing a serene little smile, which curled slightly up to the right, in deference to that same stroke that had stiffened his right arm and leg and wiped out the language functions in the left side of his brain. Periodically he would furrow his brow and make a valiant attempt to join the conversation, managing to blurt out a word or two; then, losing his momentum, he would back up, take another run at it, getting the same two words out, losing it again, trying again…and again…and again, until finally, a frustrated "Aw Hell!!" would shoot out by default and he would go silent. I always suffered through these attempts with him, trying to get inside his head and figure out where he was trying to go, so that I could fill in the words for him. Unlike my mother, I was convinced that he was still in there, capable of understanding my words even though he gave little evidence of real comprehension. The fact that he still always laughed at my jokes gave me some sort of intangible hope that he was still there. I needed him to still be there, and, as it turned out later, he didn't disappoint me.

The "Movers"

In the meantime, though, the seminary rule and curriculum gave my self-righteous inclinations fertile ground for development, and I emerged as a rather boring paradigm of piety and decorum. The liturgical movement had become popular with several of my classmates, and our class was getting a reputation for being a bunch of "movers." I attempted to read a few of the popular books on the subject, but found them ponderous and uninspiring. I had never been a big fan of ceremony and ritual, preferring my one-on-one conversations with Jesus to communal liturgies like Mass and Vespers. I could never get far enough beyond the personalities of the celebrants to be able to enter the magic of the rituals themselves, even though I went through all the motions with as much reverence and devotion as I could muster. It still always seemed like a big game of pretend to me. Others in my class seemed to derive some sort of ecstatic pleasure from the Gregorian chant, the incense, and the stiffly-choreographed rituals. I felt guilty for being so insensitive to the mystical depths of the liturgy, but I was assured by my confessor, the ever-empirical Fr. Dillon, that my reaction was not only normal but healthy, since, according to him, the liturgical movement was largely the work of soft-brained idiots and heretical modernists.

It wasn't long before the "movers" became an embattled minority at St. Joe's, constantly derided by the conventional jock types who always needed fodder for their putdowns. Things got worse when the movers added the emerging Scripture Movement to their agenda. Catholics had, up until that time, pretty much left Scripture to the Protestants, claiming that salvation came through Church Tradition, rather than through the highly suspect individual interpretation of the Scriptures. Now the movers were hauling new translations of the bible around with them, setting up elaborate scripture stands in their rooms, and telling the rest of us that we needed to read the scriptures for at least half an hour a day, that we should kiss our bible before and after we opened it, and that we should never set anything on top of it, lest we antagonize the Holy Spirit. Needless to say, the Philistine jock contingent didn't appreciate the movers' exhortations and couldn't understand why anyone in his right mind would want to read stuff that wasn't required for class. Most of the faculty sided with the jocks, seeing this new movement as a direct threat to their own authority in the classroom. Even though I wasn't temperamentally suited to this new idolization of scripture and liturgy, I found myself more and more disgusted by the "good ole boy" cynicism and narrow-mindedness of the jocks and faculty. Their reactions to the obvious excesses of the movers seemed unnecessarily mean and stupid. It was counter with the reptilian brain of the church and I didn't

Pretty soon several of my classmates expanded their interests in liturgy to fine art and set up a study group known as the "art forum." The reactionary members of the faculty immediately decided that this was just an excuse for students to ogle medieval pornography and attempted to shut it down. Such repression only added fervor to the cause, and the art forum prospered as a semi-underground guerrilla movement.

These new movements might have run their course and died away if it weren't for the fact that, at this same time, John XXIII had begun to transform the Vatican from the bastion of conservativism it had been under Pius XII to a much more progressive and open-minded institution. Suddenly, new ideas that had been long suppressed made their way into the public consciousness. John's aggiornamento heightened interest in Pierre Teilhard de Chardin's posthumously published Phenomenon of Man, which provided a philosophical framework for the "evolution of consciousness" that was just beginning to occur in the '60s. Chardin, a paleontologist of some renown, claimed his scientific studies showed that we had reached the end of biological evolution, and were now evolving in the "noosphere," the sphere of the mind. He also claimed that every cell, every molecule, every atom even, had consciousness, and that this consciousness was constantly evolving toward a greater unity. These radical ideas had been enough to get him accused of pantheism and silenced by Rome some years earlier, but he had been smart enough to entrust his writings to a colleague, rather than to the bookburners at the Holy Office, so his works were published posthumously.

Law vs. Love

The theological divide which had begun with our humorous repartee about the liturgical movement would grow into an outright war in the coming years, as the lines were more deeply drawn between the "love boys" and the "law boys." The former claimed that love was the great commandment and hence should be the basis of our spirituality; the latter claimed that obedience to the rule was the essential ingredient of spirituality, and that love would flow naturally from such submission. Supposedly, a specific event had spawned this dramatic philosophical divide: A faculty member at the major seminary had come upon a student standing at another student's door, talking to him during a silent period. The faculty member asked the student if he had gotten permission from his corridor prefect. The student said no, that he had not. The faculty member then told him to report to the Prefect of Discipline, where the student, in his defense, claimed that the other student had beckoned him to his door in a state of obvious agitation, and that he had responded immediately, feeling that the demands of Christian charity outweighed the dictates of the seminary rule in this case. The story circulated down through our ranks like a Delphic riddle, and we each solved the moral dilemma in our own fashion, unaware that our answer would eventually place us on one of two armies in the great moral battle that awaited us in the major seminary. I hedged my bet for several years, preferring ambiguity to partisanship. Only later, after I had ingenuously searched in vain for the logic behind many of the church's laws, did I come down on the side of love.

Poetry in Motion

In our Poet year, we took Latin, Greek, and Spanish, along with Poetry, Chemistry and Apologetics. The only "C" I got that year was in Poetry, from "Pop" Rock, a revered septuagenarian who had been a fixture at St. Joe's for many years. There was something about Pop that rankled me, though I realized I was alone in this reaction, since most of my classmates seemed to worship him as one of the seminary's senior deities. Try as I might, I could never quite figure out what Pop meant by "poetry;" plus, I found his habit of addressing us as "Dears" really irritating.

The one thing I do remember and appreciate from Pop's class was that he introduced us to Alan Watts and the haiku poets. This was our first indirect exposure to the Beat movement, which was thriving in Sausalito and in San Francisco's North Beach, and it awakened in me an appreciation for those who radically question the status quo, the contemporary equivalent of the Old Testament prophets.

A year or two later, Alan Watts became one of my heroes, when, as a guest lecturer at Stanford University, he said that the bible had become such an idol for people, it would be better if all bibles were burned and we let the Holy Spirit start all over again. My bible-kissing classmates were outraged at this, but I loved it, and immediately bought all his books.

In Latin class that year we read Horace, and in Greek class we struggled through Plato and Sophocles. Beansy Campbell was our Latin teacher, and seemed perfectly proportioned to instill in us an appreciation for Horace's many odes extolling the pleasures of food and drink. Our Greek teacher was Bucky O'Conner, a kindly, frail old priest who was very hard of hearing and whose hearing aid microphone was adjusted by a volume control device clipped to the front of his cassock. One of our favorite ploys was to gradually lower our voices while we were translating, until he was forced to turn the control up to full volume. At that point, John Cunningham would slam his dictionary onto the floor, causing Bucky to fly up in his chair with a terrified look on his face. I remember being rather conflicted about these pranks, feeling it was cruel to treat such a gentle and vulnerable human being this way, yet also being unable to resist the dark humor of it. Bucky was, after all, a member of the faculty and, hence, fair game.

"The Floater"

Perhaps the strangest character at the seminary was Royal B. Webster. Legend had it that Royal B had come to teach at St. Joseph's as a young priest, fresh out of the seminary, and that, after only a year or two, he had inexplicably gone quite mad and retreated to his room, never to work again. By the time we arrived at the seminary, he was an old man with a long unkempt white beard, who would be seen shuffling slowly along the corridors in his walker. His nickname was "Floater" and he spoke in a hoarse whisper, barely audible through his food-encrusted beard. Floater never came to the dining room, but ate all his meals in his room, which looked like a set from "The Munsters." The student infirmarian was assigned to bring Floater his meals, but often appointed other students to the task, just so they could experience the ambiance of Floater's room. It was a small space, jammed from floor to ceiling with junk of no particular significance or coherence. On top of his bureau was a small cake whose shellac-hard frosting was covered with dust. That, he would whisper, was his proudest possession, his ordination cake, now over 50 years old.

Floater would usually hang out in the cloister, which ran along the inside of the seminary courtyard. Most of the time it wasn't a highly trafficked route, but it connected the junior and senior study halls on the high school side of the house. It was here that young, inexperienced sixth-latiners would often have their first, unforgettable encounter with Floater.

You can imagine the scene: a kid of 14 has been at the seminary for about a week and is still scared to death of the place. All his life he's heard about how the seminary is God's elite training ground for future priests. The nuns and his parents have painted it as an intellectual and spiritual Olympus, populated by priests and teachers of outstanding virtue and intelligence. He's innocently walking along the cloister, when he encounters an etheric figure, dressed in cassock and roman collar, and sitting in a walker. The figure resembles an Old Testament prophet, with long, wispy white beard, sunken eyes, and a black cape over his bony shoulders. The prophet beckons to him with a gnarled finger, and the youngster humbly approaches, anticipating some sort of profound spiritual revelation. The figure beckons him closer yet, and he brings his face down next to that revered patriarchal mouth from which inspired words of wisdom will hopefully flow. At last the mouth opens, and a guttural "Aaarrggh" issues forth, borne on the foulest breath the young seminarian has ever encountered.

He staggers backwards, then hurries away, fleeing the awful "odor sanctitatis" which has just assailed his unworthy nostrils. Later, when he shares this experience with his peers, he is surprised to find that several of them have had similar encounters with Floater, and that his prophetic utterances are invariably indecipherable and malodorous. Thus does Floater gradually devolve from an inscrutable repository of divine wisdom to an object of pity and even derision, the quintessential Sulpician eccentric.

My own reaction to Floater was similar to that of the Sixth Latiners. I was convinced that anyone who wore a roman collar and was that old must be a bearer of spiritual insight and, hence, worthy of respect. When it came to protecting elders from the derision of youth, I was still carrying the crusader's banner I had picked up in childhood in defense of my grandmother. At first I was upset when my classmates made fun of Floater, and I was determined to probe the depths of his wisdom. Alas, despite several attempts on the cloister and in his room, I failed to find anything remotely resembling wisdom or depth in Floater, and had to admit that my more cynical classmates might have been right all along.

La Dolce Vita

Given the array of colorful characters in the seminary and the fact that the building and grounds could easily have passed for a Hollywood set, it wasn't surprising that it occurred to some of us one night that it might be fun to make a movie. Al Larkin, Conrad Gruber, Bob Carroll and I were walking around after dinner when the idea came to us, and immediately we began to see potential scenes everywhere – the tower, the courtyard, the locker room…everywhere we looked. We started getting together every night after dinner, walking around brainstorming ideas about the movie. Bob emerged as the creative director and came up with a plot – a loose story-line, strung with fragments of all his favorite scenes from Bergman, Fellini and Truffaut. At the time, I had no clue where his ideas were coming from, but years later I would be watching some classic film and suddenly experience a déjà vu as I recognized a scene that Bob had appropriated for our movie.

Bob wasn't a technical kind of guy at all, but luckily both Al and Conrad enjoyed photography and were pretty good at it, so they became the technical crew. Al was able to line up a good eight millimeter movie camera, so he became our cameraman, and Conrad filled in the other technical pieces. My own role got a little nebulous once Bob embarked on his "art film" motif. Half the time I didn't have any idea what he was talking about, so I'd just wait until he had a scene set up, then I'd start suggesting funny stuff to add to it. Often he'd ignore me, but sometimes he'd go along with my ideas. Bob had a "noire" sarcasm that could get pretty heavy and esoteric, so part of my role was to try to lighten him up by reminding him who our audience was. The filming took most of the rest of the year, and we shot the last scenes in the week just before graduation.

Bob's title for the movie was "The Sweet Life," a take-off on Fellini's "La Dolce Vita" which had just received the Legion of Decency's coveted "C" (Condemned) classification. Our movie featured an artistic loner who tries to preserve his creative identity (symbolized by a face he draws on an old beach ball) from the forces of conformity in the seminary. Throughout the film, the sound track alternates between readings from *The Rule* and "The Little City of God" and current love songs by the Everly Brothers. We shot scenes haphazardly, blindly trusting Bob's artistic vision. Sometimes he would script a scene, other times he would send Al off to film some everyday seminary occurrence. When a fire broke out in Beansy Campbell's room and the fire department arrived and started throwing his charred possessions out of the window to the courtyard below, we were right there with our camera.

The hero of the film was played by Larry Moorman, a rather depressed, though very funny guy, who eventually left the seminary to become a philosophy professor, and who, at our class reunion 25 years later, stood up and said, "I can't believe you guys are all talking about the seminary as though it was such a wonderful place. For me, it was like living in Aushwitz!!"

It was Bob who picked Larry to play the lead in "The Sweet Life," and it was a good choice. Bob evidently knew Larry's character well. He also knew, much better than I, what it was like to be an artistic outsider and to suffer from the demands of conformity in an institution like the seminary. For people like Bob and Larry, these Mysteries were anything but Joyful. Steeped as I was in my naïve equanimity, it would take me many more years to appreciate the real message and pathos of "The Sweet Life."

When we eventually showed the movie, I ran the projector and Bob ran the Wollensak reel-to-reel tape recorder. Periodically, one or the other of us would have to stop our machine to let the sound track catch up to the film, or vice versa. The tracking between machines was different every time, and so was the audience's reaction, though the majority of them, like me, laughed at the slapstick and missed the deeper meanings. Most of us weren't there yet.

Journal of the Soul

In the summer of 1960, I started keeping a journal, which I have continued, sporadically, ever since. The first entries are embarrassingly indicative of my state of mind in those early seminary years:

> *"September, 1960. It is only now, at the end of the summer, when I am beginning to get more apathetic in my own prayer life and less unattached to the things of the world, that I can really appreciate the problem of the laity. The world, like a huge magnet, seems to constantly exert a pull against the spiritually oriented, tending to force them into a state of inertia. The world stresses appearances. It is only by casting aside such appearances that we can approach God."*

There, in stark relief, I now recognize the simplistic dualism I inherited from my Grandmother, Augustine, and Mani – the struggle between light and dark, spirit and matter. This metaphysical dichotomy was the basis of our devotional life in the seminary. It was the battle we were constantly waging, fighting to retain our tenuous spiritual focus in a world of materialistic distractions. I realize now it was a schizophrenic endeavor, doomed to failure by the very nature of its presuppositions, but in the absence of a more holistic worldview, it framed all my thinking and fueled all my idealism.

Most of my journal entries seemed to occur during retreats, when my adolescent fervor bubbled up and overflowed through my pen. I wrote self-consciously, as though my words were intended for a future generation of Vatican officials who perhaps would be considering me for sainthood. I was striving for perfection, and my writing bore the mark of an uninhabited persona. There was no real "I," only the idealized and projected "I" that was striving to be "All things to all men," "Another Christ," and "The representative of God on earth." I had not yet found my voice as an autonomous individual, and would not, so long as I continued to equate any kind of authenticity with the sin of pride. Pride, we had been warned, was our most dangerous pitfall, Lucifer's weapon of choice. Our only defense against pride was humility and its corollary, absolute obedience to our superiors.

Journal: October, 1960

My first speech this year was a real masterpiece, I thought. It was my own original opinion, and I expected it to be greeted with enthusiasm and applause. Instead, Fr. Dillon exposed it as 'the typical work of a sophomore in college' – a mere opinion without any substantiation. At this my pride flared up and caused me to become quite disgusted with myself for allowing myself to be so humiliated. I should have been thankful for this warning against pride which God gave me at the beginning of the year.

I have no doubt that my first speech <u>was</u> sophomoric, and that Father Dillon was right to challenge me on it, but I find it interesting that, rather than examining my ideas and my logic, I examined my <u>conscience</u> instead, and, of course, found myself guilty. I would have done the same thing even if Fr. Dillon hadn't been a good teacher, even if he was a raving madman, because he was my superior and, as we had been told many times, *"A superior may err in commanding, but you can never err in obeying."* At age 20, as a sophomore in college, my childhood program was still intact. I was still functioning under the invisible protocols of the Catholic Operating System: Sin (Pride) > Guilt > Repentance/Submission.

Graduation

I graduated from St. Joseph's College (the minor seminary) in June, 1961. Since my eyes were still on the priesthood, this was not an endpoint for me, but merely a transition. Like most of my classmates, I was planning simply to move on to the major seminary the next year and continue my seminary training. St. Patrick's was only about twelve miles away in Menlo Park, an affluent suburb just north of Stanford University. My class graduated from St. Joseph's just after John F. Kennedy began his presidency and just before Pope John XXIII convened the Second Vatican Council. This was a time of great hope and expectation for American Catholics – we had a

Catholic in the White House, a reformer in the Vatican, and our own missionary spirit seemed suddenly to be spreading to our peers outside, who were flocking to the newly-formed Peace Corps. We were full of naïve optimism.

St. Pat's

Most of us were quite familiar with St. Patrick's by the time we left St. Joseph's, since we went over there every Spring for a barbecue with the "Patricians." We had also met many of them on Thursdays, when they would ride their bikes over to St. Joe's to visit younger guys from their parishes, or when their "house team" would come over to play against our "house team" in basketball or baseball. I didn't have many close friends at St. Pat's, mainly because there were no older seminarians in my parish and because I didn't work with any of them during the summer. That was usually where inter-class bonds were formed – during summer jobs at CYO Camp, Sunshine Camp, Hannah Boys' Center, or St. Vincent's School for Boys. In those settings, a core group would live and work together every summer, become friends, and then recruit new, younger members the next year. These groups were tightly knit and often provided a bond that was almost as primitive as membership on the Ramblers, Indians, Bears or Trojans. You had to receive a special invitation to join the staff at these places and, once there, you developed a loyalty to that group and became part of their particular culture. Each group developed its own personality, which then served as a screen for the next year's recruits. There developed, consequently, a vertical, as well as a horizontal, social integration at St. Pat's.

By the time my class got there, in 1961, St. Pat's was knee deep in the liturgical, scriptural, and catechetical movements. "The Patrician," an alumni magazine published three times a year by the seminarians, had recently changed its format and started running long pedantic articles about "Catechesis" and "The Easter Light of the Fourth Gospel," along with artsy pictures of modern chalices and Byzantine mosaics. This drove the older clergy nuts, because "The Patrician" had traditionally been their alumni magazine, and the last thing they wanted to read was a bunch of esoteric articles about scripture and liturgy. They wanted to know what was happening to their classmates in other dioceses and who had gotten hits in that year's baseball game between St. Joe's and St. Pat's. Most of the alumni had gone through the seminary at a time when you followed the rule, studied the textbook, and played sports. You didn't sit around discussing all these highbrow ideas and wearing fancy new vestments that made you look like sissies. They wondered what the hell was going on in the seminary, and why the faculty was letting it happen.

There was a battle going on, and we walked right into it. If there was a schism at St. Joe's between movers and jocks, it was nothing compared to the all-out war going on at St. Pat's, with faculty members lined up on each side, using classroom and pulpit to lob ideological grenades at each other. All this, of course, was taking place under a veneer of priestly civility and unanimity, symbolized by the black cassocks, which were the mandatory daily dress at St. Patrick's.

Uniformity

At St. Joe's we only had to wear our cassocks on Sundays, for High Mass and Vespers, so most of us had only the flimsy altar boy cassocks that our pastors had given us when we entered the seminary. At St. Pat's, the cassock was our default uniform and had to be worn at all times (except during long recreation periods when we were allowed to don our moldering "BOs"). Consequently, we had to buy a cassock that could handle a lot of wear, and possibly a second cassock to wear when our first one was at the cleaners. The best cassocks were those purchased from Wm. Thyssens & Son, Clerical Tailors, in Palo Alto. These were hand-made by Pete Thyssens, a jolly Dutchman whose little shop, founded years before by his father, was within easy walking distance from St. Patrick's. His cassocks had padded shoulders, good material, and came in either a button-down or sash style. They were also quite expensive, running about $85 in 1960.

There were two other options, either the Cabrini cassock, which could be obtained from Cabrini's Church Goods store in San Francisco, or the mail order cassocks you could buy from some sweatshop in Hong Kong. Cabrini cassocks looked great for the first three months, but then, as the fabric wore, they turned a shiny green color. We nicknamed them "Cabrini-greenies." The Hong Kong cassocks had better material, but you could never be sure they'd get your measurements right, and, if they didn't, it was a real pain to have to ship them back and forth.

I bought a button-down cassock from Pete Thyssens, figuring I could wear it every day and have it cleaned during Christmas and Easter vacations. Investing in a Thyssens cassock meant I definitely intended to stay in the seminary; otherwise, I would have hedged with a Cabrini greenie.

We also had to buy a biretta, a square black cap with three vertical tabs, the middle one always facing to the right so that it could serve as an easy handle for the many doffings required during High Mass and Vespers.

At St. Joseph's we were only required to wear our suits on Sundays, and they could be either dark blue or black. At St. Pat's the suit definitely had to be black, and we were also required to have a black "rabbie" – either a clerical shirt or shirt-front which could accommodate a roman collar. "Rabbie" actually came from "rabbet," which was a French word meaning a groove cut in the edge of something, in this case, our shirts (and, subsequently, our necks). There were two choices for roman collars. The standard collar was made of starched linen and had to be sent regularly to the laundry for cleaning and fresh starching. This meant that you would have to have at least two or three collars. The other option was to buy one of the newer collars made of plastic, which could easily be washed with soap and water. The only disadvantage with the plastic collars was their rigidity, as they often sliced like bow saws across one's Adam's apple. Nevertheless, I went with the plastic, figuring a little pain was preferable to a bunch of cleaning bills for something as stupid as a collar.

The dress requirements were spelled out in "The Common Rule of St. Patrick's Seminary," a small booklet designed to fit in a shirt pocket for easy and constant reference. Under the heading, "General Rules of Conduct in the Seminary," entry #36 read:

"All shall wear the ecclesiastical dress: that is, within the house and grounds, the cassock and roman collar; when going out, the roman collar and a black suit with coat of proper

*length. Garments of a worldly style or color are not allowed at
any time.*

*The dress prescribed by the laws of the Church for
ecclesiastics is obligatory for all in the seminary. The
seminarian who has the spirit of his vocation should deem it
an honor to wear the distinctive garb of clerics.*

*Neatness and cleanliness in dress should always be
observed out of respect for ourselves, for the community, and
for the ecclesiastical habit which we wear; but at the same
time anything savoring of vanity or worldliness should be
carefully avoided."*

There it was again, that reference to vanity, which of course meant
<u>pride</u>. We were told that our black clerical garb signified "death to the
self," and that was definitely true. It signified the death of our own
individuality, our own inner self; paradoxically, however, it also led
to an inflated sense of our external, ecclesiastical selves, since we
were now touted as "representatives of God on earth." We were men
in black, doing the will of God, and, as such, we were called to a
higher state than that of our fellow human beings. The image of
Horace's solitary plane tree (caelebs plantanus) comes to mind,
standing on a hill alone, with no messy vines attached.

The rule suggested that we kiss our cassock before stepping into
it, thus acknowledging its symbolic power. I followed that advice
religiously, trying to use every tool available in my quest for
perfection.

Mischief

As usual, the school year began with a week-long silent retreat. I
had always liked retreats and thrived on the discipline they required;
but after about the fourth day, I would start to get restless. One
afternoon, after I had exhausted my capacity for prayer and spiritual
reading, I suddenly got a mischievous urge to drill a hole through the
wall which separated me from my next door neighbor, Bob Leger.
Bob was a nervous little guy who was fun to play jokes on. He would
get embarrassed real easily, and then he'd wave his arms up and down
like a penguin, roll his eyes up in the air and let out kind of a guttural

113

groan. I was very fond of him, and had given him the nickname "Sledge."

I got a hanger out of my closet, untwisted it, and bent it around so that the curlicue part of it could function like a drill bit and the rest of it like a brace. Then I began turning it into the plaster. It made a neat little crunching sound for a while, then broke through, then hit something solid again about four inches away. I figured I had hit the other side of the hollow plaster wall, so I started turning it again. It bounced off a lathe and then chewed into the plaster again. I drilled for a few seconds, and then it broke through again only to run into something solid about two inches further on. I twisted the hanger some more, but there was no grinding sound this time, and I wasn't getting anywhere. I was stumped. What kind of wall <u>was</u> this?

I pulled the hanger out and straightened it. Then I reinserted it into the hole and pushed it straight through, being careful to keep it rigid and taut. When it stopped again, I lined it up perfectly straight and gave it a carefully directed shove. I could feel the mysterious obstruction give way a little and then the hanger broke free. A second later, there was an enormous crash in the next room. I had no idea what had happened. Only later did I learn that the hanger had come out of the wall just behind Bob's bookshelf, and my last shove had toppled it and his entire library onto the floor.

Luckily for him (and for me), he wasn't in his room at the time. Otherwise, I might have given him a heart attack. Even so, when he finally returned to his room, he was terrified to find it totally trashed, his bookshelf dumped over, books and statues strewn all over the floor. Since it was unthinkable that anyone would have risked expulsion by entering his room, he was completely befuddled, almost ready to call for an exorcism, until he noticed a tiny dot of plaster in the middle of the back panel of his bookcase. Then he noticed more plaster dust on the floor, and, looking up the wall, spotted the telltale hole. At that point his Sherlock overcame his trembling mystic and he figured out who the culprit was.

I've often wondered why this prank stands out in my mind so clearly. I think it was the first time I allowed myself to actually <u>play</u> in the seminary, to challenge its staid formality, mess with its predictable routines and fixtures, mock its medieval traditions. Up until then, I had repressed my mischievous instincts, attempting to become the mature and responsible seminarian the *Rule* prescribed. Something happened to me during that retreat. Something released in my soul. All of a sudden I began to see great humorous possibilities behind the seminary's rigid regulations and traditions.

Drilling through Bob's wall brought a great sense of excitement and adventure. I was stepping out, taking a chance, running the risk of getting caught. There was an adrenaline rush to it that was almost addictive. And Bob was the perfect foil. He was relatively new to the seminary, didn't excel in sports or studies, and was rather shy, so he didn't have a lot of friends. But he was a very sincere guy, very likeable, and laughed readily, especially at himself.

I can still hear Pat Browne admonishing me for "persecuting poor Leger," but in my mind I was only initiating Bob into the social circle of the seminary, much as Pat had done for me when I first entered, by making me the butt of his jokes in our bull sessions.

I figured Bob's popularity was growing every time I played a joke on him.

Later that year, Scott Carpenter became the second man in history to orbit the earth in a spacecraft and the entire student body was given permission to watch a live telecast of the event. Since we were seldom allowed to watch television on a regular school night, everyone jumped at the chance except me. I wasn't really interested in space, so I stayed behind and found myself all alone on a deserted corridor. Suddenly I had an inspiration. I went next door to Bob's room and quietly opened his door. Being careful not to put my foot across the threshold, I removed the pins and jimmied the door free from its hinges. Then I carried it around the corner, down the hall, and hid it in one of the janitor's closets. My heart beating, I returned to my room, turned off the lights and waited, giggling nervously in the darkness. Eventually, I heard the sound of footsteps and doors opening and closing as everyone returned in silence to their rooms. When Bob got to his doorway, he let out a guttural sound like "Erg!!" Then I heard muted voices as Bob stopped first one, then another of his classmates, to ask about his missing door. Eventually, there was quite a discussion going on out there, which came to an abrupt halt when the gravelly voice of Father Red Cronan, the corridor prefect, barked, "Okay Leger, talk!"

"Er, it's my door, Father. It's missing."

"How can you lose a door, Leger?"

About that time, there was a crash from the room across the hall. Pat Browne had been balancing precariously on his chair, watching Leger through his transom. The sight of Red Cronan suddenly arriving on the scene so terrified him that he lost his footing and crashed to the floor.

Red was now systematically interrogating Bob about his door – when had he last seen it, where did he think it might have gone, etc. Bob wasn't in any mental condition to answer any of Red's questions. He just stood there gulping and making his quirky little penguin gestures. I started to feel sorry for Bob because I hadn't intended to get him in trouble with Red, of whom he was already terrified. But I was laughing too hard and, besides, I wasn't about to go out and try to explain things to Red. Eventually Red dispatched a couple of guys to go on a search for the door, and pretty soon they found it in the janitor's closet.

The next day, everyone was standing around talking to Sledge about his door. When I walked up, he gurgled, "McAllister, I'm going to kill you!" Sledge's missing door propelled him into the social limelight and seemed to expand his circle of friends. At least that's what I told myself.

My pranks definitely made Bob more assertive. He got back at me the next Thursday by stealing my dirty laundry out of the receiving bin and then returning it to me a week later, unwashed. I was outraged when I opened my bag and found dirty laundry, and was on my way to complain to the nuns, when Bob came up smiling and said, "Oh, what a shame!" I knew then he'd gotten me, and that he probably didn't need any more of my assertiveness training.

Our mischief was what kept us free in a totalitarian situation. Without pranks and laughter, we would have gone under and become the "organization men" we had begun to read about in the pop sociology books. Mischief kept us young in what could otherwise have been a prematurely-geriatric institution. When I look back on my life, and even examine my present professional situation, I realize that I have never grown up, and am happiest when I don't have to pretend that I have. Bob was one of those people who catalyzed and appreciated my mischief-making and, for that reason, I will always remember and appreciate him as a valuable friend.

116

Choosing Confessors

The ideological battle at St. Pat's made the choice of a confessor a crucial decision. Knowing this, I had consulted ahead of time with Fr. Cornelius Burns, my former high school teacher who had recently been transferred to the faculty of St. Joe's. "Corny" was a conservative through and through, and was always very concerned about anything he considered out of the ordinary, whether ideas or people. I've often wondered if he might have been a secret member of Opus Dei. He once took me aside and warned me to be careful of my classmate, Tom Sheehan.

"Oh yes," he said. "Tom is Italian and Irish, a very dangerous and explosive combination."

Corny had opinions about everyone and was only too glad to share them. His was a Manichaean world of Good vs. Evil, and, like my grandmother, he didn't hesitate to place everyone on one side or the other. When I asked his advice about choosing a confessor at St. Pat's, he went through a lengthy description of the entire faculty, giving me an erudite, if totally biased, analysis of the strengths and weaknesses of each priest. He strongly advised that I choose Fr. William Sheehy, the oldest member of the faculty and a man widely renowned for his sanctity. I had never heard of Fr. Sheehy, though I later noticed that he had written the preface for Lyman Fenn's <u>Little City of God.</u> I followed Corny's advice, and did find Fr. Sheehy to be a very gentle and saintly confessor, but I'd only had him for about a month when he became ill and died. To be honest, I was somewhat relieved, because I had found his humble piety somewhat flat compared to my grandmother's warlike spirituality. By this time, I had a better sense of my ideological leanings and, knowing that I couldn't relate to the puffy intellectualism of any of the "movers," I again chose George Patten as my confessor, this time in the person of Father Edward "Red" Cronan. Red was an ex-military chaplain who also taught us Philosophy. He was a tough, hard-bitten, chain-smoking fanatic who believed in discipline and intimidation. Everyone was scared to death of him and many of the more liberal guys hated his guts. Just my kind of guy. He had a rough smoker's voice and a dramatic intensity that couldn't be ignored. He could also

117

be very funny, in a gruff sort of way, like the time he jumped on Bob Murnane the first week of class. He was pacing back and forth lecturing us about the philosophical method, and Murnane was sitting right in front of him, furiously taking down notes.

All of a sudden, Red stopped dead in his tracks. "Murnane!!" he barked, "Are you writing down every word I say??"

Murnane sat there immobilized and nodded his head.

Cronan looked heavenward. "Good God!!" he yelled. "Sincerity gone WILD!!"

This was the same Bob Murnane who, seven years earlier, had leapt forward as a daring champion of our eighth grade rights at St. Anselm's, and whose wild driving exploits during his freshman and sophomore summer vacations had become legendary, but who now, much to my disgust, had gradually transformed himself into an eggheaded intellectual ready to align himself with any crazy new movement that came along. I was glad to see Red shake him up a little.

Red

My classmates weren't surprised to see me pick Red as my confessor, since they had already begun to view me as some sort of spiritual Kamikaze. Red symbolized a no-nonsense approach to spirituality and the fact that he was perhaps the most unpopular confessor in the place made him somehow more attractive to me. I was still running my Grandmother's race. Like her, Red was a staunch believer in dualism, and his spiritual advising sessions always included diagrams of what looked like dumbbells – two circles with a line in between. In one circle he would write "God," or "supernatural," or "Church." In the other he would write "Man," or "natural," or "World." Then he would pontificate about how the two were diametrically opposed and how we had to constantly fight to stay in God's circle and not be distracted by the World. I remember watching his hands as he gesticulated his way through these sessions, and being captivated by the yellow nicotine stains on his fingers. Which of the two circles would his smoking habit fall in, I wondered, and did he talk to his own confessor about that?

Red taught us Philosophy the first year and History of Philosophy the second year. One day, while analyzing the illusory nature of our sense perceptions, he suddenly broke into song: "It's only a paper moon," he crooned, "floating over a cardboard sea." This was Red at his best – leaping out of his gruff persona just long enough to get a few laughs, then jumping back in, tougher than ever. None of us had ever heard the song before, and I even thought he might have made the phrases up, but then Eddie Gaffney got hold of the score and ran off copies for us so that we could sing it for Red's birthday later that year. It was one of the few times we ever saw him smile at anything besides his own jokes.

Red taught philosophy like a master sergeant in boot camp. He stuck to the book, which, unfortunately for us, was written in Latin, and he did his best to convince us that Philosophy was primarily a weapon, perfected by Thomas Aquinas, for defending the faith against heretics and fuzzy-headed liberals.

Cheech

It gradually began to dawn on us that the fuzzy-headed liberal Red had in mind was our other Philosophy professor, Fr. Bob Giguere, who was Red's absolute Nemesis on the faculty. Fr. Giguere's nickname was "Cheech," the derivation of which escapes me, other than its phonic association to a chipmonk, which may well have been his shamanic sibling. "Cheech" was a small, quivering Frenchman who spoke in a high voice, and whose openness to philosophical ambiguity was the antithesis of Red's macho sophistry. He wore his heart on his sleeve, could cry easily, was unabashedly effeminate, and yet was such an effective teacher that, at some point, he succeeded in breaking through to even the most cynical and hard-headed of us.

The Philosophy tract was split between Red and Cheech, with Red teaching us Logic, Cosmology and Psychology ("It's only a paper moon") the first year, Modern and Contemporary Philosophy the second year; and Cheech teaching us Ancient and Medieval Philosophy the first year, and Epistomology, Metaphysics and Theodicy the second. Since neither trusted the other, each would try to cover as much of the total curriculum in his own course as possible, lest we be unduly influenced by his rival. I began to feel like a spiritual and intellectual schizophrenic, attempting to remain obedient to my superiors, even when those superiors were diametrically opposed in their opinions. This became my greatest spiritual challenge during those first two years at St. Pat's. In my diary there is an entry entitled *"Reflections from the end-of-the-year retreat – First Philosophy, 1962:"*

God's Will:
A. In Studies:

1. *Be docile*
2. *Accept all systems and approaches for what they're worth. Don't adopt one exclusive of the others.*
3. *Truth is the goal. There are as many approaches to truth as there are men.*
4. *Opinions of older students are not necessarily correct. Otherwise, they would all be in complete agreement.*
5. *The new approaches are fine as long as they don't become blind and condemnatory of the older approaches.*
6. *To some minds the new approaches appeal more; to others, the older. But both types of mind must remain balanced, never excluding one approach completely.*
7. *If I have a teacher in one course whose approach I don't like, I must remember that it is God's will for me to have him – maybe to keep me balanced.*

Multiplicity

My ambiguity can perhaps best be explained by William Perry, of Harvard University, who studied the intellectual and spiritual development of college students and published a theory based on his research. According to the "Perry Scheme," students go through various stages, beginning with "dualism," a stage in which everything is seen in terms of black and white dogmatic answers. In this stage, teachers are seen as authority figures who possess the Truth and dole it out to docile students.

Only when the students have been exposed to different opinions and beliefs do they move from this dualistic certainty into the next stage, called "multiplicity." Here they begin to acknowledge the validity of diverse points of view, though they still feel there is some absolute truth out there that they will eventually discover.

The next stage is "relativism," where everything is up for grabs, nothing is certain, one idea is as valid as any other, and the student is incapable of committing himself or herself to any thing or any idea.

The final stage ("commitment") brings the student full circle, back to the point where (s)he can once again act in a committed fashion, even though (s)he is still aware that everything is basically relative.

By 1962, I had reached the "multiplicity" phase of Perry's development scheme, struggling to reconcile conflicting worldviews within the matrix of seminary spirituality. In this stage the student believes the teacher has the answer, but is withholding it so that s/he can expose the students to multiple points of view. By assuming that God Himself was bringing this chaotic array of intellectual choices into my life, I was able to maintain the illusion that there was a right answer out there, beyond all the ambiguity, but that I just hadn't grasped it yet.

It wasn't just the Philosophy department that was at war in 1961. The entire faculty had been split into factions, based on their attitude toward the new changes that were washing over the church. Frank Norris had emerged as a brilliant young liberal theologian, a reputation that would earn him an invitation to the Vatican Council and make him a very popular confessor. But not everyone liked Frank's liberal ideas, especially some of his fellow faculty members. His Nemesis was our old friend, Fr. Lyman Fenn, esteemed author of "The Little City of God," former rector of St. Joseph's, and now professor of Moral Theology at St. Patrick's. For every move Frank made in the direction of change, Lyman dug his conservative heels in a little deeper. Frank accused the conservatives of "getting stuck in the Council of Trent." Lyman parried back by calling the liberals "joy-boys of the Resurrection."

Even though I had chosen Red Cronan as my confessor, I couldn't fully commit myself to either side of this debate. If the contradictions were disconcerting to the part of me that craved certainty and dogmatism, they were also entertaining to the Irish part of me that enjoyed a good argument. It was like watching a football game, though I felt the same frustration I did whenever I had to sit and watch a game rather than participate in it. I spent a lot of time in chapel talking to Jesus about my dilemma, explaining to Him that, no disrespect intended, I really didn't care for Bible vigils and fancy new liturgies, but I didn't like the anal rubrics of the traditionalists either. He and I agreed that I would just keep it simple. I would read Thomas a` Kempis' <u>Imitation of Christ</u>, practice the presence of God, and make a lot of visits to the chapel, where He and I could just talk, without me having to worry about when to genuflect, read the Psalms, or tip my biretta.

The Good Doctor

If most of the faculty had chosen sides in this ideological battle, there was one sterling exception. Dr. Edward Philpot Mumford, a practicing Anglican, came from a long family line of medical researchers, one of whom helped establish Britain's Royal College of Physicians in the sixteenth century. Dr. Mumford had a staggering array of credentials, including a doctorate from Oxford, fellowships from Oxford and Cambridge, and numerous awards for his academic work on parasitology in the Near and Middle East. He even had a beetle named after him. Between research projects on mosquitoes and rats, he taught freshman biology at Dominican College in San Rafael and at St. Patrick's Seminary in Menlo Park. Dr. Mumford was a classic example of the sincere, but absent-minded professor. He adopted the traditional lecture method in his teaching, reading his often-abstruse notes to us at such a rapid gait that no one, not even "Sincerity-Gone-Wild" Murnane, could keep up with him. At a certain point in the lecture, when the entire class was totally lost, John Cunningham would wave his hand and say, "Doctor, could you please read your notes a little faster?" Doctor Mumford would say, "Eh…all right," adjust the glasses that were always down at the end of his nose, find where he had left off in his notes, and start reading at an even faster rate.

Part of the reason Dr. Mumford felt he had to read his notes so fast was that we were always behind in the syllabus and he was always trying to catch up. Being the gentle soul he was, he could never resist a question and could never detect the mischief that lay behind most of them. We knew that he had been strictly warned by the rector not to teach anything about evolution, so every time we

were introduced to a new life form, someone would immediateꞁy
what it had evolved from. The good doctor would get a slight smile
on his face, push his glasses back on his nose and say, "Ehh...Father
Wagner has asked me not to cover 'eevolution' in this class." Then
we would all groan and boo and act very disappointed.

When Dr. Mumford wasn't lecturing, he was either showing us 8
mm films or attempting to get us to do experiments in the adjoining
lab. The films were always fun because every time Doctor would turn
his back, John Cunningham, who ran the projector, would reverse the
direction of the film and we would be watching fish swimming
backwards or severed cells miraculously reuniting. Sometimes these
reversals would last 10 minutes or more before Dr. Mumford would
finally notice that something didn't look right.

Since we had about 40 students in the class, Dr. Mumford split us
into two groups for labs. One group would go into the lab to do
experiments and one group would stay in the adjoining lecture room
to "study our notes." He would go back and forth between the two
rooms trying to keep some sort of order. As soon as he went into one
room, half the students in the other room would sneak out the door
and go up to their rooms to take a nap. Others would pull out a deck
of cards and start playing poker.

The doctor was dealing with a bunch of adolescents, and he knew
it. He was a simple man with a good heart, and he took all our antics
in stride. For his birthday that year we presented him with a check for
$100,000 to use for biology supplies (we were constantly straining his
slim budget by smashing slide plates in the microscopes). He accepted
the bogus check and our exaggerated applause with a blush and said,
"Ehhh...that'll buy a lot of frogs."

Lord'nLady Mumford

The most memorable part of our biology course was the
anatomical dummy in the lab. It had detachable organs and stood in a
prominent position in the front of the lab. However, much to our
amusement, it had no sexual organs. These had been removed, giving
its genital area the appearance of a Barbie doll. We christened the
castrated dummy "LordnLady Mumford," and grilled the poor doctor
at length about this phenomenon, knowing that he had had nothing to

do with it, that it was just another of the bizarre restrictions imposed by the seminary faculty on his biology curriculum. We learned later that the genitals had actually been removed by our old friend Lyman Fenn and were, at that very moment, hidden in his closet for use at a later date.

When I reflect back on our biology class and the dummy that symbolized the seminary's approach to sex, my laughter shifts slowly to sadness, and then to anger, as I think about all the sexual problems that have surfaced among Catholic priests. Whatever is repressed explodes, and it is no wonder that priests who learned anatomy on a sexless dummy found themselves totally confused about their own sexuality as adults. Locked as they were into their own adolescent ignorance, fears, and twisted mystiques of sexuality, it is not surprising that the only sexual partners they felt they could resonate with were innocent adolescents and children.   Without sexual feedback from mature partners we might all be in that situation.

In 1962, when I was 21 years old, I was a lot like that dummy. I had no idea what female genitalia looked like, let alone how they worked. I wasn't even sure how my own worked. I was a celibate warrior, dutifully denying the reality of sex in my life, long before I had tasted its pleasures or understood its mythic and psychological power. In my youthful naivete, it seemed easily heroic to give up something I had never experienced, even something as integral to life as sexuality, something whose suppression was packed with such explosive dangers.

Why did the church systematically program us toward a denial of this essential part of ourselves? Partly for economic reasons, certainly. The ownership of church property reverted to Rome in the twelfth century when priests were finally driven out of their marriages and forced to deed their churches to Rome rather than to their heirs. But my intuition tells me that mandatory celibacy had a deeper, more sinister purpose. It was a way of crippling us psychologically, locking us into a pre-adolescent homosexual dependency on a similarly crippled male hierarchy. It was part of a highly sophisticated system, extremely effective, though far removed from the original teachings, and intentions, of Jesus. The Catholic Church of the 50s and 60s excoriated Communism for breaking up the family, pointing out that this was an effective mind control technique exercised by a totalitarian dictatorship. No wonder they recognized the technique. Back in 1075, when Pope Gregory VII (Hildebrand) decided to impose celibacy on his married priests, he declared, "The church cannot escape from the clutches of the laity unless priests first escape from the clutches of their wives." Then he proceeded to excommunicate any Catholics who received communion from married priests. But even these totalitarian techniques didn't work. The priests refused to leave their wives and children, and the laity supported them.

It was Gregory's successor, Urban II, who finally figured out how to break up the families of the priests. He summoned the nobles and told them he wanted them to enforce the church's new celibacy laws. Knowing they would need an incentive to perform such an unsavory task, he made them a promise. If they forced priests into celibacy, he, the pope, would give them the priests' wives and children as slaves. It was an offer they couldn't – and didn't – refuse. Our genitally-deprived dummy will attest to that fact.

Diocesan Politics

Meanwhile, the celibate clergy mushed on. In October 1961, shortly after my class first arrived at St. Patrick's, the archbishop of San Francisco died. John J. Mitty had been San Francisco's archbishop since the time I was born, and his death signaled the end of an era. As the seminary waited in suspense for news about who his successor would be, Hugh Donohue, one of Mitty's auxiliary bishops, became the temporary administrator of the archdiocese, spawning speculation that he would be named archbishop. However, in February of 1962, word came that Joseph T. McGucken, the former bishop of Sacramento, had been appointed as the new archbishop of San Francisco. More exciting, however, was the news that three new dioceses had been created, in Oakland, Stockton and Santa Rosa. Donohue was to head the Stockton diocese; Floyd Begin, former bishop of Cleveland, was moved to Oakland; and Leo T. Maher, the former chancellor of the San Francisco archdiocese, was appointed bishop of Santa Rosa.

The creation of the new dioceses had a profound effect on priests, in that it locked them forever into the diocese in which they happened to be stationed at that time. A priest who had grown up in San Francisco, but who had been temporarily appointed as an assistant pastor three hundred miles north in Eureka, probably was hoping to eventually be reassigned back to a Bay Area parish, close to his family and friends. The creation of the Santa Rosa Diocese meant he would never have that option, that he would have to develop new friendships with the priests who likewise found themselves under the jurisdiction of the bishop of Santa Rosa. These implications were not lost on us seminarians. We realized we were again being drafted on four different teams and that those teams would again exercise a major socializing influence on us.

When the announcement was first made, there was some speculation that Marin County would be part of the diocese of Santa Rosa. Jim Pulskamp and I were both excited by this prospect, since we had always visualized ourselves working in rural parishes, rather than in the inner city. When it became clear that Marin was to be included in the San Francisco Archdiocese, we were disappointed and decided we would switch to the Santa Rosa diocese. In our naivete, we assumed this would be a simple matter of contacting the new bishop of Santa Rosa and offering him our services. We soon found out, however, that our lives were not our own, that we were the property of the Archbishop of San Francisco until such time as he released us from his service. The realization that I was the equivalent of an Archbishop's serf ignited in me what I now recognize to be my first feelings of rebellion against the organized church. Others I spoke to about this didn't seem at all bothered by the fact that they were "owned" by a particular bishop. They seemed to think it gave them more value and status as individuals. I however, found it quite appalling and it made me only more determined to be released from San Francisco – just as a matter of principle, if nothing else. By this time, there were five of us interested in transferring to Santa Rosa. Mike Kenny lived in Vallejo, which had been made part of the Sacramento diocese, so he had to petition the new bishop of Sacramento, Alden Bell. The rest of us had to petition Archbishop McGuckin, but official protocol dictated that any such communication with one's bishop had to be initiated through the Seminary Rector, Father Wagner. We patiently went through this petitioning process, and then, several months later, discovered that our petitions had been lost or discarded, so we went through the whole process again. Finally, a year later, we got word that all but one of us had been released or "excardinated" from the San Francisco Archdiocese and were now free to transfer to Santa Rosa.

I was quite happy about this and felt God was definitely looking out for me by insuring that I would serve Him in the spacious countryside rather than in the crowded city. I became a little suspicious about the mysterious ways of God, however, once I met Bishop Maher. He spent his entire first meeting with us prattling on about the design of his new coat of arms. He was like a kid with a new toy, and talked so incessantly and bumptiously about his plans for the "Redwood Empire" that everyone soon began calling him "Emperor Leo." He took a royal tour of his new domain and came back with grandiose plans to build new churches and rectories up and down the coast. This didn't sit well with many of his priests, especially older pastors who had served in rural areas for many years and knew that a fancy new priest's house would only alienate them from their hard working and frugal congregations. Leo would hear no objections, however, and soon proceeded to plow millions of dollars into his grandiose building campaign. He also purchased, for himself, a comfortable mansion capping a hill in one of Santa Rosa's most affluent neighborhoods. This was his Versailles, where he could entertain his clergy in true imperial fashion and demonstrate to his well-connected neighbors that the church was an enterprise to be reckoned with.

From the start, I had serious reservations about Leo's fixation on wealth and power. I was still a Spartan by nature, much more comfortable with Jesus driving the moneychangers from the temple than with Him eating and drinking with tax-collectors. Leo's unabashed materialism didn't resonate with the ascetic tendencies I had inherited from my grandmother. I was still questing for martyrdom and Leo seemed to be more aligned with Pilate than with Stephen.

My Spartan proclivities reached their apogee when I decided, later that year, to officially join "The Pioneers," an Irish Catholic temperance society who took a lifetime vow to abstain from drink, in expiation for the "hundreds of thousands of hopeless Irish alcoholics." I had never taken a drink in my life, so this was an easy and painless way to get another merit badge for righteousness. Although Pioneer membership was offered to everyone in the seminary, only four of us actually took the oath. Our names were dutifully Irish: Moran, Kenny, O'Neill and McAllister. This was one plunge I couldn't convince Jim Pulskamp to take with me.

My misgivings about Leo's materialism were quickly overcome by my excitement about being inducted into this new male hierarchy, smaller and more accessible than the huge San Francisco archdiocese, and much more intimate. I was enthusiastically welcomed as an equal by older members of the Santa Rosa clergy, who themselves were experiencing a youthful exhilaration during this pioneering phase of the new diocese. There was something incredibly engaging and intriguing to me about this new association. Perhaps because I was convinced that I would spend the rest of my life as a priest, and that these men would be my extended family, I wanted to learn everything possible about them and about the diocese of Santa Rosa. I spent hours asking about the personalities and habits of the various priests, one of whom, I assumed, would some day be my pastor. During that summer, Mike Kenny, Jim Pulskamp and I took our own tour of the diocese, staying at various parishes up and down the coast and getting to know many of the priests. This was the beginning of a deep friendship between Mike and me. Despite the five-year difference in our age, we shared a true-believer's idealism and a dedication to what we perceived to be Jesus' most simple precepts. We vowed to each other that we would never let ourselves be tempted by the blandishments of clerical power or seduced into joining the ranks of the hierarchy. Mike violated this latter vow some years later when he was consecrated bishop of Juneau, Alaska; however, he managed to retain his idealism, integrity and simplicity in that role, and stayed sufficiently true to his values that he was never rewarded with any further hierarchical advancements. He became a committed pacifist, the only bishop who had the courage to testify on behalf of the Berrigans, and he died very unexpectedly in 1998, while on a peace mission to Jordan. It was diagnosed as an aneurysm, though I always had my doubts. Mike never smoked or drank, ran five miles a day, and had the most positive attitude I'd ever seen. Peace can be a dangerous mission.

He's the only bishop I ever trusted.

***

In those early days of the Santa Rosa diocese, I felt an exhilaration and energy I have never experienced since. Perhaps it was because I was still young and idealistic; perhaps it was because I was looking for something to fill the emotional void created by my father's stroke; perhaps it was an outlet for the sexual energy that normally would have been shared with a romantic partner. Whatever the reason, I was totally committed to this highly-charged and provocative fraternity. It both captivated and inspired me, just as it had done since I was a torchbearer in second grade. I was feeling very much at home in the temple.

The Fifth Joyful Mystery:
The Finding in the Temple

Let us contemplate, in this mystery, how the Blessed Virgin Mary after having lost (through no fault of hers) her beloved Son in Jerusalem, sought Him for the space of three days; and at length found Him in the temple, sitting in the midst of the doctors, hearing them, and asking them questions. He was then twelve years of age.

<u>The New Key Of Heaven</u>
A Complete Prayerbook for Catholics

Back in the seminary, the ideological war was still being waged. Father Giguere was doing his best to give us a personal experience of existential angst, while Red Cronan was trying to strain modern philosophy through the sieve of orthodox Thomism. Red always assigned a specific philosopher to each student in his History of Modern Philosophy course. The student had to do extensive research on that philosopher and then give a presentation to the class. Like everything else in Red's course, this occasioned a lot of anguish and trepidation among the students. Knowing this, he was very strategic in pairing philosopher to student, using this as yet another way to temper any liberal excesses he observed in individual students. His own graduate research had been devoted to Henri Bergson, a French philosopher whose <u>Creative Evolution</u>, published in 1907, had courageously suggested that energy and intuition should have philosophical precedence over matter and intellect. Red knew that Bergson was a dangerous thinker, whose ideas, in the wrong hands, could do a lot of damage to Catholic presuppositions. He wasn't about to assign this kind of French firebrand to any of the rebellious thinkers in our class, like Tom Sheehan, Ed Gaffney, Bob Carroll, Bob Murnane, or Al Larkin. Instead, he assigned Bergson to me. I was, after all, his boringly-predictable penitent, who could easily be kept in check during the course of doing research. I was also a moderate, aligned with no particular ideological camp, and showing no signs of intellectual fervor that might drive me into dangerous areas of investigation. I was a safe bet.

Tom Sheehan, perhaps the most intelligent and creative scholar in the class, whose passion lay with Heidegger and the existentialists, was assigned August Comte, the Father of Scientific Positivism.

"Elan Vital"

I had never heard of Bergson and would have preferred someone a little more boring and obscure, someone about whom my professor/confessor didn't know so much. But the next Thursday I rode my bike over to the Angelus Bookstore in Menlo Park to see what I could find on Bergson. The Angelus was an energetic little place, run by a savvy Catholic layman named Duke Douglas. Duke carried all the latest books on Catholic theology, as well as a pretty solid philosophy selection, and he did a good business in those days. Besides two hundred and fifty book-hungry seminarians, he had a fairly wide customer base among the young Catholic intelligentsia who were beginning to populate what would later be called Silicon Valley. On Duke's shelves, I found a book by Bergson entitled The Two Sources of Morality and Religion. It was an Anchor paperback and it sold for 95 cents. I decided I would start with that one, because it was cheaper, and seemed more interesting and accessible than the other Bergson book he had in stock, the thick hardback entitled "Creative Evolution."

This was the first time I had actually attempted to read an original work by a philosopher, (unless you counted reading Socrates' Apology in Greek class), and I wasn't too optimistic about my chances of finishing it. I had no idea that my brain was about to embark on the most exciting adventure of its life.

Bergson published The Two Sources late in his career, in 1932. In it I found, not only a captivating theory of morality and religion, but also a resolution of the spiritual dualism I had unconsciously been resisting since childhood. Reading Bergson was like meeting a hidden part of myself whose existence I had previously only suspected. For the first time, I realized that philosophy could change and enhance life, rather than merely analyze and categorize it. I became totally immersed in Bergson's worldview.

131

All life, he said, is pure energy, or "elan vital." And this energy flows upward and outward like water in a fountain. And just like the water in a fountain, when the energy reaches the top and begins to fall back down it meets the upcoming water and appears to be standing still. This is what we call "matter," but in reality, it's all energy.

It's the same with religion and morality, according to Bergson. They both begin with a creative impulse, a spurt of inspiration, in the form of a Jesus or a Buddha, and then they gradually fall back on themselves, become static, and crystallize into dead laws and obligations. When I read this, I was astonished. Here was a French philosopher who had died the year I was born, and he was speaking directly to me, addressing the very same issues that had bothered me since childhood, ever since I had been told that Henry Peck wasn't going to heaven because he was a Jew. Bergson was looking directly in the face of this destructive dualism, and was giving me a means to transcend it with a monistic theory of pure energy, "Elan Vital," which I immediately transposed into the Catholic concepts of Divine Love and Sanctifying Grace.

I loved Bergson's critique of intellectual concepts, probably because I was feeling overwhelmed by the constant egghead arguments that were swirling around me. Bergson held that intellectual concepts could only capture dynamic reality ("elan vital") by stopping its natural flow, much like dipping a bucket into a flowing river and pulling out now-motionless water. Only intuition, not intellect, could truly resonate with elan vital; only intuition could enter into, and honor, the present moment without immediately imposing on it the prefabricated and static concepts of "past," "future," or "clock time." Ever since my grandmother's death, I had been haunted by the insubstantial nature of time, by the fact that moments disappeared as soon as I became aware of them. Now, for the first time, I realized that the moments that were disappearing were my mental concepts of the present moment, not the living present moment itself. The living, dynamic present moment is all there is, all there ever has been, all there ever will be. And it's right NOW. I realized that intuition, the part of our consciousness which resonates with the now, was the gift of the mystics, and that it was invariably doomed to be buried under the static "past" and "future" concepts of the intellectuals and theologians. Ten years earlier, my Grandmother's death had yanked me out of the world of conventional concepts into a world of existential emptiness where no concept, no image, held any value. At the time, I had no way of appreciating the value of that experience. I was only aware of what was <u>lost</u>. Now Bergson enabled me to appreciate what I had <u>found</u> – intuition, direct perception of Being, devoid of concepts; direct awareness of God – not the god who stands outside, but the God who is the Elan Vital of the Present.

This was an unexpected spiritual by-product of what had started as just another academic assignment. I don't remember any of my classmates getting similarly inspired by the philosophers they were assigned. Bergson was a gift, generously passed on to me by Red Cronan, though he may have subsequently regretted it. He gave me an A– on my final paper, faulting me for "not using enough Thomistic sources" in my research. (Thomism was the philosophical tradition of Thomas Aquinas, which at that time was Catholicism's sole philosophical touchstone for orthodoxy.) That was Red's way of saying that I needed to treat Bergson as an object of investigation, not a model for my own thinking, and certainly not an inspiration for my own behavior. But it was too late. I had already discovered the philosophical solvent that was, even then, loosening my bonds to the seminary and to the church.

Red Cronan wasn't very popular with our class. His military style of education-by-intimidation had ceased to be welcome in the new church of John XXIII. Red must have known that his teaching career was on the downslope, because he gradually became more agitated, and his skin allergy reached a point where he started coming to class with rubber gloves over his inflamed hands. He was a chain smoker and heavy drinker, like many priests of that era, and had the gravel in his voice to prove it. It was rumored that he had suffered a nervous breakdown some years earlier and that he had thwarted treatment by attempting to psychoanalyze his own doctor. Indeed, it <u>was</u> hard to imagine Red listening to anyone, especially a shrink. Red's condition gradually got worse until, in the following year, he returned to his native East Coast and was replaced by a young philosophy professor fresh out of the seminary.

The Mediator

If there was a mediating figure on the faculty in those days, it was Fr. Gene Nicolas, who taught us English Literature and Speech, and directed the seminary's liturgical rituals. "Nick" was a "late vocation" who had entered the seminary after a stint in New Jersey's business world. He had a droll sense of humor and seemed to be above the philosophical and theological squabbles that divided the rest of the faculty. When Red Cronan left and I needed a new confessor, I chose Nick, precisely because of his openness and humor. He and I had become good friends earlier that year when I was appointed infirmarian and Nick was my supervisor. My infirmary was right across from Nick's room, and we would confer frequently about various health issues in the community. Being infirmarian was an easy job, since the only medications I was authorized to dispense were Coricidin, aspirin, and Phisohex.

Nick was also the faculty Master of Ceremonies, and this put him in a sensitive position, since the seminary's liturgy was tinder for its most intense political conflagrations. Nick had a reputation as a "progressive, but prudent" liturgist, so he played a critical moderating role in a deeply divided faculty.

Each summer there was a National Liturgical Conference, and in 1963 it was going to be held in St. Louis. Nick mentioned in class that he'd like to go and asked if anyone else was interested. Pat Browne, Mike McLaughlin and I all volunteered. Mike's dad was in the Teamsters and had connections to car rental agencies, so he volunteered to get a car for us. All we'd need was enough money for gas, food and lodging. When the time approached, Mike was unable to go, but his dad still supplied us with the car, and Pat, Nick and I took off for St. Louis. My memories of the trip are sketchy – Winnemucca the first night; Denver the second, with its endless ribbon of neon (Colfax Avenue) stretching out across the plains from the base of the Rockies; St. Thomas Seminary in Denver; some sort of monastery in Hays, Kansas; the almost-finished arch as we drove into St. Louis; and finally the Gaslight District. I remember very little about the conference itself, other than the strange name of the university dormitory where we stayed (Griesedieck Hall). Somewhere in Nebraska we were pulled over for speeding, and we got out of a ticket by shamelessly brandishing Nick's breviary and capitalizing on our priestly status. This trip is the last recollection I have of myself as a conventional seminarian. I was still going to daily Mass, saying my rosary, and armoring my soul against the seductions of "the world" in Gaslight Square. That persona would begin to change during the next year. Bergson had given me a new worldview, and I had no idea what a radical impact he was going to have on my life.

The Crack in the Armor

In my first year of theology, I innocently picked up a book my mother had ordered from the St. Thomas More Book Club. It was a biography of Martin Luther, written by an Anglican by the name of John Todd. I found it captivating, but also disturbing, after I learned that everything Luther had originally taught, and been condemned for, was now accepted by the Catholic Church. He had merely suffered the misfortune, common during that period, of being ahead of his time. I had never previously understood that Luther's real "crime" had been his objection to the scandalous sales of indulgences that were subsidizing the construction of St. Peter's Basilica. Nor had I realized that he had done everything in his power to remain a faithful son of the church. All this came as a rude awakening to me, since the only thing I had previously learned about Martin Luther (in Father O'Neill's Apologetics class) was that "he was a horny monk who married an ex-nun." These new revelations about Martin Luther pierced my orthodox armor and I began to realize that, if our teachers had been wrong about Luther, they might well have been wrong about other things as well.

About that same time, in 1963, a small book called <u>Honest to God</u> appeared, written by an Anglican bishop named John A. T. Robinson. His thesis was simple: If God is "infinite," (that is, "without limit or boundary of any kind") then how can God be "out there," separate from ourselves? In fact, how can God even be a "He," a distinct person, a Being?

That question, coming on the heels of my discovery of Bergson's Elan Vital, went right to my soul and had immediate repercussions on my spiritual life. I had always spent a lot of time in chapel, talking to

Jesus, whom I always visualized and addressed as "out there," up on the altar, in the tabernacle. After reading <u>Honest To God</u>, I found I could no longer do that, for, if God was infinite, and Jesus was God, then it was idolatrous for me to confine Him to the tabernacle. It was also idolatrous for me to think of Him as a "He." Even the notion of <u>talking</u> to God was idolatrous, because talking implied some kind of subject-object split between talker and listener. Instead of praying, I now found myself sitting in the chapel with my head spinning. I began to realize that all my religious assumptions rested on a finite infinite – a contradiction in terms – and that, in order to free God (Infinity) from my inadequate and presumptuous conceptual bonds, I had to be willing to let go of everything that I had ever believed. And then what? What would be left? Nothing. No thing. God was no thing.

Intellectually, it made sense. Emotionally, it was terrifying. I talked to others who had read the book, hoping to find someone who was going through the same spiritual crisis, but I found that my friends who had read it had kept it on an intellectual level, not letting its radical ideas challenge their Catholic preconceptions. They weren't really troubled by the book; it was just another interesting theory for them. Some even dismissed it as "lightweight," not worthy of scholarly attention. I began to suspect that several of them had only read the reviews, not the book itself. No matter. I knew now that I was on my own, cut loose from my previously secure spiritual moorings and unable to board anyone else's boat.

Bergson had given me a mystical perspective, elevating God to a principle of creative energy, permeating everything. The image of God as Elan Vital was liberating and inspiring. But it wasn't the end of my spiritual odyssey. <u>Honest to God</u> called me to the next, more challenging part of the journey – the deconstruction of all my previous images of God. I hadn't realized how emotionally bonded I was to those images, and how difficult it would be to release my childhood images and consolations. And I felt angry about having to go through such spiritual discomfort alone. I directed a lot of my anger toward those around me whom I perceived as blithely mouthing theological phrases without having the courage to examine their own preconceptions first, and I became intolerant of those whom I suspected of spiritual cowardice (which soon included everybody but myself). I could no longer take any of my courses seriously, because they all seemed hollow and irrelevant. I would sit in Scripture class, getting more and more angry about the fact that we were talking on and on about revelation and inspiration, when we had never yet figured out what we meant by "God." Until we realized that the Bible's image of God as a separate person was inadequate and basically idolatrous, we were doomed to wallow around in meaningless and arrogant speculation. Even the "exciting" new ideas pouring out of the liberal theologians were all based on the same unexamined presuppositions. All these people were begging the same basic question that had been raised in Honest to God, and I had no patience with them. The only theologian I could stomach was Paul Tillich, who had pushed the question of God far enough to conclude that the only adequate description of God was "The Ground of Being." In the process, he had also stripped Faith down to its essential elements by defining it as "Ultimate Concern." That's what faith had become for me – ultimate concern. I was committed to the search, but the answers all seemed to be eluding me. It was a very different place than where I had been six years before, when I first entered the seminary.

My attempts, during class, to ask the questions that were troubling me were met with the same kind of hostility that I imagined Luther had received. I began to be perceived as a disturber, rather than as a sincere, though admittedly bewildered, seeker, and this added to my anger and disillusionment.

As if losing my faith were not enough, I started losing my hair during this same period. This was not unexpected, since both my father and my maternal grandfather were bald, but its impact was nonetheless traumatic. At a time when the Beatles were elevating long hair to the pinnacle of youthful style, I was beginning to look more and more like Yul Brenner. Every morning as I brushed my hair and watched the cascade of blonde strands floating down into my washbasin, I was filled with depression. This was a poignant experience of death, losing a part of myself that I knew would never return. The fact that it coincided with my loss of faith only made things worse.

My confessor, Fr. Nicolaus, wasn't much help at this point, certainly not with my hair loss, but not with my loss of faith either.

He kept assuring me that I was going through a temporary "crisis of faith" which I would surely outgrow.

"Everyone experiences some kind of crisis of faith," he said, "and everyone eventually gets over it."

"I don't think this is something I'm going to get over, Father," I said.

He assured me that I would.

But I didn't.

Silicon Valley in the 60s

"Before I took drugs, I didn't know why the guys in the psycho ward at the VA Hospital were there. I didn't understand them. After I took LSD, suddenly I saw it. I saw it all. I listened to them and watched them, and I saw that what they were saying and doing was not so crazy after all."

Ken Kesey

The seminary's location in Menlo Park placed it in the center of an energy vortex that was taking place in the early 60s. Five miles to the west, Stanford University had begun construction of the world's largest and most powerful linear accelerator in 1962. About the same time, young members of a band that would eventually be called "The Grateful Dead" were practicing in their parents' garage two miles to the south, in Palo Alto; and Ken Kesey was over at Stanford working on his degree in Creative Writing. The Silicon Valley was in its infancy, and the seminary just happened to be at its epicenter.

Every evening, after dinner, we were given a talk by the seminary rector, Fr. Wagner. These were usually rather boring stream-of-consciousness monologues about the spiritual life. However, one evening in 1963, we arrived in the prayer hall to find Fr. Wagner talking to a stranger in a suit, whom he introduced as a Catholic layman from a local parish who worked as a counselor at the Veteran's Administration Hospital just down the road. Fr. Wagner told us that this gentleman had something he wanted to share with us. The man thanked Fr. Wagner and said that he had worked in the alcohol treatment section of the VA hospital for many years, and that, as we were probably aware, alcoholism was a pervasive problem among vets and very hard to cure. Recently, however, the been experimenting with a new drug, and the results astounding that he wanted to share them with us. Vets wh.. .... before been able to stop drinking seemed to totally lose their craving for alcohol when given this drug. There were other interesting things about the drug too, that he thought we might find interesting. The drug seemed to bridge the gap between the body and the soul, and it released a chemical in the brain that had previously been found only in monks who had spent many years in meditation. It seemed to be a miracle drug.

He finished by rattling off the drug's long and indecipherable name, but said it was called "LSD" for short. Father Charles McKay, the young priest who was now teaching philosophy in Red Cronan's place, immediately put up his hand.

"Yes, Father," the man said.

"I would like to officially volunteer as a test subject for this drug, if you need any more volunteers," McCabe said.

"That'd be great, Father. You're just the type of test subject we're looking for," the man said.

Then a voice came from the back of the room. Lyman Fenn, professor of Moral Theology and renowned author of <u>The Little City of God</u>, was on his feet.

"This is against the natural law," he shouted. "It should be condemned!"

If we weren't already aware of the ideological fault line that ran through the seminary, this exchange made it painfully obvious.

What we had no way of knowing at the time was that Ken Kesey, future author of "One Flew Over the Cuckoo's Nest," was currently working at that same VA hospital, precisely because of the federally-funded (and CIA-initiated) LSD experiments being conducted there. He was supplying his fellow students in Stanford's Creative Writing department with copious amounts of LSD, peyote, and mescaline from the VA's experimental storage cabinets. These students would later form the nucleus of the Merry Pranksters, a madcap group that would totally validate every fear Lyman Fenn ever had about aberrations of the natural law.

The Changing of the Guard

Other situations within the seminary were also providing Lyman with plenty of fodder for his reactionary paranoia. Inspired by Pope John's aggiornamento, the Catholic Church had started lumbering into the 20th century with all the inflated optimism of an old wino on his first snort of cocaine, often treading clumsily on the well polished shoes of people like Lyman Fenn. What many saw as simple modifications of Church practice, Lyman saw as a systematic abrasion of the rock of Peter. With a conservative's unerring instinct, Lyman saw that even slight modifications of tradition would radically alter the DNA of an absolutist structure like the Church. Once the dualistic worldview of Pius XII was undermined, the Church as Lyman knew it would cease to exist. Authority would break down; chaos would ensue. Lyman could see it happening everywhere – in the new, round-necked surplices that were replacing the old square cut style; in the way certain priests extended their hands beyond the prescribed 10 inches when they turned to say "Let us pray" (instead of "Oremus") during Mass; in the irreverent questions students were starting to ask in his moral theology classes.

Times became even harder for Lyman when his old friend and classmate, Edward "Cop" Wagner, became sick in late 1963 and eventually died in April 1964. Cop had been the seminary rector since 1957, and Lyman was his trusted confidante, well positioned to slow the pace of change in the seminary. After Cop's death, Lyman served as interim rector for a couple of months, but then a new rector, Fr. Paul Purta, was appointed in the summer of 1964. Purta was from Scranton and had a reputation as a liberal, so his appointment gave great hope to the proponents of change at St. Patrick's and moved Lyman to the sidelines, where he was relegated to playing the "devil's advocate" role.

Father Purta knew he had a tough challenge ahead of him, and he began his reign as a consummate diplomat, preaching daily homilies that acknowledged the conflicts within the seminary and the church but urged a balanced approach to healing them. At first, I was very impressed by his awareness and leadership. Only after many months, did I begin to realize that we had been hearing essentially the same homily every day, a template recitation of a straw dialectic that went something like this:

"On the one hand we see *(insert some outlandish right wing position)*; and on the other hand we see *(insert an equally outlandish left wing position)*. But if we prudently examine the facts, I think we can achieve a more balanced and insightful viewpoint *(insert Purta's own position)*."

I eventually realized that this was Fr. Purta's basic political strategy – to so caricature both the positions of the left and the right that people would have no choice but to accept his own agenda as the only reasonable point of view. It didn't take Lyman and the conservatives long to see through this ploy. It took the radicals a little longer. I don't think the liberals ever figured it out.

One of Father Purta's first moves was to liberalize the rule in an effort to reduce seminarians' isolation from the world. In preparing to initiate this policy, he set up his usual off-balance straw man:

> *Trying to be prudent with that prudence which issues in balanced action rather than in paralyzed inaction, the concerned seminary faculties welcome the suggestion that we offer the seminarian a richer intellectual environment, the cultural stimulation which comes from broader competition with a wider cross-section of the world. At the same time, these faculties would recall an ancient error: knowledge is virtue.*

"Nova et Vetera: Seminary Problems"
The Patrician, Winter 1964

Having thus framed the argument, he came up with an eminently "balanced" policy whereby he allowed us to have cars (though we couldn't keep them on the seminary grounds) and to go to "cultural events" off seminary grounds (but only with faculty permission). Lyman strongly objected to the change on many grounds, not the least of which was that wily students would soon try to argue that even rock concerts and movies should be included under the definition of "cultural events."

He was right, of course. Students did make the argument, and they often succeeded. That's not really surprising, because, about this time, the Beatles appeared on the Ed Sullivan show and elevated rock music to a new cultural status it had never previously enjoyed. Up until then, rock'n roll was regarded as a primitive activity, the domain of inner-city blacks, gyrating southerners, and moon-struck teenagers. Leave it to the Brits to give it aristocratic status.

The Beatles hit the seminary like a gale, dethroning our former favorites, the Kingston Trio, overnight. Though I wasn't immediately drawn to the Beatles (probably because they were popularizing long hair just as mine was falling out), I did sneak down, with several others, to Mike Tobin's electronics lab in the seminary basement to watch the Sullivan show on an old black and white Zenith that Mike was repairing for a faculty member.

Soon rock music became the spiritual mantra for many of the younger guys on the philosophy side of the house. Unlike us, they didn't feel the need to do battle against oppressive rules and traditions. They weren't programmed as deeply as we were, and it was easier for them to just ignore the rules, knowing, without any doubt, that the whole world was going through a profound transformation, despite the petrified structures of the seminary. Dylan had become their spiritual advisor and "the times, they were a changin."

Although, by this time, I was certainly in favor of any changes to the seminary rule, I was still fighting my own inner faith battle, and no liberalization of rules was going to help that. I began to see Father Purta's changes as liberal facades, designed to co-opt the more radical changes that needed to be made. In retrospect, I see that no changes would have satisfied me, because I was questioning the very basis of authority itself. I was fast becoming a spiritual anarchist. Once I had embraced the idea that God could not be "out there," that God was not "a person," not a "someone" who had revealed Himself only in the past, I could no longer accept the idea that authority resided in a tradition locked into that past. My God must speak intimately to me in the present, not through the dusty volumes of Vatican tradition, or even through the relatively enlightened pronouncements of Vatican II. Without realizing it, I had entered my own dark night of the soul. I had become a gnostic without knowledge, a mystic without visions. I was in the void, waiting for my own revelation.

Master of Ceremonies

To make matters worse, my confessor, Fr. Nicolas, in an attempt to re-engage my flagging commitment to matters ecclesiastical, appointed me Master of Ceremonies, which meant I was responsible for training everyone who served at the solemn high Mass on Sundays and holy days. All the seminarians had to take their turns at this and every week I had to train them, following the specifications of the *"rubrics"* – the red print in the missal which spelled out in detail every action which was supposed to accompany the official prayers and readings. This was an ill-advised move on Fr. Nicolas' part, because, by that time, I was just as cynical about the rubrics as I was about all the other regulations that were woven like steel wool through the fabric of seminary life. I did my best to deconstruct the rigid pattern of altar service, telling my charges not to worry about this or that bow, to "just pour the water, hand him the towel, and be done with it." I couldn't imagine Jesus giving a rat's ass about all the bows and genuflections that the rubrics prescribed, so part of my self-professed mission was to sabotage what I had started to consider the Nazification of the Last Supper. This didn't sit well with a lot of my trainees who were convinced I was trying to turn them into Protestants.

The War of the Socks

My zealotry had to have a target, and Paul Purta, the seminary rector, was destined to take the brunt of it. There were all sorts of issues we could have locked horns over, everything from the Vietnam war to seminary morning prayers, but the issue which brought us to the mat like two ideological sumo wrestlers was – of all things – white socks!

At the minor seminary, the nuns had issued us two nylon-mesh laundry bags, one for white socks, one for black. You put your black socks in one bag, your white socks in the other, and you secured them with big safety pins that had your laundry number on them. That way, the bags could just be thrown in with the rest of the laundry, and the socks didn't get separated. Most of us wore white socks all the time, feeling they heightened our ivy league look and, besides, everyone knew black socks were incubators for athletes' foot.

When we got to the major seminary, a lot of guys switched over to black socks, feeling they needed an accessory more resonant with the mandatory black pants and cassocks. A number of us, however, continued to wear white socks, preferring their comfort, and feeling that we were making our own more dapper, less boring, fashion statement. White socks seemed to express a certain adolescent vitality, an easy-going comfort, and a refusal to submit to the totalitarianism of black. At St. Pat's, however, there were no nylon mesh bags in which our dirty socks could form pigmentary communities. The nuns had to deal with each sock as an individual.

One day, fairly early in his reign as rector, Fr. Purta announced that we would no longer be allowed to wear white socks, because it was too much trouble for the nuns to wash both black and white socks separately. He spoke this in a voice we hadn't heard him use before, a rather nervous but stern voice that implied an edict rather than a conversation. This was suddenly not the same Fr. Purta who had been selling himself to us as the most consultative and collegial of rectors. The term "collegial" had become the watchword of the Second Vatican Council, implying a radical departure from the hierarchical authoritarianism that had become Rome's signature. Fr. Purta was known to be a collegial leader. He believed in collaboration. But there was no collaboration in this. It was an edict, directed at a small minority of us in the seminary. Why hadn't he talked to us about it? Why did he have to just dump it on us? It really rankled me, not just because I only owned two pairs of black socks, but also because it struck me as a really stupid policy, since the nuns were still washing our underwear and, if they just used some nylon bags like we had at St. Joe's, they could throw the white socks in with our Jockey shorts.

I decided to talk to the other guys who always wore white socks. They were a very diverse group, a broad cross-section of jocks, eggheads, and comedians. I talked to a lot of them and they agreed that the ruling was stupid and unfair, definitely a discriminatory act against those who happened to believe in the healthful and aesthetic aspects of white socks. Most of them, though, weren't willing to make a big deal out of it. Purta, our new liberal CEO, had them rather intimidated. To my surprise, it was Mike Sullivan, a popular, funny, jock-type, two years my senior, who agreed to come with me and talk to Fr. Purta about the idea of using nylon bags.

Mike and I ran in very different circles. In my mind, he was a member of the jock elite; a reactionary, but witty, philistine, whose social position I often mocked, but also rather envied. In his mind, I'm sure I was an eggheaded radical, whose only saving grace was that I was a passable jock who appreciated his jokes. We might have gone to our graves still clinging to these images of each other, had it not been for white socks. Those virginal socks somehow became a sacramental catalyst for us, and, buoyed up by the optimism of that new-found communion, we approached Fr. Purta, assuming that his liberal intellect would immediately grasp the logic of our suggestion.

We were wrong. He didn't even listen to our idea about the nylon bags. He cut our argument short and forcefully reiterated that it was too much work for the nuns, and that we, as future priests, should think of others instead of ourselves!

This was a powerful argument. The last thing we wanted to do was exploit the nuns, who, we all readily admitted, were much holier and more dedicated than any of the rest of us. But Fr. Purta still hadn't heard what we were saying. The bags would actually cut down the nun's work. They wouldn't have to sort <u>any</u> socks anymore. We reported back to our constituency and decided to approach him again. We must have caught him on a bad day.

This time he listened more closely to our idea.

But it didn't matter. He still insisted that the mere presence of white socks was an unreasonable burden to lay on the nuns.

"You guys are just thinking of what's convenient for you," he said. "It's my duty to look after those dedicated women."

At this point, I suggested that he mandate white socks instead of black socks, so that the nuns wouldn't have to wash anything except white stuff.

Any time Fr. Purta tried to smile, when he really didn't feel like smiling, his lip would go up at the corner, like he was nauseated, and that's how he responded to my attempt at humor – like he was going to throw up.

Once we realized he wasn't going to budge on the nylon bag idea, Mike and I pulled out our ace in the hole, the card we had hoped we wouldn't have to play, but that we assumed would win the game.

"Okay, Father, we'll wash them ourselves."

Fr. Purta slowly nodded, as though in agreement, but, as he nodded, he still had that nauseated smile, along with a vacant look in his eye, which told us he was frantically looking for a sharper weapon, something with which he could cleave our heads in two.

Finally, he cleared his throat, hesitated for a moment, and then said, "Well...uh...there's another reason why I don't want you wearing white socks."

We looked at him with an expression that said, "Huh?"

"They don't look professional," he said solemnly. "They look 'hunky.' And the modern church needs its priests to look professional. White socks just don't cut it."

Mike and I looked at each other. "Hunky??" What the heck did that mean? We'd never heard that term before.

And since when did priests have to look "professional?" My father wasn't a professional. Jesus wasn't a professional. Hell, Jesus didn't even wear socks!

We went back and told the other guys about his response. A lot them were swayed by his argument. Purta was, after all, the new kind of charismatic seminary rector that we'd all been waiting for. If he thought we needed to look more professional, then maybe we did. We all knew the church needed to become more relevant to the modern world. Maybe Harvey Cox would agree that our white socks were making us irrelevant.

I went back and thought about it a lot. What bothered me was that he hadn't been up front with us. He had tried to use the nuns to manipulate us, rather than coming right out and telling us his real agenda.

I finally learned from one of the seminarians who had grown up in Chicago that "hunky" was a term used to describe Hungarians and Poles, probably originating from "Bohunk." That's when it started to make sense to me. Father Purta was Polish. He was the first member of his family to go to college, let alone become a priest. He was proud of his accomplishments, rightly so, and he didn't want any of his seminarians wearing the white socks that would remind him of his "bohunk" relatives back in Scranton.

Okay, so that was his problem. Several of us stubbornly continued to wear our now hand-washed white socks as a protest against what

146

we saw as Purta's attempt to invade our private lives and force us to invest in Desenex. We began to use the term "hunky" back at him, using it to describe things that he liked. He'd be talking about a new liturgical vestment that had caught his fancy, and somebody would mumble under his breath, "Uh, Father, isn't that thing kinda hunky?"

At our annual Christmas show, we had Santa present him with a brand new pair of "hunky hose." He seemed to be a good sport about our joking, and he backed off his black sock campaign for a while. But I could tell it was still bothering him. A couple of weeks later, he came up and told me that he'd have no problem with us wearing white socks, just as long as we wore black socks over them. I told him that was crazy, because the black socks would hold in twice as much heat, and the white socks would only be able to breathe half as well. It wasn't a healthy alternative.

He backed off again for a while, but then one night he caught me after dinner and said he had just read a great article about West Point cadets. The author had described how the cadets wore special socks that were white on the bottom and black on top!

"West Point!?" I shot back. "That's a <u>military</u> academy. They're into discipline for discipline's sake!"

He had finally flushed out <u>my</u> real issue: Authority. He jammed his index finger hard into my chest.

"Don't forget, buddy. Once you're a priest, you're going to have to follow whatever orders the bishop gives you."

"Not if they don't make sense," I retorted. "I'll argue with him just like I'm arguing with you right now."

"We'll see," he said. And he stormed off. His liberal cool was gone. My liberal illusions were gone. We both knew that we were locked into a battle that neither of us could win.

He was right, of course. Unquestioned obedience to the bishop was still the prerequisite for being a priest. He knew that only too well, having dedicated his career to placating first one, then another, superior.

I thought about it. For me, that kind of blind obedience was no longer an option. My spiritual values had evolved in the opposite direction. For me, Jesus was a rebel, not a churchman. I would never again be able to submit to the traditional Catholicism of my ancestors. And I wasn't about to invest in a bunch of black socks.

Turnaround

That didn't mean I had to take myself so damn seriously, though. I began to detect a flaw in my position. My battle with authority had turned me into a rather testy authoritarian myself. I mean, who gets that righteously outraged over socks? In the name of tolerance, I had started getting <u>in</u>tolerant of anyone around me. I had become the very enemy I was fighting.

My mellowing, in no small part, was due to my confessor, Father Nicolaus. He had spent months trying to pry me loose from my pitbull–persistent crisis of faith. Finally one night he cleared his throat and, in his slow New Jersey drawl, said, "Greg, I have to admit I don't understand what's going on in your mind, but I think I know you well enough to know that, when you lose your sense of humah, something is wrong. And you've definitely lost your sense of humah!"

His words hit home, and I realized that he was right. I had started taking myself so seriously that I had alienated myself from friend and foe alike by projecting my own intolerance and alienation onto everyone else. I had gotten sucked into the dualism I was so determined to fight. For the first time, the comedic aspects of this seminary drama began to dawn on me, and I began to see myself more in the role of a white-socked Puck than a tragic Hamlet. I realized that it was possible for me to be who I was, and to believe what I believed, without having to convert everyone else to my opinion. I could merely play my allotted role, and, if I did so with humor and grace, I could be whoever I wanted to be. None of our roles was absolute; all were complementary. I suddenly understood the notion of the Mystical Body of Christ in Shakespearean terms. If God was the infinite Ground of Being then each person was playing God in finite costume. We were all God, and God was having a good laugh.

Once I shifted my theological lenses, the world was a good place again. I began to feel healed, at one with the world and myself, and my sense of humor did come back. I began to see the comic aspect of our seminary situation, and my previously angry political outbursts gradually evolved into satirical songs and skits. I also found my sense of childish mischief returning and only then did I realize how boringly "adult" I had allowed myself to become.

By this time I had also discovered another of Bergson's books, a small volume entitled <u>Comedy</u> in which he examined various theories of humor and concluded that comedy occurs when "the mechanical is imposed upon the human." Since much of the seminary's raison d'etre consisted in the imposition of the mechanical upon the human, I soon began to perceive Bergsonian comedy everywhere I looked. Pranks and jokes became sacred acts for me, sacramental solvents injected into the sedimentary sludge of seminary routine.

Besides providing a lot of <u>material</u> for comedy, the seminary also served as an effective <u>medium</u> for humorous communication. Everyone there shared the same experiences, lived in the same building, followed the same rules and schedule. The intense, pressure-cooker environment spawned the kind of inbred collective consciousness that guaranteed everyone would immediately "get it" whenever a joke was told or a prank pulled. You couldn't find a better incubator for humor.

The Worm

Despite the seminary's unique comedic potential, the ideological conflicts of the 60s tended to smother most attempts at humor. Finding co-conspirators for jokes became more and more difficult, and in my class, it pretty much came down to Paul Feyen and Bob Carroll. They were very different from each other, and the jokes we pulled together had different objectives. With Paul, the goal was just to create general mayhem. With Bob, it usually entailed exposing the mechanistic foibles of authority figures.

Paul and I were in town one Thursday browsing around the drug store, and we saw a rack of practical joke items, including a very realistic rubber worm. We bought it and brought it back to the seminary, not sure exactly what we were going to do with it.

It was my turn to wait tables that night, so I stuck the worm in my pocket, just in case. The dinner entrée was hot dogs and beans – those little baked beans that come in an orange sauce. This was a standard seminary meal, one badly in need of a Bergsonian goose. I watched as the beans made their way around the tables, waiting to see if anyone would raise the bean bowl, requesting seconds. It was John Meenan's table who raised the first bowl. John was a portly redhead whom we had affectionately nicknamed "Meatwagon." I swooped down on the table before any of the other waiters got there and grabbed the bean bowl from the piler's raised hand.

As a waiter, you never knew if the nuns were going to have seconds available or not. You just had to pass the bowl through a little window in the kitchen door and wait. Either they would take the bowl and return it filled or they would gesture that there was no more available. The bowl disappeared and came back full of beans. Perfect. I pulled out the worm and shoved it down into the beans until it wasn't visible. Then I returned the bowl to the table and went about my business. A few minutes later, I glanced over at Meatwagon's table, and noticed that everyone was leaning in, focused on Jack Kriel's plate. I walked by and sure enough, there was the worm, laid out on the plate. Jack was explaining that, not only was the worm <u>real</u>, but it was <u>pregnant</u>, as evidenced by the enlarged segment near one end. (Jack was taking Biology from Doctor Mumford that year, and had just finished the part about the reproductive cycle of the earthworm.) Paul's table was nearby and they were all giggling as they watched the faces of the guys on Meatwagon's table who had all stopped eating and were eyeing the worm nervously.

The meal ended, and everybody left, except the waiters, who always ate their dinner after everyone else. We were sitting there eating and I was telling them about the worm, when Father Maher, the seminary bursar, suddenly burst in and dashed through the dining room into the kitchen. I sat there for a while and then decided I'd better go see what was happening, just in case someone had reported the worm to him. By the time I entered the kitchen, he had all the little French nuns lined up and he was frantically gesturing to them with his little finger as he repeated the word "worm" over and over. The nuns were all looking at him like he was crazy, timidly shaking their heads and shrugging their shoulders.

I said as casually as I could, "Ah, Father…this wouldn't have anything to do with a worm in the beans, would it?"

He wheeled around to me and said "What do <u>you</u> know about a worm in the beans?"

"Well," I said, "it was just a little rubber worm that I put in there for a joke. It's no big deal."

"Easy for YOU to say!" he barked, then gestured an apology to the nuns and stalked out.

I looked at the nuns and shrugged. One or two of them started giggling, but the rest just stood there looking bewildered. I went back out with an even better story to tell the other waiters.

When I got to my room, there was a note under my door that read "I need to talk to you right away! – John Meenan." I went down toward his room and ran into him coming back from the infirmary with two alka-selzer tablets in his hand. He was bright red and steaming mad.

"I just want you to know that I've been throwing up since dinner because of that worm of yours!"

"Come on, John," I said. "It was just a little rubber worm."

"It may have been just a rubber worm, but when I first saw it, it was dangling from a big spoon with orange kidney beans dripping off it. It was hideous."

That really made me laugh, which only made him angrier. This was the kind of thing I lived for. Bergson would love it.

***

Bob and I usually thought up pranks as though they were scenes in one of our movies. We'd <u>see</u> the prank in our imaginations and that's how it would start. Sometimes the pranks didn't really work the way we visualized them, but that never really mattered. As long as the joke was at the expense of authority figures, just the idea of it would make us laugh.

The faculty always ate at a separate table in the dining room, up on an elevated platform. This was a mark of their authority, and hence a good target for a prank. There were always two water pitchers on the table, serving about eight faculty members. Father "Dumpy" Becker was the biggest water drinker. He usually polished off almost a full pitcher by himself. One night Bob and I imagined a very funny scene where there were guppies swimming around inside the faculty water pitchers. We saw Dumpy reaching for the water pitcher and then pulling back his hand when he saw the guppies. Or better yet, he wouldn't notice the guppies, pour a glass of water, and then slosh down one or two of them. We saw the scene clearly. It was too funny. We had to do it. On our next day off, we walked into town, found some guppies at the pet store, and brought them back in a couple of plastic bags. Just before supper, we sneaked into the refectory and, when the nuns weren't looking, we dumped the guppies into the water pitchers. Then we hustled back outside just in time for the Angelus bell. After dinner started, I stole a look up at the faculty table, expecting to see the guppies swimming around in the pitcher. There was no sign of activity. During the course of the meal, Dumpy went through his usual four glasses of water, and other members of the faculty poured themselves water without noticing anything. I looked over at Bob, a few tables away. He shrugged his shoulders and pointed toward the kitchen. The nuns must have noticed the guppies and changed the pitchers. I was irked. After all our work, the nuns had gone and ruined everything.

After dinner, Bob and I waited until the refectory had almost cleared out and then sauntered up to the profs' table to check the pitcher. There, on the bottom, covered by about an inch of water, lay the guppies. They evidently couldn't survive ice water. Dumpy had never even noticed them.

"Dumpy"

Early in 1964, Father Wagner had become seriously ill and the faculty had to call in a replacement to teach Canon Law. Fr. Edwin Becker came from a place called Egg Harbor, Michigan, and carried his 200 plus pounds in a drab wrinkled cassock. Within the week, he had earned the nickname, "Dumpy." A simple man with a gentle heart, he assumed we would share his love and respect for the Codex Canonis Legis. He was mistaken. For those of us who were beginning to question the legalistic traditions of the church, Canon Law was anathema #1. The Code of Canon Law had several thousand "canons," i.e., short legal prescriptions that governed all church behavior. These went into picayune detail about every item of church custom and tradition. By 1964, many of us had started to see the Code as an irrelevant and ridiculous farce, especially against the backdrop of Vatican II.

Dumpy's unenviable mandate was to march us through the entire Codex in two years. We were committed to stop him. We had two basic strategies. The first was to pepper him with esoteric questions about the minutiae of the law. For instance, one canon decreed that all priests were under the jurisdiction of an "Ordinary" (i.e., local bishop). The only exceptions were the "vagi" or "wanderers" who had "no fixed abode."

"Father, I know this is unlikely," someone would say, "but what if a priest were kidnapped by an alien and brought to another planet against his will? Would he have to look for a new bishop, or would he still be under the jurisdiction of his old bishop?"

Dumpy would get a slight smile on his face, happy to see we were interested enough to ask questions, and say solemnly, "Oh, well, in a case like that, I suppose…"

Usually we could eat up most of the class time with our irrelevant questions, but periodically we would come up with a better strategy:

"Father, would it be okay if we did a short dramatization of canon 459? It's such an important canon, that we thought it deserved some extra attention."

His response was always the same: "Oh, all right. Just keep it brief."

With that, several of us would exit the classroom to don costumes and pick up props. Then we would reenter with great fanfare, while someone did a dramatic reading of the canon in question. One time we asked him if we could do a dramatization of the canon entitled "the burial of a bishop." He agreed and we solemnly processed in with candle bearers, bell-ringers, a guy swinging incense, and six pallbearers carrying a full-sized wooden coffin, which had been used in one of the seminary plays, and on which we had mounted a bishop's miter. We processed around the classroom two or three times and, about the time Dumpy suggested we get back to the canons, we intoned the "Dies Irae," the Church's official funeral hymn, which took up another five minutes.

Dumpy got his revenge later in the year, during baseball season. He showed up during one of our early practice sessions and offered to hit pepper for us. The idea of Dumpy being able to get a bat past his stomach was inconceivable to us, but we figured we'd humor him, so we gave him the bat and we spread out in front of the backstop with

153

our mitts. Dumpy tucked his cassock into his sash, walked out to the pitcher's mound, and cocked the bat like a little kid who has watched a lot of Yankee games. The first ball we threw to him was low, almost in the dirt. To our amazement, he deftly dipped the bat and hit a line drive right at the thrower's ankles. We were stunned. Lucky break. But it wasn't luck. Everything we threw to him he slammed back at us, usually on a short bounce that was next to impossible to catch. No longer was Dumpy a pudgy object of scorn. He was a well-oiled machine of death and he had us where he wanted us – standing in front of the backstop with nowhere to escape. We had never seen anyone hit pepper with such dexterity and accuracy. We went back to the locker room with bruised shins and with a new respect for Dumpy's hitherto-hidden kinesthetic IQ.

***

Solemn High Mass on Sunday was just that – solemn. Which meant that any unintended deviation had the potential of unleashing a lot of repressed laughter. The faculty took turns officiating at the solemn High Mass, and the first time Dumpy officiated, the entrance hymn happened to have a refrain that went, "The King of Glory Passes on His Way." We were all singing that refrain, when we looked up and saw Dumpy, all decked out in his fancy vestments, (which made him look like an inflated Infant of Prague), solemnly processing toward the altar. Everyone went into hysterics.

Subsequently, any time Dumpy was scheduled as celebrant, we always made sure that "King of Glory" was chosen as the entrance hymn. After a couple of times, we noticed that he was wearing a slight smile on his face as he walked in (he got the joke), and we remembered pepper, and we sang louder, honoring him as the unlikely, but benevolent, king that he was.

Dumpy's royal domain was really among the squirrels in the small cemetery behind the theology wing. He regularly visited them and, in kingly fashion, dispensed liberal amounts of peanuts to his furry subjects. A few years later, when Dumpy was unceremoniously yanked away from St. Patrick's to another assignment back East, the squirrels revolted. Two days after his departure, students discovered that the squirrels had stealthily entered the laundry room across from the cemetery, crawled into the candy machines there, and consumed every bar of candy that had any vestige of peanuts in it. The king of glory had, indeed, passed on his way, but his myth lived on.

History by Threes

Father Leo Ruskowski had taught history from time immemorial and, like most of the faculty, his persona had crystalized into an easily-mimicked caricature. He spoke in a flat, inflectionless tone that resembled a Hindu chant, and he walked with his arms straight down at his sides, never moving them in synch with his feet. In class, he had a recurring mantra, which he would drone out in a low monotone: "Name three." That could be three dates, three countries, three emperors, three anything. History was one long series of trinities, and his final exams followed the same model. Needless to say, fitting everything into neat packages of three meant that he had to make some pretty esoteric leaps into the trivia of history, so his exams were almost impossible to pass, unless you had access to the multi-year backlog of old tests that had been passed down through various seminary channels. At first my conscience bothered me about using these illegal ponies and I attempted to take the tests without them. This, I found, was like trying to crack some World War II Nazi code, and I eventually gave in and agreed to study for the exams with my friend Len Duggan, who had a file containing every exam Leo had ever written. The reason everyone in our class could rationalize the use of ponies for Leo's exams was that we knew we were dealing with an alien intelligence. Leo was rumored to have been a pioneer recipient of a prefrontal lobotomy many years before, and this supposedly explained his strange, almost robot-like behavior and perhaps also his fixation on the number three.

Despite his highly predictable speech and mannerisms, Leo possessed a dry, penetrating sense of humor that often caught us off guard. Bob Leger was one of his favorite targets, perhaps because Bob would get so nervous when Leo called on him. One day, as Leo was doing his catatonic walk back and forth across the front of the classroom, he suddenly droned, "Mister Leger."

We could all hear Bob's "ulp" before he replied, "Yes, Father?"

"Name three popes between 1100 and 1250 A.D."

Bob turned all red and started hemming and hawing. "Uh, well, uh...Innocent the Third and...uh, Gregory the...Ninth, I think...and uh...Innocent the Fourth?"

Without changing his somber gait, Leo droned, "Name three more."

One of my major turning points in the seminary came while I was studying for one of Leo's final exams. I looked down at the stack of old mimeographed history tests that I had been memorizing and suddenly realized that I was totally wasting my time. I wasn't learning anything valuable about church history. All I had been doing for the last two hours was memorizing a lot of names and dates and bunching them into groups of three. It occurred to me that I now had a choice. I could spend several more hours memorizing a lot of weird triads for Leo or I could spend it trying to get some real grasp of church history. I decided that, from then on, I was going to take responsibility for my own learning. I was going to try and understand history, and, to do that, I had to stop worrying about test questions and grades any more. When I told Len about my decision, he shook his head, and told me I was nuts. I figured I was nuts either way.

Lyman

We had Lyman Fenn for moral theology that year, and our first encounter with him in the classroom drove a lot of us crazy. He believed, and taught, that the Church was the repository of infallible truths, and that it was our duty to accept and learn those truths without question. In class, he spoke in a condescending, sing-song tone that set my teeth on edge, as if he were scratching on a blackboard. His deep anger about the changes taking place in the Church was poorly masked by the tight little smile that he always wore as he sarcastically excoriated the liberals in the Church as "joy-boys of the Resurrection." In retrospect, I can see that he was a clever and effective apologist for his sector of the church, but, at the time, I viewed him only as a smug, petty reactionary. My disdain for him grew so intense that I began to feel ashamed of myself for being so closed-minded, and prayed to my now-elusive God for help. The answer I got was that I should go to class the next day with my mind and heart open, and, instead of blocking out everything Lyman was saying, I should listen carefully until I found something I could take to heart. Armed with this resolution, I went into his class with as open a mind as I could muster. We were studying the moral virtues and, on that particular day, Lyman was covering one of the lower-level virtues that helped with the practice of the big ones. I can't remember the precise virtue he was talking about, but I do remember him stressing the need for us to be forthright and honest in our dealings with others, rather than criticizing people behind their backs. Here, I thought, was God's message for me. I had never been honest with Lyman. I had reacted to him, disliked him, vilified him, but I had never been up front with him about it. I had been worse than a Pharisee in my righteous hypocrisy.

Having tapped into my ready reservoir of guilt, it was easy to convince myself that I needed to throw myself on the pyre, so that evening I went up to Lyman's room and knocked on the door. I heard his friendly "Come in!" and entered a living room whose scent and haze immediately reminded me that, for all his proper etiquette, Lyman was an addicted smoker. He greeted me from behind his desk:

"Hello, Greg. How are you?"

No sense wasting time. "Well actually, Father, I have something I really need to get off my chest."

Lyman offered me a chair and encouraged me to talk. I sat down and started apologizing. "Father, I realize that this is my problem, and I'm certainly not trying to tell you how to run your class or anything like that." I paused, he nodded, I went on. "It's just that, after what you said in class today, I realize that I need to be honest with you…about my reaction…to some of the things you say…in class.

He smiled knowingly and nodded his head, encouraging me to continue.

"Okay" I said, "I'm not saying I'm right, but, as you know, we've been exposed to a lot of new ideas in the last few years, and when you throw your barbs out, and make fun of these new ideas, well, I just find myself pulling down the shades on you. I'm not saying it's right for me to do that. I'm just saying that's what happens to me, and I…ah, just wanted you to know that that's what…ah…happens when you do that."

"Yes," he said. "I've noticed that quite a few people are pulling down the shades, especially in your class."

157

"Well, like I say, Father, I'm not trying to tell you how to teach your class. I just wanted to be honest with you about my reaction to it."

Lyman nodded and thanked me for coming forward. He said he knew it was a difficult time for the church and a difficult time for seminarians. It was also a <u>dangerous</u> time, he said, because we were about to have a schism in the Church.

"A schism? Don't you think that the Church will just get more open to different ideas and there'll be a wider spectrum of beliefs that are allowed?"

He let me rant on for another couple of minutes about my idealized vision of the new church. Then he simply said, "No. There's going to be a schism."

His friendly tone never changed during our conversation. He remained the perfect gentleman, and, as I left, he thanked me profusely for having the courage to come and talk to him, man to man. I went back to my room feeling great, optimistic about everything. Lyman and I had bonded, despite our differences, and that gave me new hope for the seminary and the church.

That hope was shattered a few months later, when a young faculty member caught me coming out of the refectory after lunch and said, "We need to talk!"

We walked off by ourselves and, when we were out of earshot of other people, he said, "What the hell happened between you and Fenn?"

"What do you mean?"

"He tried to get you clipped in the faculty meeting last night. He told us you came up to his room and tried to tell him how to run his class."

"Clipped" meant that you were turned down for orders, and it implied that you were not considered worthy of continuing on toward the priesthood. It would have meant that I wouldn't have been ordained to the orders of acolyte and exorcist at the end of the year.

The fact that the rest of the faculty hadn't gone along with Father Fenn's proposal gave me some comfort, but still, the fact that he had stabbed me in the back, after being so gracious to my face, really bothered me. I tried to get my mind around it. Did the moral virtues not apply to superiors, only to their subjects? I wouldn't have minded

if he had told me to my face, man to man, what he reall,
me. He was probably right, actually. But to pretend one thing an.
do the opposite behind my back – where was the charity or the
courage or the virtue in that? I tried my best to give him the benefit of
the doubt: In his mind, what he did was probably consistent with his
role as my superior. He was charged with training me in humility and
obedience, not sharing his feelings with me. Perhaps his role <u>required</u>
a certain amount of dissemblance when dealing with students.

It didn't matter. I had lost respect for him. In my mind, he was a
clerical coward, substituting hierarchical autism for human
communication. The fact that his cowardice was institutionalized
made him more – not less – cowardly in my eyes. By that time, I had
no forgiveness in my soul for those who had transformed the warm
human instincts of Jesus into the cold reflexes of organized religion.
If this was the Church, I no longer felt any part of it.

The Secular City

By the end of that school year (1964), I was getting worried. I had
been in the seminary for eight years now, and my crisis of faith
seemed to be getting worse rather than better, despite my confessor's
continued assurances that I'd be getting over it soon. Far from getting
over it, I was now more cynical than ever about organized religion. I
had been reading Harvey Cox's <u>Secular City</u>, and was convinced that
organized Christianity had become totally irrelevant to the modern
world, except maybe as a prophetic voice in the anti-war and civil
rights movements.

In past summers I had worked in various Catholic parishes, taking
census for the local pastor, and had enjoyed the priestly comradery in
parish houses. Now, assailed by this crisis of faith, the thought of
getting anywhere <u>near</u> a parish house was inconceivable. I was an
outsider, a skeptic who did not trust himself in the company of
traditional Catholics. I was too angry, too likely to drive well-
meaning and innocent believers into some existential hell similar to
my own. I wanted to get as far away from the Church as possible, to
take my radical brand of Christianity to the streets, to try to find
spirituality in humanity.

I had only one more year before I would be ordained to the order of subdeacon, with its mandatory vow of lifelong celibacy. I was doing my best to go into denial about the whole thing, because, even though I couldn't imagine myself in any role other than "priest," it was beginning to dawn on me that I no longer believed in organized religion, let alone celibacy.

Earlier that year, at a friend's Christmas party, I met a guy from San Francisco State who was active in the civil rights movement. He told me he was planning to work in Mississippi the next summer on the voter registration drive. I asked him if he needed any help, if there was any way I could go down there and work with him. He said that he was loosely affiliated with SNCC (Student Non-violent Coordinating Committee), and that he would have to check with them, but he didn't think there'd be any problem. We left it at that, but as the second semester progressed and my disaffection with traditional Catholicism grew, I began to consider Mississippi more seriously. The cause was certainly a righteous one, and it gave me some place to put my old "Christian warrior" energy that no longer was finding any inspiring outlets within the traditional Church. Plus, the dreaded yes-or-no decision about the priesthood was looming in my unconscious, and a dramatic martyrdom in Mississippi might just take that cross away from me. Maybe I could just get wounded down there, so that I could take an extended leave of absence from the seminary and then just forget to come back. My motives weren't totally pure.

I mentioned the Mississippi idea to Bob Carroll, who by now was going through a crisis of faith similar to my own, though on a more political and artistic level. He pounced on the idea immediately. We got hold of Rob Scoville, the guy I had met at the party, and began formulating plans to join him in Shelby, Mississippi the next summer.

Bob had emerged as the seminary's creative genius by this time and was throwing himself into a number of different projects. During Lent that year, he put together a multi-media slide show, entitled "Christ Suffers" and showed it in the chapel. No one had ever seen anything like it and, similar to everything else Bob produced, the show had a radical political message designed to create maximum discomfort in the more conservative members of the faculty and student body.

Later that year Bob and I worked closely on the Mission Carnival, a fund-raising event organized every year by the members of the Second Theology class. We chose as our theme, "Goldfinger," in deference to the James Bond books and movies that were then all the rage. Bob spent days creating a papier-mâché centerpiece for the carnival – a huge gold-painted finger that pointed skyward from the center of the room. When you looked closely at it, you noticed that it was the middle finger.

Movie Time

With as much drama as there was going on in the seminary, it wasn't surprising that "The Sweet Life" production crew decided it was time to make another movie. We were inspired first and foremost by the many great shooting locations at St. Pat's – the archbishop's palatial summer house, the deep sprawling garbage pit out in the back field, the old wooden water tower. We had sneaked into the basement of the archbishop's house several times, and the place was like a Hollywood prop room. There were all sorts of stuffed animals and birds down there that someone had donated to the seminary years before, as well as a whole collection of framed pictures – lithographs of medieval cathedrals and elegant, gilt-framed portraits of anal-looking churchmen.

The four of us kicked ideas around for a few weeks, without coming up with a solid story line. Then Bob's dad died and he went home for a few days. Because Bob and I were close friends, I was allowed to travel up to San Francisco for the funeral. It was a big event, mainly because Bob's family was related to Charley Harney, the notorious, cost over-run, developer of Candlestick Park and a heavy contributor to the archdiocese. After the funeral, the coffin was conveyed to the Catholic cemetery in Colma, where the final blessing was said and everybody lined up to offer their condolences to the family. I joined the line and, when I reached Bob, I started to shake his hand and offer my sympathies. Before I could say anything, he grabbed me in a bear hug and started whispering in my ear.

"Last night I had a dream," he whispered, "and I think I've got a plot for the movie. The two main characters are a criminal and an archbishop. We start with the criminal waking up in his room, then we cut to the archbishop in <u>his </u>room, then we…"

Bob went on for about two minutes, giving me a scene-by-scene account of the movie, while the rest of the people in line stood around waiting. It finally dawned on him where he was and he let go of me. I hadn't really been able to concentrate on everything he was saying, being in a mourning line and all, but I knew from the tone of his voice that we now had a storyline, and that I'd better go along with it. Thus began "A Ballad of the Church and the Modern World," a rather heavy-handed and slow-moving little film which, despite it's aesthetic shortcomings, was destined to plunge the seminary into a dramatic McCarthy-style witch-hunt.

It wasn't a complicated plot. The camera first focuses on a seedy-looking guy lying on a flophouse bed, chewing gum and reading a comic book. He slowly stretches, then gets up, scratches his stomach, and stretches again. Then he puts on his belt, slips his shoulder holster over his head, and puts on his jacket, his shoes, and his hat. He goes over to his dresser, dreamily inserts his finger into an unused condom, then picks up his heroin needle to see if there's anything left in it. Just before he leaves, he stops in front of a Playboy centerfold hanging on the wall, and fondly sticks his chewing gum on her ass.

The camera then shifts to a very different bedroom scene, where a very fat archbishop lies on a luxurious bed, his breviary resting on his chest. He slowly wakes up, notices his breviary, remembers to kiss it before closing it, then slowly rolls his large body off the bed. He steps into his cassock, struggles to close the sash around his midriff, then slips the chain of his large pectoral cross over his head, and dons his cape and mitre. Following the same sequence as the criminal, he checks his holy water font, slides his bishop's ring over his finger, and heads out the door, stopping briefly to plant a big kiss on the cheek of the Blessed Virgin statue near the door.

We chose Mike Anderson to play the part of the criminal. He had entered the seminary later than most of us, bringing with him a reputation for being pretty wild during his high school days. He knew how to look cool, and had a James Dean way of smoking a cigarette. To play the part of the archbishop, we chose Jack Folmer, a round, jolly guy with a good sense of humor and enough cynicism about church politics to make him enjoy parodying a greedy archbishop.

The action starts with the criminal stealing a carton of cigarettes out of a car, jumping a fence, and running off through a field of high grass. Eventually he comes to a small greenhouse, behind which looms a palatial mansion – the home of the archbishop. The criminal decides to break in through a window, and finds the archbishop up in the attic, counting a pile of money that he's stashed under the floorboards. He pulls his gun and demands the money, but the archbishop gives him a haughty look and runs away, cape flying, down a winding staircase and past a bunch of senile old priests in their rocking chairs, some of whom are asleep, others who are just too daffy to understand his cries for help. The chase, winds through the house and eventually ends up in the basement, amidst the menagerie of stuffed animals and portraits of anal churchmen. After a battle of wills, during which the archbishop gets righteously piqued enough to attack his intruder with a stuffed owl, the criminal finally loses his cool and shoots the archbishop, who, after doing a dramatic death-crawl past a whole gallery of grim-faced churchmen, dies nose-to-nose with a weather-beaten pelican.

The cook upstairs hears the shot and stops stirring the soup long enough to put down his theology book and call the police. Three detectives in overcoats drive up, jump out with guns drawn and take off after the criminal. They chase him down the road and shoot him just as he's running toward the garbage pit, causing him to topple in amidst the old bottles and tree clippings.

The scene then changes radically, as we hear Gregorian chant and see a funeral procession wending its way along the archbishop's veranda and down the stairs. There are about twenty seminarians in cassock and surplice, carrying a variety of prayer books, lilies, stuffed animals, etc., followed by a thurifer who waves a smoking incense burner over the casket carried by six pallbearers.

The actors in this scene included a wide spectrum of seminary types, conservative to liberal to radical. All I told them was that we were making a movie and we needed them to be in a funeral procession. Most of them asked no questions about the overall plot, and we certainly didn't feel the need to tell them. It was a last minute scramble, because our summer vacation was about to start, and this was the only day we could shoot the scene. So we grabbed whomever we could. To complicate things, the archbishop himself was due to arrive at his house sometime that afternoon, so we had to post a lookout near the front gate of the seminary. We didn't want the archbishop driving up and seeing a funeral procession on his porch – especially one with a bishop's miter mounted on top of the coffin.

The procession slowly winds off the porch and down the back service road, which runs right next to the garbage pit, where the police have just retrieved the body of the criminal and put it into a wheelbarrow. Just as the procession reaches the pit, a gardener on a tractor comes driving through, separating the casket and pallbearers from the rest of the procession. At this point, the police are wheeling the dead body of the crook off in the wheelbarrow, and they end up in the procession right behind the guy with the incense.

The last scene, accompanied by the words of the then-popular song, "We'll build a world of our own, that no one else can share," is a long shot which pans front to back along the procession, focusing on the thurifer, who is now dutifully incensing the wheelbarrow, while the pallbearers with the casket are running to catch up and get back in line.

Bob and I worked all summer editing the film and recording the sound track, which we would have to play separately on a tape recorder. The film was regular 8mm, and our editing equipment was primitive, so our splices often broke and had to be reglued. We finally finished editing the movie near the end of July, just before we were scheduled to go to Mississippi. We decided we would wait to show it until we got back.

Mississippi

Bob and I knew that neither of our mothers would have been capable of handling the truth about our Mississippi adventure, so we devised a story about going on an extended camping trip with several other seminarians whom our mothers had never met, during which time we would be away from telephones and not able to call. We gave them another friend's number, in case of an emergency (which, of course, in our youthful fog, we were sure couldn't happen) and brought him in as a co-conspirator for the cover story. That way we could call him once in a while and make sure everything was okay.

Had they known where we were going, our mothers would have had good reason to worry. The summer before, in 1964, three young civil rights workers had been murdered in Mississippi. Others had been murdered in Alabama and Georgia. The Klan was still operating openly, and the government had done little to stop them. The violence had been triggered by the Civil Rights Act of 1964, which barred segregation in public places and forbade discrimination in voter registration. White bigots were outraged. Their autonomy had again been crushed by the North.

Bob and I showed up at the Greyhound station in San Francisco, tickets in hand for our two-and-a-half day trip to Shelby, Mississippi. The first thing we noticed was that morning's Chronicle in the newsstand. Its headlines blared the story of a massive riot that had erupted the night before in the Watts section of Los Angeles. Watts was one of the poorest areas in the country, with unemployment among blacks at 14 %, and little or no public transportation. A traffic arrest had ignited a riot by angry residents and buildings were being looted and burned. The riot continued for five days, so at every bus stop along our trip, we anxiously scanned the local papers for more details.

Bob and I had a lot of time to talk during the bus ride and, at one point, he said to me, in his intense, nouveau-socialist tone, "Greg, I come from a wealthy family and have a lot more money than you do, so I'm going to pay for most of the expenses on this trip." I tried to object, but Bob would have none of it. He'd thought about it and that was that. You didn't argue with Bob once he'd made up his mind about something. I told him, okay, that was fine with me if he wanted to do it. We were both socialists at heart.

We also talked a lot about politics and civil rights…and about how they applied to the seminary. Actually, I was the one who talked about the seminary. Bob talked mainly about politics. On some unconscious level, he had already left the seminary.

The trip is a blur of large and small Greyhound stations with smelly bathrooms and sad little cafeterias. Often the stops would come in the middle of the night and we'd be wrenched from sleep by the static of the driver's microphone: "Next stop, Henrietta, Oklahoma. We'll be here approximately 45 minutes. Limited dining services are available."

We finally got off the bus in Memphis, and had to spend several hours waiting for a local bus to Shelby, so we wandered over to a downtown café. It was dinnertime and the place was pretty full. Everyone was watching an old black and white television mounted on a shelf just under a small confederate flag. When I looked up at it, I was amazed to see what they were watching – "Amos and Andy!" There wasn't a black face in the crowd, but everyone there was laughing really hard at the Kingfish. Bob and I looked at each other as if to say, "Who ARE these people, anyway?" We didn't have a clue. Not yet anyway.

The next day we arrived at Shelby in the late morning. It was muggy and hot, but we stepped off the bus into an attractive little southern town with whitewashed houses, green lawns and well-swept sidewalks. Rob had given us an address where to find him, so we started walking in that direction. After we'd walked a few blocks, everything changed. Abruptly, the roads were no longer paved and there were no longer any streetlights or sidewalks. There were open drainage ditches on the sides of the road instead of buried culverts. Most of the houses were still neat and tidy, but the public infrastructure was non-existent. We had entered the "Negro" side of Shelby. We found out later from Rob Scoville that, even though these people paid the same taxes as their white counterparts, they received no city services. The sewage system didn't extend to their part of town, many of the houses had no indoor plumbing, and some even lacked electricity. This was the South of the 60s, and that's just the way it was.

The blacks in Shelby had their own community, totally separate from that of the whites. Many of the poorer blacks worked in the cotton fields all summer, whole families spending long hours in the hot sun to earn a few pennies per pound of cotton picked. Others owned small businesses, which served the black community that was not welcome in white establishments (even though the recent law had forbidden any overt segregation). And then there were the black aristocrats, usually school principals or ministers, who had cut their deals with the white overlords, promising to keep their black brothers and sisters in line in exchange for the good life.

We finally found the house where Rob was staying, a little four-room clapboard place that had been divided in half, with Rob living on one side and a black family on the other. There were two small rooms on each side and a rickety little back porch that overlooked a swampy creek that ran behind the house. On one end of the porch there was a refrigerator and a wash basin, which served everyone in the house. On the other end of the porch was an outhouse whose pit was always full of swamp water from the creek. The family next door consisted of a mother and about nine kids, ranging in age from 6 months to 12 years. There was one bed in the place and a bunch of blankets, which the kids would pull out every night and sleep on. Their mother and her current lover got the bed.

We'd go to sleep every night with our t-shirts over our heads to keep the mosquitoes off. I remember waking up one hot, humid morning, looking up at a fat mosquito trying to force his proboscis through my Fruit of the Loom netting, while the sounds of "I Love Lucy" came from the other side of the wall. The kids were over there, sprawled out on their blankets, watching Lucy and Desi on their old black and white TV set, the only modern appliance in the place.

"The seeds of revolution!" I thought. "What must these kids think about America?"

Shortly after our arrival in Shelby, Bob and I walked downtown to check things out. Being the naïve seminarians we were, we nodded a friendly "hello" to everyone we passed on the street. No one responded. They just stared back at us, not with any hint of welcome, nor of curiosity, just dull hatred. They already knew who we were and why we were there, and they hated our guts. I'd never experienced flat-out hatred before, and it was awful. I don't know what I had expected, but it wasn't this. Being a pacifist, committed to love and non-violence, I had assumed that, no matter how deep the problem, it could be worked out with a little good will and patience. But maybe not with these people. Not with that kind of hatred in their eyes.

After that experience, we pretty much stayed within the black community, though we did venture over to the Catholic Church that first Sunday morning, expecting to find a few good Catholic liberals who would sympathize with our cause. No such luck. We got the same reception there that we had gotten on the street. Most of these proper church-going people wouldn't talk to us at all, and those who did told us that race relations had nothing to do with religion and that we should be ashamed of ourselves for coming down here as Catholic seminarians to stir up trouble and get involved with something that was none of our business. This was the first time in my life I felt like an outsider in a Catholic church. It wouldn't be the last.

Not that the black churches were much better. The next Sunday, we went over to the Pentecostal church that most of the poor blacks regularly attended. The small clapboard church was locked when we got there and forty or fifty folks, all dressed in their threadbare Sunday finest, were waiting in the hot sun, fanning themselves with whatever they had handy. Finally, after about forty-five minutes, the pastor and his driver cruised up in a brand new Lincoln. The pastor weighed about 300 pounds, and wore a fancy tailored suit. He pried himself out of the car, muttered some excuse for being late, and lumbered over toward the locked church. Bob caught up with him and asked if it would be okay if we made an announcement to the congregation about the voter registration drive scheduled for the coming week. The pastor kept walking and shook his head. "No politics in the house of the Lord."

We decided to go into the church anyway, because we were curious about what a black Pentecostal service would be like. The choir processed in first, in step to a jaunty hymn, and I was impressed by how sexy they looked, compared to the Catholic choirs I'd been used to. They went on to belt out a few hymns while the pastor nodded away in his oversized chair. Then he got up and, in a deep ministerial voice, started talking about how he'd been under the weather, down with a bad cold, and that medicine was very expensive these days, so everyone needed to be generous and give whatever they could. These were about the poorest people I'd ever seen in my life, but, when the collection was taken, they all dug in and tossed their coins in the basket. Then the choir sang another hymn, the pastor stood up and read some scripture, and then motioned to the ushers to take up another collection. More singing, more scripture, another collection, then a long rambling sermon about how the Lord rewards cheerful givers. Then another collection. I couldn't believe it. Once in a while, Catholic churches would take up a second collection for some special cause like the missions, but never more than two. This guy knew no shame. He kept going, until he had taken up SEVEN collections. I guess he figured the more collections he took, the more money he would make, but it seemed to me that the congregation had his number. I noticed that no one put more than a few coins in at a time. They were pacing themselves for what they knew would be a long gauntlet of greed.

Bob and I were disgusted by his performance, but we were guests, so we just sat there waiting for the fiasco to end. But then came the distinctly Pentecostal part of the service, when the pastor, his collection baskets safely filled, called upon the Holy Spirit "to descend upon this generous and faithful congregation and inspire them with Your Word."

"Is anyone moved by the Spirit to speak?" he wailed, his eyes half closed in bloated ecstasy.

There was a moment of silence. No one made a move. They all seemed too intimidated by his pervasive presence.

Another moment went by, and then I saw Bob slowly rise to his feet, his eyes closed as though he were experiencing some sort of mystical vision. He paused for a moment, and then, raising his arms heavenward, he crooned out some quote from St. Paul in a voice so deep and resonant that everyone in the church went totally silent, as though they were listening to the Spirit himself. I was sitting across from the pastor, and as soon as he heard Bob's voice, he opened his eyes just a slit and I could see nervous little pupils darting around under those big turtle lids. Bob paused dramatically after his quote from St. Paul, and then deftly linked early Christianity to present day Mississippi, and the oppression of Old Testament law to the oppression of the White power structure. He moved fast. By the time the pastor figured out what was happening, Bob had convinced the congregation that St. Paul wanted them to register to vote the next day.

***

I was shocked by the reactionary role that black churches played in the South. Up until then, I had watched Martin Luther King and other black ministers on television, and had assumed that religion was the fire behind the whole civil rights movement. Once I got to Shelby, though, and saw the churches there, I had to revise my opinion. Most of the black ministers were puppets, preaching and believing a brand of roll-over-and-die Christianity that guaranteed black subservience and fear. I spent two hours one afternoon, on the porch of a retired black minister, arguing about whether it was "Christian" to be involved in civil rights. He kept coming back to his favorite quote from St. Paul: "Slaves be obedient to your master." That was his mantra and he wasn't about to change it. God had created blacks as slaves and only by accepting God's will could they be saved. This was just another version of my grandmother's salvation-through-self-denial, and that minister spoke for many of the older blacks who saw the Civil Rights movement as prideful rebellion, tantamount to Adam's original sin in the Garden of Eden. Contrary to my previous, naive assumptions, the black Church was not united in favor of the civil rights movement. Many preferred the status quo. The black Church was, after all, an integral part of organized religion, and I was beginning to realize that organized religion almost always defaulted to the status quo.

Besides working on voter registration, SNCC conducted non-violent workshops for young blacks who were involved in sit-ins and demonstrations. Such workshops would usually be held on Saturdays in one of the nearby towns, such as Clarksdale or Greenwood. We were using an old green pickup that someone had donated to SNCC. It wasn't in very good shape and the steering wheel had about five inches of play in it, so you'd constantly have to correct to the right, then to the left, as you wove down the road. We used it to transport folks down to the voter registration center in Jackson, or to bring kids to the non-violent workshops.

One Saturday, I had about six teenage boys in the back of the truck and I was driving down to Greenwood for a workshop. Suddenly I heard some noise from the kids and a new yellow Impala came speeding up and started to pass me. I was concentrating on the steering wheel, trying to keep the truck in my lane, so I didn't pay much attention to the Impala until it cut sharply in front of me, causing me to hit the brakes suddenly. Then I noticed it was full of white guys, ranging in age from about 17 to 50, all of whom were looking at me with that by-now-familiar hateful stare. This was the Klan, I realized, out on their weekend maneuvers.

They pulled over to the shoulder and allowed me to pass, but then they come up behind me again. They pulled alongside, this time yelling obscenities and giving us the finger. Then they pulled behind me again.

Here I was, all by myself with a truck full of young kids, and the Klan was trying to run me off the road. Given my commitment to non-violence, the only near-pragmatic idea I could muster was that my untimely death on this lonely highway might add fuel to the civil rights movement. Then I realized that this was a rather selfish thought, since I had six youngsters in the truck who weren't nearly as committed to martyrdom as I.

"Lord, help me!" I prayed, surprising myself by this sudden reversion to a childhood relationship with God. "Show me what to do!"

I looked in the rear-view mirror and saw the Impala right on my tail, with burly guys hanging out the windows yelling and shaking their fists. Then I saw one of my kids bend over and come up with an empty coke bottle in his hand. He waved it at the Impala for a minute and then let it fly in their direction. I watched the bottle arcing gracefully toward the Impala; then I saw smoke erupt under the front tires, as the Impala dipped suddenly down toward the asphalt and went into a banana-shaped skid, escaping the shattering coke bottle by inches.

"Oh Jesus!" I thought. "We're done for."

I watched the Impala grow smaller in my mirror as I floored the gas pedal. They were still back there. They hadn't started to chase us. And then...then they turned around!! And drove off in the opposite direction!!

"Whew! Thanks, Lord!" I exhaled, realizing I hadn't been breathing for the last minute and a half. Then I suddenly got it, as though Jesus were personally whispering in my ear, patiently explaining things to me.

"There's theory, and then there's communication!!"

Those kids had effectively communicated with the Klan – by threatening their car's new paint job. All my theorizing up in the front seat hadn't accomplished anything. I drove on with my hands shaking, but also murmuring my thanks to Jesus for teaching me a crucial lesson.

This challenge to my dogmatic pacifism came in the knick of time, because a few days later we began to hear from our black friends that the Klan was planning to bomb our house. People in the black community were concerned enough about our welfare that they offered to put us up in different homes, and they evacuated the mom and kids from of the other half of our house. Up until this time, I had been pretty detached and passive about everything, doing whatever needed to be done, but taking little initiative. But something about getting that revelation from Jesus in the truck impelled me to feel that this was now my responsibility. I had seen how the Klan dealt with a coke bottle thrown by a teenager. They weren't invincible.

It was a Thursday when we first heard about the Klan's threats. The bombing would probably happen that weekend, when the Klan had time to drink a lot of beers to bloat their courage. The three of us decided we better stay away from the house that Friday night, so we went to one of the little dance joints that were the center of life in the black neighborhood. They were just little places, with a dance floor, a juke-box and a bar that served beer and burgers. The burgers were good, but I noticed that they didn't taste like the hamburgers I was used to, and I eventually figured out it was because they were made out of ground pork, not ground <u>beef</u>! And what I first thought were potato chips actually were fried pork rinds. Everything in this place was brand new to me, and I suddenly realized that this was about as far removed from the Catholic Church and the seminary as I had ever been. It was also safely removed from the potential bombsite we were calling home in Shelby!

I loved watching the dancers. They were totally uninhibited, especially the girls, who seemed to be taken over by the music as though it was flowing through their veins. One of them finally got up her courage, came over, and didn't <u>ask</u>, but <u>challenged</u> me to dance with her. I would have given anything to get out on the dance floor and move with her, but I was still my grandmother's son, still locked into my head, and incapable of responding to anything so primitive – and innocent – as rhythm. So I just smiled and said, "No thanks, I don't know how." She looked at me as though I was an alien.

She was right.

But even though I couldn't unlock my feet to dance, my brain was jumping all over the place that night. My recent adventure with the Klan had revealed them to be a lot less threatening than they first appeared, much like guys I had known in the seminary, who were tough jock types on the outside, but scared little boys underneath. I watched the lithe bodies moving so rhythmically on the dance floor, and thought of those beer-bellied Klansmen and their unimaginative bomb threats.

We managed to stay up the whole night, which wasn't that hard, because there was no 2 a.m. curfew, like in California. These folks danced all night. When it started to get light, we walked back to our house, half expecting to see a smoldering pile of rubble. But the house was untouched. The Klan must have decided to wait for Saturday night.

I took a short nap, then told Bob that I was going to take a walk, and I headed downtown. It was about 10 a.m. by now and Main Street was getting busy, everyone out doing their Saturday shopping. I walked down to the hardware store, which I noticed had a lot of cars and trucks in front of it. I took a deep breath, opened the screen door and stepped inside. The place was crowded, and, as I entered, I might as well have been Jack Palance in "Shane." Everything went totally silent, and nobody moved.

The guy behind the counter looked up at me, excused himself to the customer he was waiting on, and said in a loud Southern drawl, "Can Ah help you?"

He knew he couldn't refuse to wait on me, because, for all he knew, I might be one of those federal lawyers who had come down to mess with folks like him. But he wanted to get me out of his store as fast as possible. Everyone in the store just stood where they were, giving me that dull stare. My heart was beating, so hard that I thought it was going to explode, but I was on the Lord's overdrive, so I walked slowly and deliberately down the aisle and up to the counter. When I got there, I looked the cashier in the eye and said real loud, in my best Southern, macho drawl, "Ah'd like a box of them twenty-two shells, please."

The guy gave me an incredulous look, then caught himself and pulled a box of shells off the shelf. "Two dollahs and fifty nine cents," he said.

I paid him, said "Thankya, Sir," and then sauntered out, trying to look as much like John Wayne as I could. As I closed the screen door behind me, I heard everyone break into nervous chatter, and I thought to myself, "Ten minutes at the most before our friends in the Klan hear about this."

I went back and told Bob what I'd done. He looked at me like I was crazy. He didn't think it was a good idea, because it violated the principle of non-violence and it might escalate things with the Klan.

I told him I wasn't sure it was a good idea either, but that we had to do something and that's the only thing that I'd come up with. Bob didn't like other people doing things that he hadn't approved. He was a bit of a control freak, like lots of creative people are. He bitched about it for a while, making it sound like I'd jeopardized the entire Civil Rights movement.

I didn't care. I'd been God-struck. And besides, it <u>was</u> kind of funny.

Besides that, it worked. We didn't get any more bomb threats.

***

But the Klan didn't go away. They kept showing up everywhere we went. One night, after a meeting, we were dropping some freedom-riders off in Greenwood, about 50 miles southeast of Shelby. It was late, pretty close to midnight, and as we entered town and turned onto Main Street, we saw about thirty white guys standing there in a tight little knot, looking down the street like they were getting ready for a gang fight. They all had their sleeves rolled up and their arms folded, biceps flexed. We drove past them and headed down Main Street, to the "Negro" part of town, where we saw a bunch of black guys standing on the porch of an old hotel. The whole thing looked like the set from "High Noon," so we asked them what was going on. They said that, earlier in the evening, a couple of white teenagers had run into a couple of black kids on the street and one of the whites had pulled a knife. A fight ensued and one of the black kids had hit the knife-wielding white kid on the head with a coke bottle and done enough damage to put him in the hospital. Word had spread quickly, and the Klan had gathered up at the end of the street, waiting to hear if the kid was okay or not. Supposedly, if the word came back that he wasn't okay, they were going to shoot up the black part of town.

The leader of the blacks was a guy named Davis, and he was the first black person I'd ever seen carrying a gun. He was active in the civil rights movement and had been committed to non-violence, but his house had been shot up the week before, so he was no longer embracing pacifism as his sole strategy.

We waited for about an hour, everyone worried about what the word from the hospital would be. Periodically, the sheriff would cruise down the street and drive slowly past the hotel, sometimes stopping to talk to Davis or one of the other guys. I noticed a guy in a fancy new car who was driving right behind him. The guy was about 40 and had a tough James Dean look – hair back in a duck tail, cigarette hanging out of his mouth, short-sleeved shirt rolled up to show off his muscles. I asked the guy next to me who he was.

"That's the Grand Dragon," he said.

"You're kidding!" I said. "The sheriff escorts the Grand Dragon of the Klan through your neighborhood?"

"What do you think?" he said, and smiled.

Back inside the hotel, I met a white college kid from New York who had been working for SNCC in Greenwood. He was bright and tough, and he told me about how he had been stopped by the cops a month before, charged with not having a Mississippi driver's license, and thrown in jail, where he'd been introduced to the other white prisoners as a "freedom rider" and had the shit beaten out of him.

"Make sure you're always with somebody," he said. "Don't ever go out by yourself."

It was nearly two A.M. when word finally came from the hospital that the kid was all right. The Klan gradually disappeared and we started toward the truck to drive back to Shelby.

"No way," said Davis. "You get five miles out of town and they'll be waiting for you. You can spend the night at my house and go back in the morning."

So we spent the night at the Davis house, sleeping on the floor where the rest of his family had slept for the last week, after Klan gunfire had shattered all his windows.

Everything about Mississippi had been mind-boggling to me. For one thing, I had never spent any time around black people before I got to Shelby. In Marin County, where I grew up, all the blacks lived in Marin City, a collection of wartime barracks just north of Sausalito

175

originally built to house shipyard employees during World War II. All the black kids from Marin City went to Tamalpais High School in Mill Valley, so I had little contact with them, except watching them beat the hell out of us in football. The only blacks I knew were a couple of classmates at Marin Catholic who had been recruited on sports scholarships, and Matty, our cleaning lady, who came to our house every other week after my mom went back to teaching. There wasn't one black seminarian during the whole nine years I was there.

This absence of minorities in my life may explain why I was so unaware of racial discrimination and so unprepared for what I would see in Mississippi. The only stories I had heard about discrimination concerned the injustices inflicted upon the Indian tribes by the U S Government. My grandfather had spent a lot of time with the Sioux in North Dakota and was painfully aware of how they had been mistreated. He had handed that awareness down to my mother, who always made sure her students learned about broken treaties and stolen lands in their Social Studies lessons. Though my family was relatively conservative about most issues, religious and political, they were definitely liberals when it came to Native American issues, and it was this small liberal window that enabled me to appreciate the righteousness of the Civil Rights movement.

But being theoretically aware of injustice was one thing. Seeing Mississippi-brand injustice face-to-face was another. One Sunday, we got word that one of the black women in town had been arrested and was being held in jail. There were two jails in Shelby, one for whites and one for negroes. The white jail was a well-built two-story building near the police department headquarters. The negro jail was a low brick structure out on the edge of town next to the swamp. There were no window panes in the negro jail, only bars. There was no heat, no electricity, no running water. The beds were moldy old straw mattresses, infested with snakes and rats from the nearby swamp. There weren't even any guards on duty. When we arrived at the jail, we saw the woman standing at the door, clutching the bars, afraid to go any further back into the damp, dark room. She still had on her best Sunday clothes, because she had been arrested on her way home from church. She had been charged with stealing ten dollars from her employer, an elderly white woman, who, everyone agreed, was senile enough to misplace a ten dollar bill. The black woman was a pillar of her church, a devoted wife and mother, for whom stealing would be unconscionable. Nevertheless, the Shelby police arrested her simply on the word of her employer and locked her up, with their usual disregard for due process. When prisoners were locked in this jail, they were totally on their own, and had to depend on friends even for food and water. We brought her a hamburger and a coke, but she said she was too upset and frightened to eat.

She didn't get out of jail until the next day, after spending the entire night gripping the bars at the door, lest she have to deal with the sounds scurrying in the dark behind her.

***

We weren't always able to follow our policy of never going out alone. One morning, Rob had planned to pick up a local black leader and drive him to a SNCC meeting in Jackson. Unfortunately, the man was sick when he got there, so he decided to drive down by himself. When he didn't come home that night, Bob and I began to worry. There were very few phones in town, especially in the black section, but we started asking around to see if anyone had heard anything. Finally, late in the morning, we heard that a neighbor had gotten a call. Rob had been arrested the night before and was being held in jail down in Clarksdale. He needed us to come down and bail him out. He had been there all night, he said, and he was worried that he might be in real danger if he didn't get out soon. Bail was $36.

The jail in Clarksdale was well known among civil rights activists, because that was where black prisoners were routinely tortured with cattle prods. We left immediately, and, when we got there, we had to go through a lot of bureaucratic paperwork before the jailor finally sent someone down to release Rob from his cell. While they were gone, I asked the jailor about the $36 charge. I had noticed that the traffic fine was only $17, so I asked him about the rest of the bill.

He sat back in his chair and drawled out, "Waall, you got 11 dollars jail cell fee, four dollars meal fee, and four dollars court fee."

I knew from the earlier message from Rob that he had been given nothing to eat, had never appeared before a judge, and had spent the night sitting in a holding cell with two drunken red-necks who threatened to kill him with a broken mirror. I mentioned this to the jailor.

He leaned back in his chair, laughed, and said, "Waall, you know how it works...you boys come down here, stir up all this trouble,...you got to be ready to take whatever comes to you."

That seemed like a pretty honest answer, so I just smiled and said, "Yeah, I guess you're right."

We left Mississippi shortly after that, and on the bus ride home I thought about all the people who lived in Shelby, for whom these events weren't just fodder for stories, but sources of ongoing pain and hardship. I thought about the courageous grandmothers in Shelby who rode fifty miles in the back of our old pickup truck to register to vote, even though the local welfare office had threatened to cut off their families' surplus food allocation if they registered. I thought of the family living in the two rooms next to us and wondered how the kids would ever reconcile the disparity between their hard, dirty floor and that other comfortable world they were watching on television. I thought of the joyous, uninhibited dancing in that little burger shack and I wondered how I would ever reconcile such freedom with my return to the seminary.

My presence in Mississippi in 1965 didn't contribute much to the civil rights movement. But it sure changed my life forever.

Re-entry

My conversations with Jesus became more intense during and after my Mississippi trip. I was gradually getting comfortable with the Jesus who disdained the organized church of his time, who castigated the Pharisees for their hypocrisy, and who drove the money-changers from the temple with righteous indignation. I was beginning to realize that priesthood was not synonymous with organized religion. In fact, I was beginning to feel that the two might be antithetical for me. Try as I might, I couldn't imagine Jesus wearing a roman collar and functioning as a clergyman in an organized church.

My disaffection with the organized church reached a symbolic zenith shortly after my return from Mississippi, when a few of us went to visit a priest friend who had recently been transferred from my parish to an inner city parish in San Francisco. He was a big, cynical guy who took great delight in shattering the idealistic illusions of his seminary proteges by exposing us to the "realities" of the priesthood. He regularly told us scandalous stories about priests he had known. He bragged about how he made $300 in Mass stipends on Mothers' Day alone. He prided himself as a traditionalist who lived by the book, not getting involved in anything that smacked of "fanaticism." He had no use for his peers who worked with the poor, or who dedicated themselves to migrant worker ministries or other "causes." He fancied himself a pragmatist who never got sidetracked by any kind of theoretical or idealistic nonsense.

He was in his glory at the new inner-city parish. His pastor, whose paranoia was legendary, had issued him a ring of house keys that would have made a jailor wince, as well as a small wrist-strapped billy-club which he tucked inconspicuously under the sleeve of his clerical suit – protection from his parishioners who lived on the streets. The pastor had installed a target range in the basement of the priests' house, and practiced his marksmanship daily in preparation for his favorite nocturnal activity – leaning out his bedroom window and shooting his BB gun at any drunks who might be loitering on the church steps.

I was dazed when I heard this. Priests armed against their parishioners, a pastor <u>shooting</u>, rather than <u>feeding</u>, his flock? What kind of twisted, psychotic religion was this? Had these guys never read the Gospels? Did they even remember who Jesus was?

Earlier, when we walked up to the rectory, we had been confronted by a locked iron gate, with a sign on it saying that anyone who wished to see a priest should go to an adjacent telephone booth and call a certain number. We went to the phone booth, and were amazed to find it was a pay phone, and that we needed a dime. We paid our money and dialed the number, and a gruff male voice asked what we wanted. After we told him we were seminarians here to see the assistant pastor, he got a little more polite and told us to go over by the gate. He came out the rectory door a moment later and unlocked the huge gate. We found out later he was an off-duty cop, hired to defend the wall between church and state.

The inside of the place was just as cold and eerie as the outside. There were four priests living in the narrow five-story building (six stories, if you counted the shooting gallery in the basement), and each priest lived on a separate floor, accessible only by elevator. The pastor lived on the top floor, from which he could perform his sniper activities, and the first floor housed the dining room, where the sullen community met for occasional meals.

At another time in my life I might have been amused, or perhaps saddened, by such a scene. In 1965, I was outraged. The place symbolized everything that I felt was wrong with Catholicism. When we got back in the car, my seminary friends joked about the experience with the same cynicism that the place itself reflected. I couldn't share their laughter, and I suddenly realized there were many things I could no longer share with them. I no longer shared their goals, their values, or their assumptions about God and the church. I had become an outsider, a heretical quisling within the system. It was a lonely role, though at the same time, strangely exhilarating. I was once again my grandmother's protege, fighting a world full of apathy and sloth. I could feel her warrior energy in my veins, even though I suspected she would neither recognize, nor approve, my current battle flag.

Of course it had dawned on me that my anger and disillusionment with the church might eventually necessitate my leaving the seminary, but it was still impossible for me to consciously entertain that idea. After all, hadn't I always been the perfect seminarian, the one everyone thought of as the ideal priest? And wasn't I still following Jesus' call to His kind of priesthood? Who <u>was</u> I, if not a priest? The alternative was inconceivable. I was in a state of profound clerical denial.

The MOVIE

On the bus back from Mississippi, Bob and I had talked about our movie and decided to hold a preview showing before we got back to the seminary. We held it in my mother's basement, and about fifteen people attended, including Mike Anderson who had played the role of the criminal. Mike brought his mother with him, and his cousin who was a priest from San Francisco. The cousin didn't say much that night, but he evidently went back and told all his priest friends that some guys in the seminary had made a dirty movie about the archbishop.

We had no idea these rumors were circulating through the archdiocese, so, a month or so later, we scheduled an "underground" viewing of the movie in the basement of the seminary, open to anyone who wanted to see it. A lot of the guys who had bit parts in the movie came to see it, along with a few others who, unbeknownst to us, had heard the horror stories from the priests' rumor network. About a week later, things exploded. Some of the guys who had been in the movie were upset and said that, if they had known what the whole thing was about, they never would have agreed to be in it. Others, acting on behalf of priest friends horrified by the gossip, became self-appointed inquisitors. Only then did we realize what a wide impact our movie was having – especially among those who hadn't seen it. We even heard that someone had leaked word to the archbishop.

Things quickly escalated and pretty soon there was a whole bunch of guys demanding that we destroy the movie. We of course refused, on the grounds of artistic freedom and free speech. They, in turn, threatened to go to Fr. Purta, who, like the archbishop, had already heard rumors about the movie, but was hoping he wouldn't have to deal with it in his official capacity as rector. There followed a series of emotional meetings between those of us who made the movie and the eight to ten guys who were hell-bent on having it destroyed. Things got so heated at one point that Bob and I thought someone might get hysterical enough to try to steal the film, so I left a dummy canister on my desk and hid the real one.

The debate raged on for days. At one point, my classmate, Jim Kidder (presently a monsignor in the Sacramento diocese), cornered me in the hall. He had his own well-reasoned slant on the situation. The movie should be destroyed, he said, because we had featured a condom in it. That meant we had <u>purchased</u> a condom, and purchasing a condom was a sin, because condoms were inherently evil, having a sinful act as their only purpose. I told him there was at least one other purpose for a condom, which was not evil – its use as a prop in a movie. He assured me that if I kept thinking that way, I'd end up in Hell.

The negotiations continued, and we offered to put a disclaimer at the beginning of the movie saying that many of the actors had been unaware of the full context of the movie, and consequently wished to disassociate themselves from it. This did not satisfy the moral crusaders in the group. They still wanted the movie destroyed. We refused, and the stalemate continued.

Finally, they gave us an ultimatum. Either we agreed to destroy the movie by the end of the week, or they would send a delegation to Fr. Purta and officially tell him the whole story. This would have the effect of forcing Purta to act, and that meant those of us who made the movie would probably be expelled. We still refused, feeling that a simple disclaimer was a fair solution. The standoff continued through the week. On Thursday they scheduled an appointment with Fr. Purta for the following Saturday morning. The countdown began.

On Friday, the situation suddenly changed. Jack Folmer had played the part of the archbishop and had known the movie's whole story from the beginning. Initially, he'd been squarely on our side of the debate, but as the meetings went on and the threats grew more serious, the tension got to him and he abruptly announced that he had changed his mind and now regretted what he had done. An emergency meeting was called for that night, just before the Saturday deadline with Fr. Purta. I was off campus that evening and couldn't attend the meeting, but when I returned later I found two notes under my door. One was from Bob and one was from Ken Kelzer, a classmate who had had a minor role in the movie and was now spearheading the opposition. Bob's note was short and upbeat, reveling in what he called "this cliff-hanging diplomacy." Ken's note was long and somber, outlining the points of agreement that had emerged from the meeting:

1. *We all agreed that Folmer's rights are to be considered very strongly.*
2. *If Jack calls for drastic action, Bob would call a moratorium on the thing and spell out in writing whom he would show the movie to.*

He went on to say,

Tomorrow at 8:30 A.M. the debate will be presented to Fr. Purta in his office. The appointment is already made. Those present will be: Klaas, Folmer, Isola, and I. Bob and Al refuse to come. You may come if you like. We are going to present *the <u>whole</u> case, including the naming of names, and discussing the content of the film if Fr. Purta asks any questions. I realize this is not very fair to you because you haven't had much time to think it over, about going to Fr. Purta. Perhaps we should apologize, but at this stage apologies don't mean much anymore. See you in the morning. Ken."*

I, like Bob, was enjoying the drama of the debate. This was a something I felt sure about, something worth fighting for. In my mind, it was symbolic of the central issue facing the seminary and the church: freedom vs. fear and authoritarianism. I went to bed that night feeling incredibly alive. I would go to the meeting the next day, and I would argue our case. It would actually be easier without Bob being there, because his cynicism often put others on the defensive. I wanted to confront this issue alone, without having to defend whatever bizarre issues Bob might want to drag into the discussion. I wanted it to be a simple case of whether the movie should be destroyed or not, whether the right of free speech would be protected. I was looking forward to putting Fr. Purta on the spot, to see how his balancing act would work this time.

Unfortunately, I never got my chance. Jack told us early the next morning that the movie was jeopardizing his mental health, and that if we didn't do something, he would have to leave the seminary. That made it a different ballgame. Jack had been involved in the movie from the start, and if he was that distraught by what was happening, we would do whatever was necessary to placate his fears, short of destroying the movie. We quickly made a proposal: We would agree not to show the movie for a period of five years. That was the length of time it would take for anyone who had been in the movie to be ordained. We made it clear that this was an offer made out of respect for Jack, not in response to what we considered the unreasonable inquisitorial demands of the others. They accepted our offer and cancelled their meeting with Fr. Purta. We signed a moratorium, promising not to show the movie for five years.

We kept our word. Jack went on to be ordained a priest and then got a degree in Canon Law. Mike Anderson left the seminary and became a film cameraman. Everything seemed to work out fine.

The whole crisis was a wonderful experience for me. It forced me to examine my own basic beliefs and to deal with those whose beliefs were different from mine. I realized that many of those opposed to the movie honestly considered it something evil, and, consistent with our Catholic warrior upbringing, evil must be destroyed. So it was natural for them to want the movie destroyed. Five years earlier, I no doubt would have been one of them, leading the charge against "immorality and blasphemy." Now I was a different person, but I understood where they were coming from, and I respected their sincerity. Some of them seemed to respect my sincerity as well, and we reached the point where we could differ radically without impugning each other's motives. I reached that point with Ken Kelzer, Jack Folmer, and, I think, Jack O'Neill, who, when he agreed to drive the tractor in the last scene of the movie, was totally unaware of the rest of the plot, and felt he had been conned into doing something he didn't agree with. He was right, and I admitted that to him, though I also told him that we purposely didn't reveal the plot to any of the supporting actors, because we didn't want to start a lot of rumors that might jeopardize the whole project. I told him I would give a disclaimer every time we showed it, taking him off the hook. Jack held his ground that the movie should be destroyed; I held my ground that it shouldn't; but the two of us kept a level of personal trust between us that helped keep the rest of the negotiations from blowing up.

My Life as a Politician

When we had returned to the seminary in September, I was poignantly aware of Tom Sheehan's absence. Tom had decided to leave after being "clipped" three months earlier, at the end of Second Theology. Being "clipped" meant that the faculty had refused to call him to orders, signifying that they did not think he was a viable candidate for the priesthood. I was deeply angered by this. Tom had been our class president since first high, and was one of the brightest guys who ever went through the seminary. His fierce intellect had intimidated those members of the faculty who still equated learning with parrotry, and they had done their best to drive him away. Being clipped was the last straw for Tom. He decided to leave the seminary to pursue an academic career in philosophy. His departure fed my anger at the faculty, who had begun, increasingly, to resemble grotesque cartoon figures.

The class held an election to replace Tom as class president, and, to my surprise, I was elected. For me, the timing was right. I had come back from Mississippi with the poignant realization that, just as blacks in the south were denied their right to due process, we seminarians were also denied such rights. We could be expelled at any time, with no explanation, unable to defend ourselves from unidentified accusers. We were still expected to obey rules that made no sense to us. *"A superior may err in commanding, but you can never err in obeying"* was still the underlying philosophy of the faculty, even in our supposedly progressive Vatican II seminary. I now had a mission – – to introduce due process rights into the hitherto authoritarian structure of the seminary.

On the bus back from Mississippi, Bob and I had talked a lot about what needed to be changed in the seminary. In many ways, Bob was my mentor, always more astute (and more trenchant) politically than I. We had both been radicalized by our experiences in Mississippi, and we both had lost any fear we previously had of being thrown out of the seminary.

In retrospect, I can see that I was actually courting martyrdom at that time. I still felt called to a radical priesthood, but I no longer trusted organized religion. I was hoping that the seminary would play the role of Pontius Pilate and wash its hands of me. That would relieve me from the dreaded decision that was hovering like a black cloud just outside my consciousness. Even though I had become totally disenchanted with Catholicism, I was unable to imagine myself in any other profession than priest.

The first thing Bob and I did when we got back was craft a very diplomatic letter to Father Purta. We thanked him in detail for all the modifications he had made in the seminary rule. We also thanked him for his openness to new ideas and for his Vatican II leadership qualities. Then we socked it to him. We listed off about twenty-five issues that we still wanted him to deal with, most of them relating to due process rights for students.

He wasn't fooled by our flattery. He politely thanked us for our input and proceeded to ignore our letter. He knew the archbishop wasn't about to buy into "civil rights" within his seminary.

Father Purta had set up a "presidents' council" the year before, so that he could meet monthly with all six class presidents and discuss issues with them. As class president, I used this forum to drive the due process agenda that Bob and I had formulated. Father Purta soon tired of my persistent reduction of every issue to a matter of student rights, but the four younger presidents started to find these ideas rather intriguing. The only president older than me was Jerry Kennedy, who had already been ordained a deacon and was going to be ordained as a priest in a few months. The last thing he was interested in was seminary reform. He dismissed my due process ideas as "shit disturbing" and tried to direct the meetings to less controversial topics. By this time, however, change was in the air, and, increasingly, Jerry's conservatism fell on respectful, but deaf, ears.

During this time, I was running on an energy that was as unfamiliar to me as it was disturbing to my classmates and teachers. I had suddenly become consumed with destroying what I perceived to be the smug authoritarianism that permeated the church. I had watched the bishops at the Vatican Council talk eloquently about restoring the gospel ideals of collegiality and openness and then, true to form, get sidetracked by their own timidity and back down. I found, however, that I could no longer back down. My former pietism had taken a distinctly activist turn. I had gone from John of the Cross to Savonarola without passing go.

Up to this time in my life, I had always been plagued by self-doubt, probably due to the emphasis placed on humility by my grandmother, and all her warnings about the sin of pride. Now, however, I felt strangely self-assured about what I was doing, as though I was being called by Jesus to a different kind of priesthood, one more like His own – totally outside the confines of organized religion. I was more at peace with myself, less angry at others. I realized that my views had become heretical, both to the egg-headed liberals and to the procrustean conservatives within the church, and this gave me a new sense of freedom.

I didn't realize the depth of that freedom until one evening I stood before the mirror in my room and decided to exorcise the demon of Father Leonard. Smiling at my reflection, and feeling very much at one with God, I joyfully masturbated for the first time in ten years. I didn't fantasize a sexual partner (at that point I didn't know enough to even create such a fantasy), but simply reveled in the physical and spiritual experience of freedom. I had broken some powerful internal shackle and I was treated to the orgasm of release. Sex remained mysterious, but it was no longer shameful. Mani and Augustine had been given their walking papers – finally.

The movie controversy had convinced me that we needed to address the issue of human rights in the seminary. Though my anti-movie peers couldn't really be accused of mounting a full-scale witch-hunt, they had definitely demanded a book burning, and had arranged the equivalent of an *auto-de-fe* for us. I realized that they still believed what we had been taught in our Christian Apologetics class: that an inquisition was always justified to protect the church from heretics; and that the rights of individuals were always to be subordinated to the needs of the church. If the deadlock had persisted and the movie had been officially denounced to Fr. Purta, he would probably have felt obliged to throw the four of us out. For Bob and me, expulsion would have been an easy pitch into the briar patch, but for Al and Conrad it would have been devastating. Both had already spent eleven years of their lives preparing for the priesthood (and indeed both have gone on to serve the church as priests for over 35 years now). Nevertheless, they could have been thrown out, without any due process recourse. It seemed to me that, as priests, we could champion the rights of others all we wanted, but if we couldn't recognize, and demand, our <u>own</u> rights from the church, we were merely programmed functionaries. I kept up my due process monologue in the presidents' council, until, eventually, the other presidents agreed that the students needed an official voice with the faculty. We decided to form a "student body" and elect a president who could act as an advocate for all seminarians, not merely members of his own class.

This was a radical departure from the seminary's traditional top-down governance structure, but a precedent had been set the year before, when Fr. Purta, following Vatican II's mandate, had approved the election of a student "Liturgical Commission." This group consisted of representatives from each class and was empowered to make decisions in that most politically-explosive arena – the liturgy. They had proceeded to make sweeping changes in key ceremonies, such as the Palm Sunday and Holy Week celebrations. This wholesale surrender of power to students drove the more conservative faculty members crazy, especially when they themselves were assigned as celebrants for liturgies that they considered to be sissy theatricals. Only their own commitment to obedience kept them from revolting. Paul Purta was their superior, after all, despite his dangerous liberal tendencies, and he was always careful to couch all his decisions in unassailable Vatican II rhetoric. Paradoxically, their own vow of obedience required them to submit to a process that they felt would ultimately destroy the very foundations of that vow. In this sense, they became martyrs to modernity.

Father Purta, on the other hand, had embraced modernity and was emerging as an enlightened leader and administrator, precisely because of his adaptability to change and his seeming finesse in handling this dangerous and unpredictable "new breed" of seminarians. He was astute enough to know that his trading-stock with the archbishop depended on his success in managing any potential student revolutions through wise managerial techniques. Better for him to channel student unrest into manageable bureaucratic structures than to let it fester into anarchy beneath the surface. The archbishop had heard all the horror stories about seminary unrest and had read Andrew Greeley's dramatic descriptions of rebellious seminarians, so, despite his own conservatism, he was prepared to let Father Purta make whatever liberal concessions were necessary to keep the lid on things.

One of the members of the liturgical commission was a young guy named Dennis Lucey. Dennis was the best argument I've ever seen for reincarnation, in that he seemed to have walked into the seminary fresh from about three previous lives as medieval churchmen. He knew more Latin than most of the faculty, could sing long passages of Gregorian chant by memory, and, best of all, had developed a perfect imitation of the archbishop. Not only could he mimic the archbishop's voice and intonations, but his thought processes and sentence structures as well. He became a minor celebrity in the seminary for his archbishop imitation, to the point that even Father Purta would stop him on the corridor and kneel to kiss his imaginary ring, so that Dennis would launch into his archbishop imitation for him.

Father Purta saw the student body election as a litmus test to see just how far the students were willing to go. He and I had crossed swords all year, and he knew my position well, but he still considered me an impractical idealist with very little grasp of the "Real-Politik" within which the church operated. I symbolized one end of the scale, which he, as the Archbishop's fulcrum, had to keep delicately balanced. He was sure that, despite my popularity with the radical fringe, I didn't have the support of the student body as a whole. I didn't think I did either, but it didn't matter at that point. The only light that had penetrated my "dark night of the soul" was a vision of Jesus driving moneychangers from the temple, standing up to the Pharisees, and protecting the poor and weak. That was the essence of the church I now believed in, and I really didn't care if I had the support of the rest of the student body or not. In fact, I knew I didn't have much support in my own class, because all the other "disturbers," including Bob, had left by then, and my remaining classmates had all started thinking that I had gone quite mad. I did have some allies among the younger students, who didn't seem to be as brainwashed by seminary tradition as guys of my vintage. Phil DeAndrade who had been expelled a few years earlier for possession of a paperback novel, had returned with a healthy skepticism about the authoritarian structure of the seminary, and he introduced me to several of his younger drinking buddies who were also pushing for change in the seminary. By that point, I had taken off my Pioneer (temperance society) pin, and had begun drinking contraband beer at the King's Table Pizza Parlor in Palo Alto.

The student body election evolved into a watershed event for the seminary. Emotions ran high, and it was anyone's guess how it would turn out. There were five of us running, so the chance of splitting the vote was high. I was the only avowed radical on the ballot, and the others spanned the political spectrum, with Tony Isola, who had found his conservative voice during the movie conflict, representing the right wing. There were three middle-of-the-road candidates: Mike Murray, a classmate of mine; Bob Nixon, the president of the class behind us, and Jack Isaacs, a Second Philosopher three years younger than I. Jerry Kennedy, the president of the Deacon class, and until then the titular head of the student body, was in charge of overseeing the election and counting the ballots. He had made no bones about his opposition to me.

The election was held on March 13, 1966, and that evening Jerry posted the results:

McAllister -79
Murray   -19
Nixon   -17
Isola   -10
Isaacs   -8
Votes cast -133
Needed to win -67
Gregory McAllister is the first President of the Student Council – March 13, 1966 -jfk

Jerry's omission of anything even approaching congratulations was unlike him, and it eloquently expressed his disgust over the results.

I was amazed by the vote. I had gotten a clear mandate from the student body, something I had not really expected. It was the only "ordination" I would ever fully value.

"EverySeminarian"

The election occurred about ten days before Archbishop McGucken was scheduled to come down to the seminary for his Silver Anniversary celebration. Father Purta told me that, as the new student body president, I would be expected to present a gift to the archbishop on behalf of the students, and he also asked me to come up with some sort of entertainment for him. I learned from Gil Mata, a classmate of mine who was also a confidant of Father Purta, that Purta was really hoping that we put on some kind of obnoxious skit, so that he (Purta) could say, "See what I have to deal with, Archbishop?"

I spent a long time thinking about what to do for the archbishop, and even spent a lot of time in chapel, talking it over with my elusive Godhead. Finally it came to me – a skit in which we would make fun of everybody, ourselves included, a skit that would serve as a catharsis for all the pent-up anger and anxiety that everyone was feeling. It would be in the form of a medieval morality play, and we would call it "Everyseminarian."

The seminary was such a tightly-knit institution that type-casting was easy. You knew exactly who should play what roles, and you also knew who could improvise the lines if need be. There were six characters in the play. Three were abstract qualities (Timidity, Rashness, and Balance) and three were human characters (Everyseminarian, the Rector [Fr. Purta], and the Archbishop). The play begins with Timidity and Rashness on stage. I cast Leonard Duggan, the epitome of prudent planning, as Rashness, and Joe Taranto, an explosive Italian, as Timidity. Everyseminarian was played by John Van Hagen, a happy-go-lucky guy from the deacon class with whom everyone could identify. As he enters the stage, Everyseminarian is assaulted, first by Rashness, then by Timidity, then by Rashness again, after which he impulsively knocks on the door of the Rector. When the rector (played by Gil Mata) invites him in, he plunges through the door and demands that seminarians be allowed to keep dogs in their rooms. The rector is sitting in a chair, with Dame Balance hovering behind him like a guardian angel. Dame Balance was played by Bob Johnson, who stood six-three and weighed around 250 pounds. He was draped in a white sheet and held a broomstick with plates hanging from either end, like the scales of justice. Gil Mata was a confidant of Father Purta and had helped him write many of his speeches, so he knew his mannerisms and thought processes well. He responds to Everyseminarian in typical Purta fashion, assuring him that he totally understands what he is saying, and that he agrees that pets are God's creatures and wonderful companions and he can certainly understand why students would want to have them in their rooms...(as he talks, he leans further and further to the left, until he is almost ready to fall off his chair. At that point, Dame Balance gives him a good whack on the left shoulder, reversing his direction back toward the center).

"...But, on the other hand, we must consider...". (He slowly pendulums back toward the right, giving the opposing argument, until he almost falls off his chair on that side and Balance nudges him back toward the center again.)

"But I think we need to search for some balance in this matter." The rector then thanks Everyseminarian for coming to him and says it represents a good first attempt at communication. Everyseminarian thanks him profusely and backs awkwardly out of his office. After he's gone, the rector flies into a rage: "What is the <u>matter</u> with these people!!" Dame Balance runs away.

I was watching the archbishop closely during this part, and he was chuckling under his breath. Father Purta, on the other hand, had turned beet-red, even though still managing a forced smile.

The second act opens with the rector being assailed by Rashness and Timidity, as he debates whether to bring the matter to the archbishop or not. He vacillates back and forth between them, until he finally explodes and cries out for Balance. Balance rushes in and shoes Rashness and Timidity out of the room.

The third act begins with the Rector entering the archbishop's office to tell him about Everyseminarian's demand. Everyone in the seminary, except Archbishop McGucken, is familiar with Dennis Lucey's imitation of the archbishop, so when Dennis stands up and greets the rector in McGucken's unmistakable brogue, the whole place goes into hysterics; then they all catch themselves and look nervously at the archbishop who, fortunately, cracks a big smile as he hears Dennis' imitation for the first time.

Then the rector, with the prodding of Dame Balance, gives a carefully modulated account of Everyseminarian's demand for dogs in the rooms. At that point, the archbishop's phone rings and he excuses himself to answer it.

"Hello? Oh yes, Leo. How's everything up in the empire?" (Bishop Maher is evidently on the phone, asking the archbishop's advice about something.)

The archbishop listens, nodding his head, and eventually says, "Well, you know what they say, Leo – 'Roma locuta est, causa finita est'"

There's a slight pause, after which the archbishop frowns and says, "What do you mean 'what does that mean'?"

At this point, the real archbishop lets out a loud guffaw (Leo's ignorance of Latin was legendary) and the tension totally drains from the room. Everyone starts laughing together.

I looked around and I knew that we had done it. We had exorcised the demon of fear and distrust that had previously existed between ourselves and the archbishop. We had created a catharsis and it was incredibly liberating. Even Father Purta was smiling now, despite the fact that we had roasted his management style in our skit.

This may have been the high point of my seminary career, the time when I felt most true to my priestly vocation. It was the time when I came to realize that my God was a God of humor, and that Faith for me was primarily an act of humility in which human beings were able to acknowledge our comic human finitude.

The Emperor and I

It had been three years since Leo Maher had been made bishop of the new Santa Rosa diocese, and over two years since Jim Pulskamp and I had officially transferred into his diocese. During that time, Bishop Maher had distinguished himself as a big spender, launching a massive building program up and down the Redwood Empire. He insisted on spending millions of dollars on new rectories, even when many rural pastors objected that such lavish displays of wealth would only alienate them from their working class parishioners. He created new parishes, built new high schools, remodeled or replaced existing churches. His was a church of prestige and power and, consistent with this vision, he bought himself a luxurious mansion atop a hill in a wealthy section of Santa Rosa. He was an exciting and dynamic leader, definitely going places in the Church.

Bishop Maher and I had always gotten along, and he had even made indirect inquiries through Mike Kenny about whether I would be interested in going to Rome to study. (I politely declined, saying I was already so disillusioned with the organized church that I feared going to Rome would push me over the edge.) Jim Pulskamp, Greg Klaas and I had been invited to dinner at the annual priests' retreat in 1965, and after dinner I was standing on the porch when Bishop Maher came out, flanked by a couple of his chancery office colleagues.

"How are you, Greg? How are things going?" he said, beaming a big smile.

His question seemed genuine, so I told him the truth.

"Well actually, Bishop, there's something that's been bothering me."

He sounded very concerned when he said, "And what's that?"

"Well, Bishop," I blurted, "I know we don't take a vow of poverty as diocesan priests, but I've always thought that we were supposed to live according to the <u>spirit</u> of poverty."

He shook his head in the affirmative.

"And…well, I'm just having a lot of trouble reconciling the spirit of poverty with your building program."

His face got bright red and he flashed an anger I hadn't seen in him before. He got right in my face: "Greg, you don't understand <u>anything</u>! We have to show people that the Catholic Church is not a fly-by-night institution! It's here to stay! That's why I bought that house on top of that hill. Do you know who my neighbors are?" He started listing off bank presidents, judges, winery owners, corporate executives. "We have to show these people that the Church is a player!"

I put up my hand in a gesture of surrender. "Okay, Bishop, I understand."

He turned and began shaking the hands of the other priests who were now coming out the door.

I was shaken and bewildered. I had wanted him to empathize with my conflict, to give me some sort of spiritual perspective that would enable me to respect him as my religious superior and support what he was doing. I hadn't expected him to get defensive and call me stupid. And I certainly hadn't expected him to argue his position solely on corporate economics.

I was still very naïve.

Many years later, I realized that this event was a real turning point for me. Never again after that would I mistake the organized church for the church of Jesus, and never again would I trust a bureaucrat with my soul.

Double Standard

I had a short term as student body president, because we had agreed the annual elections should be held in May, and consequently, the initial March election was just to get things going. Nonetheless, during that brief window of time, I did my best to push through as many changes as possible. I wasn't always temperate in this endeavor, and news of my activity evidently reached Bishop Maher, because one day his Chancellor, Jerry Cox, appeared at my door and said he wanted to talk to me. Jerry was a pretty straight-forward guy, so he got right to the point.

"Greg," he said, "you're supposed to be ordained as a deacon in a few weeks, but the bishop isn't sure if he should ordain you or not. He's heard about all the radical stuff you're doing in the seminary and he's wondering if you really want to be a priest."

That was a good question, and I was glad he asked it. I'd been wondering if the bishop was oblivious to what was going on in the seminary, and I was relieved to hear he wasn't.

"I don't really know, Jerry. I still feel called to the priesthood, but I don't know if it's a good fit for me or not. No one here in the seminary really knows what the parish is like, and none of you guys in the parishes know what we're thinking in the seminary these days. The last thing I want to do is go out there and offend all the little old ladies, and hopefully I won't, but I have no way of knowing unless I try it. I guess that's why I'd like to become a deacon – so I can function like a priest for awhile and see if it works."

I knew this was a real stretch, since, at that time, bishops never ordained anyone a deacon unless they were sure he was going to be a priest, so I added, "I'll totally understand if the bishop decides he doesn't want to ordain me a deacon." That's what I was secretly hoping.

Jerry looked a little perplexed, then shrugged his big shoulders. "What the hell," he said. "I'll tell him, and we'll see what he says."

Then he looked at me, as if trying to decide whether he could trust me or not. He must have decided he could, because he leaned over, and, in a conspiratorial voice, said, "You know, Greg, maybe you can explain something to me. I really don't understand what's going on in the seminary these days. When I was in the seminary...shit...we went out with girls...but we knew it was <u>wrong!</u> Today, guys go out with girls, and they don't think it's wrong! They don't feel guilty about it! I just don't understand that kind of attitude!!"

I was hit by at least three different emotions simultaneously. First, I was flattered that he had leveled with me and was genuinely asking my opinion. Secondly, I felt a tinge of jealousy toward him and the other guys he was talking about, because I had never gone out with girls – not because I thought it was wrong, but because I was too damned shy and too caught up in my egg-headed crisis of faith to have the hutzpah to do anything that normal. Thirdly, and this was the emotion that carried the day, I was outraged by what I saw as the double standard behind his question.

"Damn it, Jerry. That's just what really pisses us off in the seminary – the double standard in the church. You guys never really question anything. You just do things and then feel guilty about them and go to confession. If it's wrong, don't do it; but if it isn't really wrong, then don't slink around feeling guilty about it. Just do it. That's why you don't understand what's going on in the seminary. You've never questioned anything in your life!!"

Jerry put up his hands defensively. "Okay, okay. I think I see what you mean."

It was 20 years before I saw Jerry again. I ran into him at the Catholic Social Services office in San Francisco, where he was employed as the director. He had left the priesthood several years before, had married, and had a couple of kids, but was still working for the Church. I asked him if he remembered that day when he came to my room on behalf of the bishop. He got a blank look on his big Irish face and said, "No, I guess I don't."

So I told him the story. He still didn't remember.

"I?…said <u>that</u>!?" he gulped, and we had a good laugh about how life changes one's attitudes…and memories.

The Oath

I was really hoping that the bishop would find my rationale for becoming a deacon totally ridiculous and refuse to ordain me. I was still looking for an easy out. I hadn't managed to get injured in Mississippi; Father Purta hadn't thrown me out for making the movie; and Father Fenn hadn't been able to persuade the faculty to clip me. Things were getting down to the wire, but the idea of making a decision based on my <u>own</u> desires and preferences was inconceivable. No matter how radical I had become, how aware of basic human rights, how liberated from the old ideas of blind obedience to authority, still, the idea of making a "selfish" choice based only on my own preferences was beyond my capabilities. I still felt that God would intervene somehow. If not in the form of a bullet, or a bishop, or a faculty member, He would nevertheless find <u>some</u> way to intervene.

But time was running short. In a couple of weeks, I was to be ordained as a deacon. And being a deacon wasn't so bad, because you could preach and counsel people and get involved in social causes. But, in order to become a deacon, you first had to become a <u>sub</u>deacon, and that was where they got you. That was where you had to take the vow of celibacy and promise never to have sex for the rest of your life.

Now granted, never having had sex, I wasn't really that concerned about giving it up. Since I had no idea what I was missing, it was still relatively easy to do without it. It was the "rest of your life" part that bothered me. If I had changed as completely as I had over the last three years, what could I expect for the future? There was no way I could commit to do or be something for the rest of my life. Not when I remembered who I had been when I entered the seminary, and compared that person to the person I was now. It was ridiculous.

Celibacy had also become for me the ultimate symbol of ecclesiastical totalitarianism, and there was no way I could take that vow. I had done some historical research and found out that celibacy only became a church law around 1100 A.D. Before then, most priests were married, had children, and owned their own churches, which they deeded to their sons, who often became priests in turn. It was only when Rome became hungry for centralized power that celibacy was invoked as a way to break the family bond and confiscate the property of her priests. Celibacy was thus just another tactic of control by a "Mother" Church, who was beginning to look more like a castrated Father to me. I had done my best to buy into the various liberal rationales for celibacy that had been presented to us in the seminary, like Adrian Van Kaam's lofty theory of "sublimation," but they always seemed a bit flaccid. Now I knew why. They were simply prefabricated attempts to make the best out of a corrupt system of economic and political oppression, not too different from Father O'Neill's rationalization of the Inquisition as "the best gift the heretic ever knew."

There was very little opposition to celibacy in 1966, certainly none from the other members of my class, who, in my mind, were obliviously drifting closer and closer to this Niagara Falls of the soul.

There was no one I could talk to about my feelings that this was a ridiculous and unreasonable prerequisite for priesthood. For most, it was just one of those things that had always been there, something you did to symbolize your loyalty to the Church. Questioning it was unheard of in our fraternity of sexual martyrs.

I had only heard my bishop mention celibacy once, and that wasn't really to defend it as a way of life, but rather to use it as a rationale for his own, and others', drinking: "If priests are going to give up women, we need some kind of compensation," he pronounced, holding up his scotch and water. It sounded rather appealing at the time, but, even then, I suspected that Dewars wasn't always going to work as a substitute for my freedom.

As ordination approached, I started having strange dreams, all involving a long ditch in which I was forced to walk. Gradually the ditch would grow deeper, then constrict and turn into a grave. I was starting to feel very claustrophobic.

Nevertheless, I continued to struggle with my decision. I still felt like God was calling me to the priesthood, even though I no longer believed in organized religion. I wanted to help people deal with their spiritual questions, but I was afraid that my own doubts would only compound their confusion. I certainly didn't want to take a vow of celibacy, but without becoming a deacon and experiencing life in the parish, I didn't feel I could make a good decision. I felt like I was tied to the train tracks, and a locomotive was rushing toward me.

Finally, a few weeks before we were scheduled to take the vow of celibacy, I made up my mind: I would fake the vow. Thanks to my theological training, I had a legal loophole: I would go through the motions, but I would not <u>intentionally</u> take the vow. It was an unreasonable requirement and, consequently, I figured I would be perfectly justified in feigning compliance, in order to achieve the higher end of becoming a deacon, since that was the only way I was going to know whether God was calling me to be a priest. My faith may have been in shambles, but my casuistry was intact.

I carefully drafted a statement, then, during Easter vacation, brought it down to a notary in Kentfield who, after she read it, tried her best not to appear as bewildered as she no doubt was.

To Whom It May Concern:

I, J. Gregory McAllister, at the approach of my ordination to the subdiaconate, feel impelled to officially record my attitude toward vows in general and the vow of celibacy in particular.

I feel that a vow can be, at best, a promise made at a given point in time and space. As such, it says, in effect, "As far as I can see right now, I will do such-and-such in the future." However, there can be no certainty that such will be the case, nor should there be, for "to live is to change." I consider openness to reality to be tantamount to openness to God's will and I am unwilling to confine God's will by imposing an a priori mold on my life by swearing that I will remain unchanged in certain aspects of that life.

I am not suggesting that this is objectively right for all. I am merely saying that the concept of a permanent vow does not fit within my act of faith. In other words, I do not believe in the possibility, or in the binding force, of permanent vows.

Consequently, with regard to the law of celibacy, I do not believe in the binding force or in the spiritual efficacy of the vow. I sign it only because it is demanded (underline>unreasonably, I feel) for priesthood. I intend no permanent vow.

Signed,
J. Gregory McAllister

The statement was notarized by "Clarissa Day Gillis, Notary Public, 5/12/66"

I believe it was a Thursday when we were scheduled to take the oath, because it seems like we didn't have class that day. (Thursdays and Sundays were our weekly holidays.) It was around 10 in the morning when our class of soon-to-be-deacons gathered outside the Theology classroom, each armed with the bible of his choice, on which he would swear a vow of perpetual celibacy. I remember looking around, checking which edition of the bible each of my classmates chose to bring. It was important, in 1966, which translation of the bible you chose, because it put you on a certain team. If you

199

were a liberal, you carried the New Jerusalem Bible; if you were a moderate, perhaps the Knox translation. If you wanted to flaunt your conservatism, you arrived with a dog-eared copy of the Douay Rheims.

There weren't many surprises. My classmates were quite predictable by then. Predictability was, after all, one of the requirements of ordination.

I can't remember which translation of the bible I brought, probably because, by that time, I had begun to consider the bible another form of idolatry. If God was really infinite, then revelation couldn't be confined to the bible. It couldn't be confined to the past either. It had to be going on all the time – in every culture, within every person in the present moment. So how could we presume to limit God and revelation by swearing on a book to do (or not do) something for the rest of our lives? How could I be sure that God wouldn't inspire me to fall in love or get married later in life? The more I thought about it, the more it seemed to me that vows were a form of prideful arrogance, tantamount to Adam's original sin of wanting to know good and evil.

I felt like an extraterrestrial, standing there, thinking these thoughts. My classmates were all chattering about their upcoming ordination to the priesthood, now scarcely a year away: Who was going to assist them at their first Mass? What were their invitations going look like? How many people were they going to invite? What kind of chalice were they going to buy?

And I was standing there thinking about faking the vow of celibacy.

As I looked around at my exuberant classmates, I felt like an imposter; worse than that, a quisling. They all looked so resolved, so committed, so settled.

I also felt a tinge of jealousy. This, after all, had been my goal too. For the last nine years, I had been just as committed as they were. Why, after all that time and effort, couldn't I share their excitement? Why did I have to be tortured by all these questions? Why couldn't I just have accepted things the way they did? Then I could be standing here, thrilled and excited about taking this warrior's oath that I had dreamed of as a child.

I found myself talking to Jesus, even though I didn't know where to find Him, and even though I wasn't absolutely sure he was there at all.

"This is really weird," I said to Him.

He didn't say anything, but I thought I heard some laughter from His direction.

Finally Father Fenn arrived with an armload of papers. He was smiling his usual brittle little smile through clenched teeth. He had a reputation among the older clergy for being "the perfect priest" and, in a 1940s, Bing Crosby kind of way, he <u>was</u> the perfect priest. He was precise in his diction and in his dress, a regular but moderate drinker, a chain smoker at a time when smoking was still considered cool, a better than average golfer, and a skilled defender of the faith who was not above using any means necessary to humiliate his (and God's) adversaries. He was admired by some of my classmates, despised by others, feared by most. He was the leader of the "law" faction of the faculty, those who felt that obedience was more essential than compassion in a priest. He was here to administer the oath of celibacy and his tight smile told us that he relished the role.

Sex was Father Fenn's official domain, because he taught the "de sexu" ("concerning sex") tract in moral theology to the ordained deacons during their last year in the seminary. Previously, our only formal exposure to sex in the seminary had occurred in the college biology course taught four years earlier by the eccentric Anglican entomologist, Dr. Edward Philpot Mumford. Dr. Mumford was forbidden by seminary officials to discuss either evolution or sex in his class, and was expected to illustrate human biology to us on an anatomical dummy that was missing its genitals.

The genitals had not been thrown away. Unknown to us, they had been stored in Fr. Fenn's closet, awaiting the time, six years later, when Fr. Fenn would bring them to his "de sexu" class in a brown paper bag. A fitting way to transport those ill-fated conveyors of original sin.

We had certainly not seen the rubber genitals yet when we gathered on that Thursday morning to take the vow of celibacy. Nor had we yet experienced Father Fenn's enlightened insights into the mysteries of sex. That would come next year, after we had taken the vow of celibacy and renounced sex for life.

Fr. Fenn ushered us into the one of the classrooms and told us to take a seat. Then he passed around a sheet of paper containing the oath and a place for our signature. I was feeling strangely excited now, almost like some undercover FBI agent at a communist cell meeting. Father Fenn was talking to us in his pedantic sing-song voice, emphasizing what an important step this was in our progress toward priesthood, and how it would place us in an elite corps of men who had made the ultimate personal sacrifice. Our oath, he said, would trigger an outpouring of God's grace, which would give us the strength to live out our celibate commitment. I heard the words, and they stung and then bounced off me like small hailstones; for they were not really addressed to me. My God was no longer the Church's God, and, right now, my God was calling me to do something very different from what Father Fenn was talking about.

Father Fenn, now in a gentler voice, bade us place our hands on the bibles which rested on our desks, and repeat the oath after him. I placed my right hand so that it hovered about a sixteenth of an inch over the bible. I wasn't really touching it, but, from Lyman's perspective in the front of the room, it looked that way. My left hand was in my lap and I crossed my fingers, as a further protection against whatever invisible magic this ritual might possess. Then, as my classmates repeated the vow in unison, my voice wasn't among them. I merely mouthed the words, careful not to let any air actually connect with my vocal cords and escape through my lips. It seemed to me that Father Fenn was staring right at me during most of the vow, so I made eye contact with him at the end of each phrase, figuring this was the best way to keep him from watching my lips.

When we had finished saying the oath, we were instructed to sign it and put it on his desk. I knew there was no way around this part, but, since I had already signed and notarized a disclaimer, I felt no qualms about going through yet another motion.

I walked out of the classroom, and tried to avoid the banter of my classmates, who were doing their adolescent best to dismiss the gravity of what they had just done. As I listened to their laughter, I realized, with a great deal of sadness, that I was no longer one of them.

For the next couple of weeks, I was in a fog. On the one hand, I looked forward to being ordained a deacon; on the other, I dreaded it.

I continued to have that recurring dream of the long, narrow ditch and I had begun to suspect that ordination was the entry to that ditch, the beginning of a constricted lifestyle which would spell the end of my personal freedom.

On the other hand, I still felt called to the priesthood and couldn't imagine myself doing anything other than devoting my life to the principles of Jesus. But that's what was so confusing: Everything about the organized church seemed to belie the teachings of Jesus. The thought of Jesus running around in a roman collar, saying Mass, hearing confessions in a little box, living in a "rectory" seemed utterly ridiculous to me. There was an individuality and an anonymity to Jesus' priesthood that seemed antithetical to the conventions and uniformity of the Catholic Church.

I prayed for some sort of revelation. Maybe the ordination ceremony would bring me some sort of mystical insight. Maybe I would feel the power of the Spirit through the words of the bishop and everything would make sense. Maybe. And maybe not.

Ordination

The ordination took place in Santa Rosa. There were three of us ordained that evening. Besides myself, there was Jim Pulskamp, my friend since boyhood, and Greg Klaas, an older guy who had joined our class a year earlier, after a career as a probation officer in Los Angeles. My mom was there alone, because my dad was back in the hospital, having suffered yet another series of minor strokes. It was a surreal experience, and I don't remember much of it, except lying prostrate in a white robe, my face to the floor, as the choir and congregation sang the Litany of Saints over me, invoking the blessings of all the saints and angels, one by one. That was a dramatic moment for me, hearing all those voices calling down blessings on my behalf. I realized then that I trusted the prayers of the laity more than the ministrations of the bishop. We lay on the floor for a long time, and I found myself getting distracted, wondering if the dust on the carpet was going to make me sneeze.

I don't remember the rest of the ceremony, and that strikes me as strange, since my memory for most other things is good. I think by that time I had begun to see liturgy and ceremony as just another means to program submission, and I was blocking out whatever part of it I could. Perhaps for that reason, my hopes for a revelation went unanswered. I received no sudden infusion of energy or insight during my ordination ceremony.

A Mission from God

I woke up the next morning tired and depressed, having dreamed about the ditch again. However, I did have a mission that day that got me out of bed early. I was going to bring my Dad communion in the hospital. If nothing else, this single act would make my ordination worthwhile. At that time, only a deacon or a priest was allowed to transport the consecrated host, in its tiny gold "pix," to the sick. I had arranged with my pastor, Father "Red" O'Connell, that I would bring my dad communion after the morning Mass at our parish. "Red" was the uncle of Jerry Kennedy, the president of the class ahead of me, who felt (rightly so) that I was challenging everything that he and the traditional clergy believed in. I knew Jerry had poisoned the wells on me with his uncle, because, during the past year, Red's attitude toward me had gradually changed from warm to icy. Nevertheless, I was now a deacon, and he wasn't about to deny me the right to take communion to my Dad. I met him in the sacristy after Mass, and we exchanged frosty pleasantries. Then he opened the door to the sanctuary for me and said, "I hope you know what you're doing." Jerry definitely had primed him for this, and I felt anger boil up inside me, but I went past him into the sanctuary without responding. He stood there, still holding the door open, staring at me. He was daring me make a mistake, to miss a genuflection, to fail to fulfill the letter of the rubrics.

All I could think of was Jesus and my Dad. Red's presence at the door was not going to distract me from the essential meaning of what I was doing. I would do it the way Jesus would have done it. I got to the bottom of the altar stairs where the first genuflection was supposed to take place. I hesitated for a brief moment, but then went up the stairs to the altar without genuflecting. I was now in front of the tabernacle where the second genuflection was specified by the rubrics. I was talking to Jesus now, and I didn't care if Red was shooting daggers at me or not. Jesus had never wanted to be a king with people genuflecting to Him, and I felt like He was there with me, helping me resist the automatic Roman kneebend that had been programmed into me since childhood. I opened the tabernacle and again resisted the required genuflection. The pix was inside, a small circular object on a cord. It resembled a pocket watch or a locket. I put one of the consecrated wafers inside the pix and snapped it shut. Then I put the cord around my neck so that the pix hung on my chest, just inside my clerical coat. I locked the tabernacle, turned and walked down the altar toward the door, which Red was still propping open. His face was throbbing a deep red and I was sure I was going to get a full barrel of his legendary rage. When I reached the door, he thrust his face next to mine, teeth bared, ready to tear into me, but then his eyes traveled down to the pix around my neck, and we both had a sudden realization. According to official church law, it was forbidden to talk to anyone who was carrying the pix. Red, being the traditionalist he was, had no outlet for his rage. All he could do was glare at me. I nodded to him and went out to my car, feeling like St. Tarsisius fleeing the Romans with the host clutched to his bosom.

I had been to see my Dad in the hospital the day before, and on the way to his room, I had done my usual seminarian thing, greeting all the nurses and orderlies I passed. Most of them had responded cheerfully. Now, I came down the same hall, dressed in my black suit and roman collar, and again said hello to the same nurses and orderlies. Instead of meeting my eyes, as they had done the day before, they got only as far as my roman collar, and then barked an automatic "G'morning, Father," "G'morning, Father." I was aghast. No one recognized me from the day before, and no one was really talking to me as a person. I was running a gauntlet of "g'morning, father's," and the further I went down that corridor, the more it started looking like the long, straight ditch of my dreams.

When I reached my dad's room, he was slumped over in his wheelchair, only the restraining belts keeping him upright. He looked up at me, raised his right eyebrow as if to say, "What's this?" and gave me his crooked little smile. I put a small stole around my neck (a stole resembles a narrow scarf and is the official badge of office for deacons), and explained to him that I had brought him communion. He nodded, and automatically stuck out his tongue to receive the host when I held it out to him and said, "The body of Christ."

Afterwards, I felt I needed to explain things to him, to warn him, perhaps, not to get his hopes up. It had been seven years since his stroke, seven years since he had been able to speak, and before that all he could talk about was his son who was studying to be a priest. In case he still felt that way, I wanted to prepare him, to cushion him, in case I decided not to be a priest.

"You're probably wondering why I'm dressed up like this," I said. His eyes met mine and the smile remained. I had no idea if he was going to be able to understand what I was about to say, but I was determined to try to communicate it to him. "Last night I was ordained a deacon…and that's the last step before becoming a priest. But…(I was groping for words now)…but I'm not <u>sure</u> I'm going to become a priest."

He looked at me with his tired, grey-blue eyes, smiled, and, without hesitating or stumbling on his words, said, "You'll never be a priest!"

I couldn't believe it. This was his first coherent sentence in eight years, and he <u>understood</u>!

I blurted back, "Why? Am I so much like you?"

"Yep," he said without hesitation, and then his eyes lost focus and he slid back behind the shroud of the stroke.

It was exactly what I needed – an affirmation from my father, my wonderful father, whom I had so dearly loved and respected, and whose absence had been so devastating for me during the past eight years. He had managed to reappear, just for a moment, when I most needed him. He had sensed my conflict, and he intuitively knew that I had been disappointed in my search for father figures in the church. Perhaps he too had been disappointed, and perhaps that's why he was able to break through his veil with such vigor and assurance.

I felt an incredible sense of relief, and, at the end of my visit, I kissed my dad and thanked him for who he was and what he had given me. I also told him how proud I was that he thought I was like him. He smiled his crooked little smile and nodded.

When I got home, I related the story to my mother, but she pretended not to believe it. She dismissed it as some sort of projection on my part. She was too crushed by my father's absence in her own life to be able to imagine him playing an active role in mine. She was also painfully aware of my ambiguity about the priesthood and was intuitively dreading my decision. Despite her best efforts to remain detached, she had come to enjoy the deference shown to her as the mother of a future priest, and my dad's pronouncement jeopardized that status.

A few years later, when her wounds over my departure had healed, she told me a story that might explain my dad's surprising pronouncement that day. Back in the early '50s, St. Sebastian's parish had been broken off from St. Anselm's parish to accommodate the growing population of Greenbrae, an affluent new development just east of Kentfield. Kentfield was included within the boundaries of the new parish, much to my parents' regret. They would have preferred to remain in St. Anselm's, where all their old friends were, but they were obliged by church law to become members of St. Sebastian's. The new parish had no church, so we had to use the nearby chapel at Marin Catholic High School until we could build our own church. In 1953, we got a new pastor, Father Harry Leonard, who had previously been the head of the Catholic Youth Organization in the archdiocese. He was an affable guy with a lot of contacts in the diocese, and the bishop figured he would be able to tap into the wealth of Greenbrae and get a new church built. From the start, my mother had little use for Father Leonard. In her mind he was too much of a blowhard, and she resented the fact that he spent all his time cultivating the young wealthy in Greenbrae and ignoring the old guard from St. Anselm's. My dad didn't seem to notice, and bonded easily with the young guys from Greenbrae who were active in parish activities.

Father Leonard got up in the pulpit one Sunday and triumphantly announced that finally, after three long years, we were going to build our own church. This would be a great challenge, he said, but St. Sebastian's parish was up to it. This was Father Leonard, the old CYO coach, at his best, motivating his team before the big game. Then he laid out his strategy. He had, he said, assembled "the finest men of the parish" into a committee that would go around and collect pledges from all parishoners. He kept praising these "fine men" and encouraged everyone to reach deep in their pockets when one of them appeared on their doorstep. He then dramatically read the names of the "finest men of the parish." As my mother feared, his list included only young guys from Greenbrae, and my dad's name wasn't among them, despite the fact that he had been active in all the parish functions and had previously been the president of the Men's Club at St. Anselm's. After Mass, my mother, knowing how hurt my dad was over being excluded from the committee, told him what she thought of Father Leonard, and how it was simply inexcusable that he would overlook someone like my dad, who had devoted so much time and energy to the church. My dad said to forget it, that it was no big deal.

Evidently, some of the other guys on the committee had also noticed that my dad wasn't on the list and went to Father Leonard during the next week to tell him that he had omitted a key person from the committee. The next Sunday, as my folks were walking out of church after Mass, Father Leonard came running out of the sacristy, still dressed in his alb.

He rushed up to my dad, clapped him on the shoulder and said, "Joe, Joe, an oversight on my part. I really want you to be part of the team."

My mother said that my dad's eyes turned "steel grey" as he looked at Father Leonard. Then he said, "Father, you can go to hell."

It wasn't too long after this that my dad had his stroke and lost his ability to talk. An act of God? Or a classic case of the Catholic Operating System crashing when an Irishman performs an illegal function that violates his childhood program? Whatever the cause of his affliction, my dad managed to silently survive for eight years, and I like to think that he even succeeded in repairing his own program code during that time – to the point where he could help me change mine.

Deaconate

As deacons, we were assigned to work in a parish over the summer. My assignment was to St. Rose Church, the original parish church in Santa Rosa. Bishop Maher had chosen St. Rose as the launching pad for his new building campaign, and had added a brand new addition to the beautiful old stone church, as well as building a huge new rectory that was reputed to have cost the scandalous sum of $250,000.

I had been told by friends in the diocese that the pastor of St. Rose, Monsignor Walter Tappe, had specifically requested that I be stationed there, so that he could "straighten me out." Monsignor

Tappe had been well-known in the old San Francisco Archdiocese as the longtime editor of the Catholic Monitor. He was still widely regarded as a scholar, and took himself very seriously in that role. Evidently he had heard that I was an intellectual (something I found quite laughable), and so he was anxious to sharpen his mental sword on me. He was known as a cautious liberal, mainly because he, unlike most of the priests of his generation, actually tried to keep up with the new theological ideas that were proliferating after Vatican II. He would typically spend six to seven hours a day reading liberal theologians like Hans Kung, Cardinal Suenens and Edward Schillibeeckx. I later realized he didn't agree with much of what they were saying, but he read them nonetheless, perhaps out of a sense of duty in his self-appointed role as protector of the faith.

Because of his love for books, he designed his study as the "holy of holies" in his new rectory. It was a large circular room, with teak wood paneling, a large oak desk, polished bookcases, and a thick carpet. On the day I arrived at St. Rose, this was the room into which he ushered me for our first official conference. I remember sitting across the room from him, hearing his voice bouncing across that luxuriant carpet, as he thundered, "Gregory! The problem with young priests today is that they have <u>lost</u>...the <u>spirit</u>...of <u>POVERTY</u>!" He boomed out these words with such dramatic intensity, and such utter conviction, that I felt like I had just lost my mind. I had come in there determined not to make any more negative judgments about the bishop's lavish spending policies, even though I knew that wasn't going to be easy, because of my unfortunate habit of asking myself "What would Jesus do in this situation?" Anyway, I was doing my best to visualize Jesus' bare feet on Monsignor Tappe's carpet, when he came out with that line about the spirit of poverty. For a minute I really thought God was playing a joke on me, (and even now I'm not sure S/He wasn't). But I sat there nodding (which is what Monsignor's Italian bombast always seemed to require), and didn't say a word.

He went on to explain that, as part of my training in poverty and humility, I would be assigned to two parish organizations, the St. Vincent de Paul Society and the Legion of Mary. The former was a charitable organization, which raised money for the poor. The latter was a very traditional group, dedicated to promoting devotion to Mary by praying the rosary every day. I cringed when Monsignor gave me the Legion of Mary assignment, imagining a bunch of pugnacious old battleaxes who would report back to him about everything I said and did. I figured he was setting me up. Actually, to my surprise, the Legion turned out to be a wonderful group of people whose sincerity and warmth impressed me deeply.

There were several other priests living in the rectory. Jim Gaffey was a young, square-jawed Irishman who had already begun to earn a name for himself as a church historian. He taught at the local Catholic high school and had a room at the rectory. Despite his youth and exposure to modern ideas, he had managed to retain the unwavering conservatism of his San Francisco roots, and was even now beginning to develop traces of that absent-mindedness often associated with the bumptious professoriate. On the infrequent occasions when he would attempt to cook a meal for himself, he would invariably forget about the stove hood and bang his head on it. One evening, after we had been discussing Church issues for some time, Jim turned to me with a very serious look on his face and said, "Greg, I really like you, and I respect your sincerity, but, in all honesty, I have to tell you that I think you're a heretic."

Dennis Clark was only a year or two older than I, and had just arrived in Santa Rosa from the San Diego diocese, a trophy from one of Bishop Maher's recruiting safaris. Dennis was from a wealthy Southern California family and had an aristocratic bearing that often rubbed people the wrong way. He had a caustic sense of humor, and tended to be fairly conservative, but he didn't take himself as seriously as Gaffey, and was fun to joke around with. He was the first guy I had ever met who had a personal credit account at Brooks Brothers men's store, and his good-natured and unabashed defense of his own high-end lifestyle helped to soften my self-righteous criticism of the bishop's spending habits.

Mal Costa was the assistant pastor, six years my senior, and one of the most delightful guys I ever met. Mal's patience and compassion were legendary, and he was the glue that held the parish together, because the other three priests were always managing to tick someone off and Mal was the person who always patched things up. He had a wonderful sense of humor, punctuated by a deep, hearty laugh, and he gradually became my mentor at St. Rose. I confided to him all my uncertainties and reservations about organized religion, many of which he shared himself. Mal was very fond of Monsignor Tappe, and that fondness enabled him to understand his foibles to the point where he developed a hysterical stand-up imitation of him. Any time I'd return to the rectory depressed about the state of the church, Mal would crease his brow, pull his glasses off in a dramatic sweep and declare in Monsignor's most grave, apocalyptic, tone, "Gregory! The trouble with young priests today is that...they've lost...their sense...of humor!" Then we'd both go into hysterics.

Awakening of the Heart

Though I found the fraternity and interaction of the priests very enjoyable, I found myself equally intrigued by another presence in the rectory. During the evenings and on weekends, the parish employed local high school girls to answer the rectory phone and take messages. The first week I was there, I met Marie, and I soon found myself anticipating which days she would be there, enjoying the glint in her blue Irish eyes and the enthusiasm she brought to our conversations. I found that I had more in common with her than I did with most of my priestly colleagues, whose clerical baggage I often found depressing. I got a fresh perspective from Marie, not just because she was nine years younger than I, but also because she saw things through feminine eyes, a perspective which was both foreign and fascinating to me, especially since I never had sisters (let alone girlfriends). She had gone to Catholic school until her junior year of high school, but then had decided to part company with the nuns and attend the local public school. She had a bit of a rebellious streak, which was compounded by having an identical twin sister, and the two of them had finally come to loggerheads with the nuns at Ursuline High. She was rebelling against many of the same things I was, so we formed an instant bond. She also gave me a different perspective on the clergy. I learned what the parishioners really thought about the bishop and the pastor, how the teenage girls of the parish ranked the young priests, and who really called the shots in the rectory. Her insights enabled me to appreciate the human complexity and beauty of the whole experience instead of reducing everything to my usual simplistic categories of "liberal" and "conservative."

211

I felt enlivened around Marie, and only very gradually did I begin to suspect that such a feeling might be related to sexual attraction. One night, as I was drifting off to sleep, pleasantly embracing thoughts of Marie in my celibate bed, I was given a profound revelation. At that moment, for the first time in my 25 years, I actually understood why my penis was getting long and hard, and where it was intended to fit. I never had a clue before that night.

Of course, I immediately went into denial and did my best to push this possibility out of my mind. However, I did find myself savoring the glimmer of adventure it had awakened in my soul. Perhaps my life really could change on some unimaginably radical level. Perhaps I, the unwilling but thoroughly programmed celibate, was a physical and sexual being after all. An ember was glowing now, and it gave me blind hope and a strange courage. I would throw myself into this work as a deacon, and God would let me know which direction I should follow.

Life in The Rectory

I found the rectory life constricting. First of all, I had never lived in such fancy surroundings, and the sterile luxury of my room made me uncomfortable. Plus, I was expected to show up for three meals a day, unless I had a good excuse, in which case I was supposed to inform Monsignor ahead of time. It's true, I was used to a meal schedule at the seminary, but the meals at St. Rose were different. They were basically opportunities for Monsignor Tappe to pontificate about all the articles and books he had read that day. He loved to talk – preach, really; so our meals often resembled the silent meals in the seminary where we were forced to listen to someone read a suitably boring book at us. Monsignor would come in primed to talk, and would gradually reach an emotional crescendo in which he would sweep off his glasses and use them to punctuate his favorite refrain: "Boys, the trouble with _____s today is that they've lost the spirit of _____!!" At every meal, a new group was castigated for lacking one of the essential virtues. We would sit attentively through these fulminations, obedient sons of an eccentric father, trying desperately not to look at each other for fear of bursting into laughter, but carefully storing away his exact words, inflections, and expressions, so that later, over a scotch and soda, we could regale each other with faithful imitations of our lovable superior.

My fears about being perceived as a radical heretic by the members of the Legion of Mary disappeared after I realized that all they expected me to do was show up in my roman collar and say the rosary with them. The commander-in-chief of the group was a handsome fellow by the name of Everett Clary, who turned out to be Marie's uncle.

"All his brothers call him 'The Saint,'" she said. "He's kind of a religious fanatic, but otherwise he's a really nice guy."

In truth, Everett was an extremely nice guy, who patiently led his legion of five elderly women through the decades of the rosary once a week. Once I got to know him, I realized that he was a lot like me, and that his religious conservatism was but the opposite side of that same coin of idealism I carried in my own soul.

One of the most colorful members of the parish was a woman named Helen Halpin. Helen was British, in her 60s, and almost certainly a convert to Catholicism, judging by her near fanaticism in the practice of her faith. She was one of the few parishioners who attended Monsignor Tappe's daily Mass, where he always subjected the small congregation to a homily distilled from his previous day's reading and mealtime proclamations. Helen was a very traditional Catholic, who considered Monsignor Tappe to be a liberal windbag. To make her point, she would always bring to Mass a copy of The Wanderer, the most right-wing Catholic newspaper in America. As soon as Monsignor turned around to begin his homily, she would sit back, put her feet up on the kneeler, unfurl The Wanderer, and begin reading. It drove Monsignor Tappe crazy. He, who seldom discussed, let alone criticized, any of the parishioners, would come storming into breakfast growling about "that woman."

Helen had a son named Joe who was away at college studying music. He had evidently inherited his mother's eccentric bravado, because one day a letter arrived from Joe addressed to "The Priests of St. Rose Parish." It simply stated, "IF you can answer the following questions to my satisfaction, I MAY return to the Catholic Church." A list of ten questions followed, starting with one that read, "I have heard that the blood of St. Januarius changes from 75 to 98.6 degrees each year on his feast day. Is this true?" Subsequent questions were similar, mentioning obscure accounts of bizarre miracles and demanding to know if they were true and if Catholics had to believe them. Finally, at the very end of the list, was appended the simple question, "What about birth control?"

Joe's letter said that he would appear at the rectory on Monday of the next week, when he returned home for the summer break. Mal Costa read the letter aloud to us at lunch, and then, amidst a lot of laughter, handed it to me and said, "I think this is something you should handle, Greg."

I was waiting for Joe when he arrived the next Monday, right on time. I introduced myself, ushered him into one of the small rooms reserved for counseling sessions, and invited him to sit down.

"Did you get my questions?" he immediately asked.

I said "yes," and pulled the list out of my coat pocket. I had no idea what to expect from Joe, since I hadn't even heard of several of the miracles he had listed. I decided just to be frank with him. I told him that I knew nothing about St. Januarius's blood heating up every year, nor about the rest of the reputed miracles, but that he was free to believe them or not, since the Church had never declared miracles as articles of faith.

"And as far as the last question," I said, "there's some difference of opinion. The official Church position seems to be that birth control is a sin, but many priests today feel that it should be a matter of personal conscience, and I would agree with that latter opinion."

I expected him to launch into a conservative tirade over that response, but he merely thanked me and left. It had been a lot easier than I had thought it would be.

That evening several of us were up in Mal's room having a drink, when the phone rang. He answered it, listened for a moment, then motioned me to put my ear to the receiver. I could hear Helen's shrill voice, even from a couple feet away.

"That Father McAllister has ruined my son! I'm canceling my contributions to the church! I've torn up my Sunday envelopes! I'm finished with you and I hope you all get sick from those figs I brought you yesterday!"

Mal was doing his best not to laugh, but managed to calm Helen down enough to get her to agree to come in the next day and discuss things. When he hung up, he and the others were laughing a lot harder than I was. This is exactly what I had feared – that my radical ideas would just stir things up and upset the people for whom the church was a necessary crutch. Mal was still laughing really hard when he told me that I, not he, would meet with Helen the next day.

"Oh great," I thought. "After talking to me, she's liable to end up in a mental hospital."

She arrived promptly at 10 o-clock the next morning. I met her in the front office and invited her to come down to the same room where I had met with her son the day before. She looked around, expecting to see Mal or one of the other priests, but then, when she realized I was the only one there, she reluctantly followed me down the hall. I sat behind the small desk, so that, if she lunged for my throat, there'd be something between us.

"Helen," I started, "I understand you're upset with me."

She looked past me at the wall and launched into a monologue. "I don't know what's become of the Church today,' she said. "It used to be, you'd ask a priest something, and you'd get an answer. Now all they ever say is 'I don't know, I don't know, I don't know.'"

Her British accent, coupled with her sing-song inflection of "I don't know," gave the phrase a humorous mantra-like quality that made it stand out from the rest of her machine gun monologue.

"Every priest I meet these days, all he can say is 'I don't know, I don't know, I don't know.' No one knows anything!!...Except Father Persano. He's the only one I respect. Now don't get me wrong. I don't like him. But I do respect him. One time I was in the confessional with him, and I was confessing my sins, and I kept repeating the same sin over and over again (I guess I was being a little scrupulous) and he finally yelled at me – right in the confessional, he yelled, 'Helen, shut up!!' right there in the confessional. Well I was very angry at him for that. In fact, I was so angry that, the next day when he was in church saying his breviary, I sneaked up behind him and yelled in his ear, 'I hope you die in mortal sin and go to hell!' I was that mad at him. But all the same, I respect him, because he didn't just say, 'I don't know, I don't know, I don't know.'"

Helen kept rattling on, still looking at the wall, and her words started feeling like hailstones bouncing off my head. The barrage continued for another thirty seconds, and I realized she might never stop. She might just go on talking forever. So I took a deep breath, paused, and then yelled out at the top of my voice, "HELEN, SHUT UP!!!"

She stopped and looked at me with wild eyes. A long second passed. Then, simultaneously, we both burst into hysterics.

We walked out of the rectory arm in arm, and remained close friends for the rest of my stay at St. Rose's – much to Monsignor Tappe's utter bewilderment. Because he lacked a sense of humor himself, he was never able to discover Helen's. She was one of the wittiest, most intelligent women I ever met, but she wasn't about to show that card to a blowhard contemporary like Monsignor Tappe who took himself so seriously that he never got her jokes.

A few months later, after I had decided to leave the seminary, I went back up to Santa Rosa and visited Helen at her house. She poured me a pre-mixed martini out of a can, and we sat and laughed for a couple of hours – under her fig tree. She told me, with tears in her eyes, that she was sorry to see me leave, that the Church needed priests like me. I was sad too, because I knew that, despite my best intentions, I would probably never see her again.

"Father"

My breakthrough with Helen convinced me that I probably could function as a priest, that most people in the church valued relationships a lot more than they feared ideology. Nevertheless, I found that a lot of people wanted to restrict that relationship to a parent-child model.

The title "Father" really bothered me, and I did my best to dispel it, almost begging people to call me "Greg," rather than "Father." I didn't feel like I was ready to be a father – either biological or spiritual. All I had were questions, and fathers were supposed to have answers. Nonetheless, most people would succeed in calling me "Greg" only two or three times. Then they'd regress back to their childhood dependence on the church and start calling me "Father" again.

One place where being called "Father" actually came in handy was the county jail. Shortly after I arrived at St. Rose, a Hispanic woman called the rectory and begged me to help her. She had been jailed the night before, after her social worker discovered that her estranged husband had returned to town and that she hadn't reported this to the welfare office. Since her husband was technically her only means of support, and since her welfare check was only intended to cover her during his absence, then, according to the social worker, she was guilty of welfare fraud for not reporting his return. Unfortunately, the social worker hadn't bothered to check if the woman had actually seen her husband, or even known that he had returned. Instead, based only on the fact that the husband had been arrested in Santa Rosa, her social worker assumed that she and her husband had been together. As a result, her two daughters had been taken from her and sent to a county foster facility, and she herself had been sent to Sonoma County jail, ironically the same jail where her husband was being held.

According to the woman, she had had no knowledge of her husband's return. He had not contacted her or the kids, and he certainly hadn't given them any money. I told her I'd come to see her that afternoon and that, after that, I'd see what I could do. This was one time I didn't mind wearing the roman collar, since all the people in the jail were wearing uniforms of one sort or another, and the ones wearing badges saw my collar, politely addressed me as "Father" and let me go wherever I wanted. This was a new experience for me, and I decided that, in the pursuit of justice, the roman collar might have a use after all.

The woman was young and attractive, though very distraught about her children being taken away from her. I collected all the information I could from her – her husband's name, any relatives she had in town, where her kids were, where she lived. She said she had a brother in town who was a successful businessman and that he might be useful as a character witness. She also suggested that I go out to her house and talk to a friend of her husband who had been renting a room at their house for some time, and could testify about her fitness as a mother.

I started with her husband, John, who was in the other wing of the jail. I had no problem getting to see him after I told the guard that I was the family priest. We met in a small conference room. When I told him what had happened to his wife, he was remorseful. "Yeah. I came back to town a couple of weeks ago, and I should have called her, but I didn't. I got a job over on the other side of town, and I never even talked to her or the kids. I feel real bad about that."

I asked him where he had been working and wrote down the name he gave me. It was a trailer manufacturer.

During the next week, I followed up on all my leads. I talked to the woman's brother, who was an up-and-coming Chicano businessman in town. He didn't want to get involved. His sister had never amounted to anything, he said, though he had to admit that she was a devoted mother. She just didn't have any sense when it came to men.

I could tell he wasn't going to be much help.

I also talked to the trailer manufacturer, who corroborated the husband's story about when he had returned to town and how long he'd been employed. He said he wasn't even aware that John was married, and that he'd never mentioned having kids.

Then I went out and saw the kids, about 6 and 8, at the foster center. They were scared and confused and wanted to know how long it would be before they could see their mom and go back home. I told them I thought everything would be fine, they just had to be patient for another day or two.

I drove out to the woman's house and knocked on the door of the little room around back. The renter answered it and seemed relieved that I was trying to help.

"I was living here with them before John split, and I've just stayed around, because I like the kids and I can help around the house. John and I are friends, but he can be a real jerk. He never even called her when he came back to town, and he hasn't done anything to help her out with the kids. This is really crazy, her being arrested. She didn't do anything wrong."

Based on all this information, I called the courthouse to arrange a meeting with the judge and the social worker. We met the next afternoon in Judge Murphy's chambers. The social worker was a woman in her 50s, fashionably dressed in a yellow and blue outfit, complete with a broad-rimmed yellow hat with a feather in it. She looked like she had just come from a Junior League luncheon. I thanked the judge for his time, and proceeded to lay out all the information I had gathered. The social worker squirmed in her chair while I was talking and made a few cynical comments to the judge about "those types of people." When I finished, Judge Murphy kept writing for a couple more moments, then put his pen down and peered over his glasses at me.

"Well Father, certainly you're not so naïve as to think that that man would be living in her house and they wouldn't be sleeping together."

At first I had no idea what he was talking about. Then I understood and I looked over at the social worker who was earnestly nodding her support of the judge's assumption.

That did it. I mustered the most authoritative voice I could, and said to the judge, "Well, Your Honor, as I understand it, the way you play the game – in terms of the law – people are innocent until proven guilty. And I haven't seen any proof that he was sleeping with her. The way I play the game – in terms of morality – I don't see as how that matters at all. All that matters is that she and her kids shouldn't be in jail."

I could tell the judge didn't like my response, because he abruptly terminated our meeting, thanked me for my input, and said he would look into the matter.

I went back to the rectory feeling inadequate and angry. But later that evening, the woman called from her home to thank me for my help. Judge Murphy's sense of justice had evidently overridden his Catholic prudery. She had been released that afternoon.

Though I felt good about getting her out of jail, and had started to accept the fact that the collar had a good use after all, I still felt out of place in the rectory. Life was too secure, too predictable, too shielded from reality. I stood in the middle of my room one afternoon and made a deal with Jesus. I told Him I felt like I had been thrust into a privileged position without paying my dues. I was living in a luxurious house, with a cook and a housekeeper. I was getting three meals a day, had a car at my disposal, was being treated with deference everywhere I went.

"I feel like I've been elevated to the top of the pile without earning it," I said to my vague divine mentor. "It doesn't feel right. Let me experience the bottom. Then I'll be willing to be a priest."

The rest of my stint at St. Rose was made up of hospital visitations, occasional dinner invitations at parishioners' houses, regular lectures by Monsignor Tappe in his study, and two Sunday

219

sermons. My mother came up to St. Rose's for both of my sermons, and I introduced her to the other priests in the rectory. She immediately bonded with Mal Costa and, during one of their talks, asked him if he didn't think I should get some psychiatric help, since I seemed so confused and troubled. He assured her I was fine, that I was just "finding myself."

Had she asked any of the other priests, she no doubt would have gotten a different answer, but Mal was dealing with many of the same questions I was, and, in fact, he himself would decide to leave the priesthood a few years later.

My mother was poignantly aware of the struggle I was going through, and she was doing her best to keep her own anxieties and fears to herself. She kept assuring me that my decision was between me and God, not something I should base on other people's expectations, including her own.

Decision

Decide [Latin. Decidere, decisus; de + caedere to cut, cut off.]

Deciding was easier said than done. All my life, I had been programmed to live up to others' expectations. That's what the church was all about – live for others, die to yourself. Now, I found I could no longer do this. I felt like I was being smothered by others' expectations. I had to start doing what I wanted to do. The problem was I couldn't get in <u>touch</u> with what I wanted to do. I could rebel. I could complain. I could subvert. But I couldn't cut the cord and be myself. I didn't know who the "I" was that might be capable of wanting something.

As I look back on this, I realize that I was attempting to make a decision for which I had no tools. In order to muster the strength to break with my past, I had to tap into my feelings and emotions. I had to <u>want</u> a change, not just <u>think</u> I wanted it. My Catholic Operating System had locked me into my mind and out of my emotions. Feelings, after all, were the selfish impulses that had to be repressed if you were going to be a competent priestlike person. Decisions were made by the mind, not by emotion and feelings.

I did my best to <u>reason</u> to a decision. I sat down and wrote "pro" on one side of a sheet of paper and "con" on the other side. Then I listed all the reasons for staying on one side and for leaving on the other. It was a total bust. The sides ended up equal. I stopped trusting reason.

I finished my six weeks internship as a deacon and returned home. I had only about two weeks before I was due back to the seminary to start my last year. Every night I tossed and turned, wrestling with the decision; but still the mental stalemate continued. How could I leave after all those many years? On the other hand, how could I stay? Who *was* I, if not a priest? I had no other identity. But how could I stand working for a church I no longer trusted? How could Jesus be calling me to be a priest, knowing that I no longer believed in the Church?

Well, I reasoned, he didn't stay in <u>His</u> church either.

When my mind failed to give me any resolution, I prayed again to my elusive God. I knew I needed a nudge from outside. Nine years earlier, I had experienced a "voice" as I was falling to sleep. It had come from somewhere outside my conscious mind, and I had assumed it was Jesus, or God, calling me to the seminary. It had broken through my mental carapace, and had inspired me to do something adventuresome and out of the ordinary. It would take a similar voice to release me from my present impasse.

The voice came early one morning, just before I woke up. It spoke a simple permission: "You really want to get out. It's okay. Just leave." It seemed so simple. Once it happened, I no longer had any doubts. I got up, and went into the kitchen, where my mother was cutting up oranges for breakfast.

"I've decided," I told her. "I'm leaving."

She looked at me, nodded, then sat down, trying her best to retain her composure. She retained it for a while, asking me responsible questions like "What are you going to do?" "Are you going to continue your education?" "Where will you live?"

Then she broke down; and said she thought she better go away for a few days, by herself.

I had just ripped her soul from its moorings. I had uprooted my own soul as well, but I had a new life to look forward to. She was experiencing only emptiness and death. I realized then why my decision had been so painful and so long in coming. Unconsciously, I had been protecting her from this terrible moment.

My mom spent the next few days with her sister-in-law, and I spent the time formalizing my departure from the seminary. I called Mal Costa, told him about my decision, and asked him to set up a meeting for me with Monsignor Tappe; I called the chancery office and arranged a meeting with the bishop; I called the seminary and left a message for Fr. Nicolaus. Then I started writing letters. I wrote to parishioners I'd gotten to know at St. Rose; to old family friends who'd known me since childhood and had followed my seminary career from the beginning; to seminary friends with whom I'd shared my radical ideas; and to Marie, who in the last six weeks had become my closest confidante. Some letters were easier to write than others, depending on the recipient's ability to understand and empathize with my decision.

My meeting with the bishop was cordial. He had, of course, already heard about my decision from Monsignor Tappe, and he seemed rather relieved. He asked me my plans and I told him that I was going to look for a job in San Francisco.

"Good!" he said. "That's just what you need. Your problem is you think too much. You need to go out and get a job."

"Well, I'm also signed up in a Master's program at San Francisco State," I said, "so I'll only be working part time."

He furrowed his brow. I could tell he didn't like that idea.

"Well Greg, now that you've left the seminary, you'll probably start to be interested in young women – after you get your dispensation, of course. But I don't think you'll find any suitable young women at San Francisco State. I think you should look somewhere like Lone Mountain College. There are a lot of fine young Catholic women there and it's very important that you find someone who has the same interests as you. For instance, if a young woman were interested in opera you could be pretty sure."

"Opera?!" I interrupted. "I don't know anything about opera." (I had a bizarre image of myself, standing on the lawn at Lone Mountain College, launching an aria up at the dormitory windows and waiting for a soprano response.)

"Well, you know what I mean," said the bishop. "If not opera, something else having to do with art and culture."

The idea of Leo Maher lecturing anyone on romance, art or culture struck me as pretty funny, but I found myself unexpectedly grateful to him for caring enough to make the attempt, and I thanked him as I left. (As fate would have it, he was partially right, as I ended up teaching at Lone Mountain a few years later and did find several women there who shared my interests.)

During the next week, I began to get responses from my letters. Most of them were supportive, telling me they were sorry to hear I was leaving, because I would have made a wonderful priest, but that they wished me success in whatever I decided to do. A few, like my godmother, expressed their disappointment in me and implied that I should be ashamed of myself for being so selfish and letting God down. Many of my seminary friends wrote surprisingly heartfelt letters, reminiscing about our times together and telling me that they would miss me. Marie's letter, which I had eagerly awaited, congratulated me for making a difficult decision; then went on in euphoric terms about our search for truth and the changes it demands.

She understood. She knew exactly what I was going though. I was leaving a place, a career, an institution, a social circle, a belief system; but I was also taking my next step in the search for the grail. This was my spiritual path and, despite my sadness over having to leave so much of myself behind, I was infected by curiosity and enthusiasm about what was to come next. Just as Jesus had left the organized church of his youth, I was leaving traditional Catholicism, in response to that inner voice which I had come to acknowledge as God. The voice was loud and clear at that time. I assumed, naively, that it would always be loud and clear.

Thus ended the Joyful Mysteries of my rosary. I realize now that they coincided almost exactly with my initial state of celibacy, a state which shielded me from those deep heartfelt emotions that resist mental conquest and stubbornly occupy the heart and stomach, refusing to budge until fully experienced and accepted. These are the emotions of the Sorrowful Mysteries.

As a deacon I had finally found my Self in the Temple and, when I did, I no longer felt at home there. I told Jesus that I didn't feel right living in such luxurious surroundings, that I wanted to experience the bottom before I would feel worthy to be a priest.

You have to be careful of what you ask for. Before I knew it, the Sorrowful Mysteries were upon me.

ABOUT THE AUTHOR

J. G. McAllister is a native of northern California, who entered a Catholic seminary at age sixteen and left nine years later at age twenty-five. His seminary tenure coincided with the reign of Pope John XXIII, whose ideas sparked a period of revolutionary change in the Catholic Church. Those were years of turbulent idealism for seminarians, the "Joyful Mysteries" of McAllister's Irish Catholic rosary.

After leaving the seminary as a deacon in 1966, he has worked as a college instructor, bartender, restaurant manager, truck driver, career and education counselor, and tuition benefits administrator. He has two grown children, Elan Vital and Shane, and presently resides in a one-room cottage near a pond, where he is reflecting on the Sorrowful Mysteries and attempting to live the Glorious.

Printed in the United States
202125BV00002B/166-183/A